SATURDAY NIGHT PETER

SATURDAY NIGHT PETER

PETER KAY

CENTURY · LONDON

Published by Century 2009

2 4 6 8 10 9 7 5 3 1

First published in Great Britain in 2009 by
Century
The Random House Group Limited
20 Vauxhall Bridge Road
London SW1V 2SA

www.randomhouse.co.uk

Addresses for companies within The Random House Group Limited can be found at:
www.randomhouse.co.uk/offices.htm

The Random House Group Limited Reg. No. 954009

A CIP catalogue record for this book
is available from the British Library.

ISBN 9781846053634 (Hardback)
ISBN 9781846053641 (Trade paperback)

The Random House Group Limited supports The Forest Stewardship Council
(FSC),the leading international forest certification organisation. All our titles that
are printed on Greenpeace-approved FSC certified paper carry the FSC logo.
Our paper procurement policy can be found at: www.rbooks.co.uk/environment

Mixed Sources
Product group from well-managed
forests and other controlled sources
www.fsc.org Cert no. TT-COC-2139
© 1996 Forest Stewardship Council
FSC

Typeset by Palimpsest Book Production Limited,
Grangemouth, Stirlingshire

Printed and bound in the UK by
CPI Mackays, Chatham ME5 8TD

Acknowledgements

The author and publishers would like to thank the following copyright-holders for permission to reproduce images in this book:

The many faces of Peter Kay at the Frog and Bucket © Martin Pope.

Peter Kay on Bolton backstreets © Nigel Hillier/UNP.

City Life magazine cover © MEN Syndication.

Peter Kay with Yamaha-ha © Eamonn Clarke.

Photographs of the Frog & Bucket © Paul Jones – www.pauljones-photographer.com.

DVD cover images courtesy of Universal Pictures.

Newspaper cuttings reproduced by courtesy of the *Bolton News*, formerly the *Bolton Evening News*.

The author and publishers have made all reasonable efforts to contact copyright-holders for permission, and apologise for any omissions or errors in the form of credits given. Corrections may be made to future printings.

For Finley and Stanley

Contents

Chapter One

Her Majesty's Gravy

The Northern Ballet School is situated next door to Greggs the bakers. It's a bizarre juxtaposition and if you drive up Oxford Road at lunchtime you can regularly see hordes of beefy ballerinas queuing up for Steak Bakes in their tutus. Inside the school is the Dancehouse Theatre, where I'd been booked at short notice by Agraman – The Human Anagram to perform my stand-up as part of the annual Manchester Comedy Festival.

I was scheduled to be the opening act for John Thomson, the comedy actor who was experiencing the dizzy heights of success after appearances in the highly acclaimed *Cold Feet* and alongside Steve Coogan in *Paul Calf's Video Diaries*. I'd never seen him do stand-up before and thought I may never get the chance, as with only ten minutes left to show time he still hadn't arrived. 'He's still filming,' panicked Agraman (– The Human Anagram) (I have to give him his full title – it's comedy law), as he clipped his house-brick-sized mobile phone back on to his chosen belt loop.

'Peter, could you do me a favour, could you pad it out a

bit?'* he said to me as I stood nervously in the wings, spying on the arriving audience through a pinhole gap in the curtains.

'Er . . . well . . . ?' was my reluctant response.

This was only my second ever fully professional gig, in front of the largest crowd I'd ever played to. The Dancehouse holds over four hundred people, as far as I was concerned it was Wembley Stadium. I'd be lucky if I could remember my fifteen minutes of material let alone do any 'padding'.

I'd been honing my material all week, during both of my part-time jobs, working as a cinema usher and as a steward at the Manchester Arena. Not a single customer had been spared my selfish and shameless attempts to try and crowbar my act into any given conversation. I'd completely ruined Gabrielle for a couple from Halifax by bombarding them with my observations on the O. J. Simpson trial and the disappearance of white dog shit.

But how else was I going to practise my stand-up? Since winning the North West Comedian of the Year three weeks previously my life had been turned upside down. With both a booking for a Labour Club in Glossop and an interview for my local free paper, suddenly I found I was a man in demand! Winning the competition may have declared me a 'professional stand-up' to the powers that book, but I still had to rehearse my material before I presented it to the world. I was a total perfectionist, still am, the fact that you're reading the thirty-eighth draft of this first chapter proves my point.

The thought of 'padding it out' now sent me into a panic. But

* By the way, 'Could you pad it out' is one of the worst things you can ever say to a stand-up comedian, it's right up there with 'Can I pay you next week' and 'Get off, you're shit'.

reluctantly I agreed to his plea and before I had time to even contemplate just how I could possibly extend what material I had, Agraman (– The Human Anagram) was centre stage introducing me as 'the prestigious winner of the 1996 North West Comedian of the Year, ladies and gentlemen, he's come all the way from Bolton at very short notice, please would you give a very warm welcome to Peter Kay.'

I walked on stage to the sound of applause and left my 'other me' in the wings. Now when I say 'other me' please let me explain: I don't suffer from schizophrenia but every time I ever perform stand-up I get a bizarre out-of-body experience. Part of me takes to the stage yet I always leave another part of me in the wings, watching. The only thing I can compare it to is that advert they used to show on TV for Lockets, you know the throat lozenge that helps aid the symptoms of colds and flu? It featured a farmer sat on bales of hay, who magically splits into two. One half of him says, 'Sore throat?', while his other half nods sympathetically adding, 'Runny nose.' 'Try Lockets!' says the patronising voiceover offering hope. And Hey Presto! They both pop a honey Locket into each of their mouths and before you can say 'Swine flu' they're back out fighting 'blue tongue' or whatever else is top of the 'crops' that week.*

Whilst I may not suck a lozenge on stage, I've found this out-of-body experience has remained with me throughout the years and as much as I truly admire the part of me that can perform stand-up, the other part of me finds it completely terrifying. The question is which one of them is real? Ooooooh, that's a bit deep for Chapter One.

* That was a truly awful and lazy joke. I'd like to offer my sincerest apologies to both you the reader and the publishers, I promise I'll try harder.

I watched in astonishment as the other me walked on and proceeded to sit on the edge of the stage. What was I doing? This really wasn't the normal comedic etiquette but immediately it created a much more relaxed atmosphere in the theatre. Ahhh, I thought to myself, he's padding it out. Apparently Danny Kaye did a similar thing when he first played the London Palladium in the fifties. Sitting with his legs dangling over the orchestra pit, sipping a cup of tea, he told anecdotes of his life, working in Hollywood. I admired that technique and thought, What the hell, we roughly shared the same last name.

So how are you? You don't mind if I sit down, do you? I'm knackered, it's been non-stop since winning the competition. I've never won anything in my life. Except once I won a copy of that film Mask *on video, I like Jim Carrey an' all but it turned out to be that other version of* Mask, *the one with Cher and The Elephant Man on a motorbike. And you know what my prize was for winning the competition? A four and a half litre bottle of whisky, I don't even drink, I'm tee-total. And it's one of those huge bottles, it's sitting in the kitchen at home. I'm dying to pour it down the sink just so I can start filling the bottle back up with 2p's. My mum and dad used to have one of those, a huge whisky bottle in the corner of the front room. In went the loose change and shrapnel every week and then every year, just before Christmas, out came those polythene banking bags and you start coppering up on the carpet. Stacking your change, 'Five twos is ten, Ten tens is a pound, bag it up,' my dad would shout, 'quick, son, bag it up.' I was the bagger. I'd hover round my dad with my bag ready. Five hours we'd be counting. Five hours for £8.60. Then he'd go to the off-licence and buy a bottle of whisky.*

Like I said, I'd been rehearsing my material all week and had no idea I was going to do this. But that's what happens when the adrenalin takes over, it can take you to places you never dreamed you'd go. And go with the flow you must, because down that route lies the excitement, down there lies the secret ingredient that makes each and every performance you give unique.

So there I was, positioned on the edge of the stage chatting to the audience. As with most of my early stand-up I recorded my performance that night on my Dictaphone. I used to archive all of my stand-up so I could study it later and check what worked and what didn't; it also used to come in handy for keeping a record of what material I performed and when, so if I returned to the same club I could change my material accordingly. I've just listened back to my performance at the Dancehouse that night once again and I was shocked at how high my voice sounds for a 23-year-old. I thought the tape must have warped over the years or something.

I'm also amazed at how confident I come across, as this was only my second ever professional booking. My first had been the previous Sunday at Manchester's legendary Boardwalk – they've got one of those blue plaques on the wall outside now as it was home to one of Oasis' first ever gigs.

I can't believe I forgot to bring my Dictaphone for that very first performance so the only memory I really have is being on the bill with a comedian called Frankie Doodle, who is the son of TV's own Jimmy Cricket. I remember Frankie being quite a gentle, polite bloke who had a series of visual gags; one of them involved him pulling out a package made out of newspapers, the kind you use for Pass the Parcel. He furiously began to unwrap it for what seemed like an eternity due to the deafening silence in the room. He'd tear away at the layers, finally revealing a large pair of comic scissors which he held up to the audience, once again in silence. He's since given up comedy and entered the priesthood. This isn't a joke, he really has.

I honestly can't remember what material I did my first night at the Boardwalk. You'd think it would be up there with the first time I ever had sex or completed a Rubik's Cube,* but I think I was that nervous I've blanked it out. My other overriding memory is that for a fifteen-minute performance Agraman (– The Human Anagram) paid me £35, which was twice as much as I got for working a full week in both my part-time jobs.

Coincidentally I had to ask Mrs Hayworth, the cinema manager, if I could finish my shift early so I could go and play my second gig at the Dancehouse as I usually worked until 7 p.m. on a Saturday. Thankfully she obliged, meaning I was spared the arduous task of having to sweep up a screen full of popcorn left by two hundred sweaty kids who'd been watching *The Indian in the Cupboard*.† I can still vividly recall the flutter of butterflies in my stomach as I took off my usher's bow tie and headed towards the train station in the rain.

I actually told the audience that night all about Mrs Hayworth letting me bunk off early so I could do the show. In fact I kept on padding it out until I heard an exaggerated cough from the wings and turned to see Agraman (– The Human Anagram) with his thumbs aloft and John Thomson stood by the side of him beaming like a Cheshire Cat (if indeed they do beam). It turned

---

* I never actually ever did, I just peeled the stickers off R Julie's while she was out at the cinema watching *Mad Max 2*. She was underage, I know, but my uncle Tony sneaked her in backwards through the fire door.
† Which was a film incidentally and not a children's entertainer.

out my material didn't need that much padding after all and I was very relieved to see him.

I chatted to John backstage during the interval. He was a lovely man, I was in awe of him as a comedian and his success had been an inspiration to me. He'd used stand-up to break into the world of comic acting and that's exactly where I wanted to go. I'd managed to get myself a local acting agent after completing the HND in Media Performance I did at the University of Salford but I quickly realised that the acting world was brutal enough without me limiting myself to just taking comic roles. After seeing John Thomson's and Steve Coogan's success I decided to follow a similar path. And now just four months after receiving my diploma here I was, supporting John on stage in a comedy festival. It was a huge moment for me.

It was also the first time I'd ever met anybody really famous before, apart from Sir Jimmy Savile at the Bolton Marathon in 1982. Even then we didn't really meet, he just threw a wave in our general direction as he jogged past, flanked either side by minders. Three hours we stood waiting in the piss rain and all we got to show for it was a photo of the back of his head as he ran off.

I also once bumped into a local TV celebrity called Bob Greaves while I was out shopping. He was famous for reading the news on *Granada Reports* and having his genitals sniffed by an elephant on *It'll be Alright on the Night*. I've no idea which one he's most proud of, you'd have to ask him.

I also spent a few hours chasing Rod Hull and Emu around Bolton Town Hall in an effort to get his autograph but was eventually told by security that his reluctance to sign anything was due to the simple fact that his writing hand was up the bird.

Oh, and Jon Pertwee, it's all coming back to me now. He was on the back of a carnival float dressed as Worzel Gummidge and I'd tried to touch his straw as he came past. Casually, he leaned forward and, smiling, he snapped, 'Get off, you little fucker', but in Worzel's voice. I leapt back in fear and then I watched in shock as he sped off at 4 mph. I should have grassed him up to the Crowman.

What surprised me about John Thomson was how nervous he was before going on stage. Pacing back and forth in the wings with a fag in his mouth, mumbling his act to himself in between drags. He confessed it had always been like this and that it never got any easier. I was relieved to find that it wasn't just me who suffered with nerves but was shocked to discover that it wouldn't get any easier. I'd been under the misguided assumption that experience and success would calm the nerves, that they would eventually pass just like with any other job, but I quickly started to realise that being a stand-up isn't like any other job. It's just you, on your own in front of an audience, and you've got nowhere to hide.

John had nothing to worry about, his act was brilliant and the audience loved him. His comic timing and talent for mimicry is incredible. He'd cleverly constructed a showcase for his talents, with his impressions displaying the range of voices he had. I quickly saw that there was a lot more to the man than the characters he'd portrayed so far on TV. Basically he always seemed to play himself in roles when in fact he was clearly capable of playing anybody. I sat on a chair in the wings, soaking up the opportunity to study him at work.

It was also an education playing in a theatre for the first time. It was such a different vibe to the brief experiences I'd had playing clubs. When I first came on stage I was thrown by how attentive the audience were. In clubs it felt as if you had to fight for their attention. There were so many other distractions when you played a club, for a kick-off the audience is usually in what they call cabaret-style seating, round tables and chairs with candles sat in wine bottles which was all the rage in the mid-nineties.

The candles often came in handy as an act would soon discover how well they were being received (or not) by the amount of hot wax that was flicked at them by the audience. This trial by hot wax, rather than fire, was harsh but fair; however, it soon became apparent that naked flames and comedy should never mix. This was highlighted for me during a Christmas party for the C.I.D. one night in Burnley when a drunken detective inspector tried to set fire to the stage during an act. I was compèring that night and remember pleading to the bar staff, 'Who should we call?' As we already had three hundred police officers in the building, the correct answer quickly turned out to be the fire brigade. Luckily I managed to get paid and leg it as chaos ensued at the fire assembly point outside Abrakebabra.

Another difference between performing in a theatre as opposed to a club was how quickly the level of laughter died off. It really threw me. Don't get me wrong, my material went down well at the Dancehouse and the laughs were strong that night but I'd previously found that when I performed in a club the laughter seemed to linger for a lot longer. I'd never noticed the laughter tailing off due to the general hub-bub in the room.

I started compèring regularly at a comedy club in Manchester and for some reason the audience for the first hour on Friday nights were always painfully quiet. So I hit upon an idea. I went to my local library and hired a sound-effects CD that featured a variety of different atmospheres – shops, airports etc. I listened to the interior pub atmosphere and it sounded just like the busy club. It was four minutes long and I thought if I could get the sound man to put the track on repeat and play it very low for that first half an hour then it might just relax the audience. So he did just that, I came on stage and it worked beautifully right up until about two minutes in and somebody on the track won on a fruit machine. Everybody in the club looked round to see who the lucky person was, only to find there wasn't a fruit machine. Confused, they turned back to me, and although I was in a mild panic I successfully managed to distract them until four minutes later (and with the CD on repeat) the lucky bastard won again. What a fool, I hadn't played the track all the way through, had I? And why should I? Never in a million years would I have expected to hear the musical fanfares of an invisible jackpot.

'Stop the track,' I shamefully shouted to the sound man, and he did so immediately, thereby revealing the deafening silence I'd been trying my best to disguise. I attempted to explain what I'd been trying to do. But they just stared at me more confused than ever and everything I said just made me sound like a moron who hung around public libraries listening to sound-effects CDs, which of course was the truth. A few seconds later I felt the first splatter of hot wax on my cheek.

Hosting a comedy night and being a compère was a role that I quickly fell into working as a stand-up. I enjoyed it because it was a lot less pressure than having to perform an act for a solid twenty minutes. It also gave me the opportunity to try out any new material that I'd written during the week and if it didn't get a laugh I just brought on a comedian. Being a compère also meant regular work and luckily I managed to get a booking as one of the resident compères at a local club called the Frog & Bucket. There were quite a few comedy nights in and around Manchester in the mid-nineties but the Frog & Bucket was the only fully-fledged comedy club. Previously a Yates Wine Lodge, it could easily hold up to three hundred and fifty sweaty punters on the weekend, a figure that would easily have doubled if the manager Dave Perkin could have found a way around the health and safety regulations.

The Frog & Bucket was a chaotic circus of drunken laughter and loud music. Then there was the unforgettable aroma of the place. Stale beer soaked through a wooden floor combined with the stench of over a billion cigarettes. I can still taste it. This was in the days before the smoking ban, and when the club was full on a hot Saturday night, the nicotine-stained sweat used to drip into my eyes and blind me. It was almost as painful as the hot wax. The place used to be roasting all the time too. I'm sure Dave Perkin used to turn the heating up full to sell more drink.

The club was on two levels. A grand spiral staircase led up to the balcony directly overlooking the stage. This was acknowledged as the VIP area (Very Ignorant People who often saw fit to talk during the show because they felt they were above the rest of the audience and they were too, about fifteen foot). They also had a hatch leading to a kitchen that served a variety of foods such as potato wedges, curly fries, potato wedges with cheese, and curly fries with cheese. One of the standard lines the compères used when having to advertise the serving of the food was 'and please avoid the dips as it's the chef's last night'.

So suddenly here I was, cinema usher/steward by day, stand-up comedian by night. Thrust into an exciting world of comedy. Winning the North West Comedian of the Year competition meant that I was able to leapfrog the usual rigmarole that comes with establishing yourself as a stand-up comedian. I never had to endure the painful route of touting my wares at open-mic nights. I never had to perform at open spots for free in an effort to get a booking. But I was thrown in at the deep end. Winning meant I went straight to the top of the bill. It really was sink or swim. But thanks to a large amount of material gathered over fourteen part-time jobs, I quickly learned the backstroke.

I felt like The Karate Kid when he's unwittingly taught by Mr Miyagi. He has him sanding his deck and painting his fence, waxing on and waxing off. And he isn't happy – just like me when I was working at Netto and Top Rank Bingo, I wasn't happy, hottest summer for fifty-three years and I was working shifts. 'I want to learn karate, Mr Miyagi, not paint your goddamn fence,' said Daniel-san. Then Mr Miyagi says, 'Paint the fence', 'Sand the deck,' and suddenly a stunned Daniel-san says, 'Oh, Mr Miyagi, you've taught me karate.'

The similarity between Daniel-san's situation and my own was spooky. There I was thinking I was trapped in these mundane part-time jobs for ever, when unbeknownst to me, they were actually arming me with all the stand-up material I'd ever need.

Finally being able to make people laugh on stage instead of in some work canteen was the beginning of a very happy and creative time for me. I used to thrive on the opportunity to perform each week. I lived for the weekend and being up on that stage, and I used to love the buzz I'd get on a Saturday afternoon, knowing that I had a gig that night, a combination of butterflies and excitement.

Every Saturday I went through the same ritual before heading off for a gig – when I say ritual it wasn't a black mass or anything but just a particular routine. I'd cycle home from the cinema as fast as I could. I lived at the top of a hill. It used to take me four minutes to get to work and over forty-five to get home – that hill was a killer, my friends. Dashing into the house I'd promptly place my tea order with my mum, who'd be sat watching the *Brookside* Omnibus, and then I'd run in the shower (though why I ran after all that cycling I'll never know).

Saturday teatimes meant it was always chips and something with beans or peas. The something could be a number of things and usually they'd be breaded, ranging from McCain's Cauliflower Cheese Grills to Findus Crispy Pancakes (minced beef and onion). But since I'd started earning some extra money from stand-up I'd become a bit of culinary snob and had started opting for Chicken Kievs.

It took two songs to have a shower; my tracks of choice were usually 'Xanadu' – Olivia Newton-John, and 'Kiss from a Rose' – Seal (or the full version of 'Bat Out of Hell' if I was feeling frisky), then a quick spray of Insignia, a splash of Kouros and I was ready for anything. After vaulting the stairs I'd position myself on the old pouffe in the front room (he never minded), where I'd simultaneously try to shine my shoes and eat my Kiev whilst watching *Noel's House Party*. Now there's a fella who knows how to please people on a Saturday night. Mr Blobby and Grab a Grand up Crinkly Bottom. Young bucks, take note and get on YouTube for a few tips from the master.

Back upstairs, I'd put on a whistle and flute (and my suit as well). I always wore a suit, nice shirt, no tie. It was important to look smart. Some comedians wore what they arrived in but I always felt the need to get ready. I tried doing stand-up a few times in jeans and trainers but I always felt a bit scruffy. I would already have devised a crib sheet with bullet points of key words that linked my material together, and there are a couple of examples on the next page.*

My notes were all I needed, one of the benefits of being a stand-up was that there was no lugging huge dirty great pieces of equipment up fire escapes for me. All I needed was a couple of sheets of A4 tucked into my trouser pocket and I was away. Then I'd kiss my mum goodbye, assure her that I had my keys and leg it down to the bus stop on the main road. It was times like that I really wished I had a car. It had taken me six years and five attempts to finally pass my driving test and now I couldn't afford one. It was very frustrating. I used to have to invite my friends who had cars to gigs, 'Do you fancy coming to this gig with me?', and once they'd said yes, I would ask if they didn't mind giving me a lift. Cheeky, I know, but I thought it was a good deal: they got a night out, I got a lift home.

I knew the times of the buses off by heart – I knew the times but whether they actually turned up was a different story. Three would come at once. I still had my bus pass left over from uni, it'd expired three months previously but when I flashed it to the driver I'd deliberately place my finger over the date. Most of the time they never even looked but occasionally they'd ask for a closer inspection only to discover it was out of date. I'd have to act all surprised and pay up the 75p fare. I knew my acting training would eventually come in handy.

* I'm afraid you'll have to make do with a shitty black and white photocopy. Apparently the colour stuff can only go in the middle of the book. I don't make the rules. If I'd wanted colour in Chapter One the lady at the publishers said they'd have to send it off to the Far East 'in advance'. I thought she said 'in a van' but clearly I misheard her. I thought she was being a bit specific.

FROG   Fri/Sat 8/9th August

Are Friends Electric?
Summer Old People Meaning
Play out / Water Fights / Manfredi / Mr. Freeze
Mr. S. Oftee. 🎤
Welcome to the Pleasure Dome, the Frog and Bucket the biggest
and Brightest comedy club on Oldham St. We've got a
fantastic show for you tonight 35 Minutes of entertainment
spread over a 3hr Show.
I'd like to welcome on stage

DAD CRABS Yal
Council Sound / Blackpool - Alan Bradley
Pleasure Beach - Revelation (Jim'll Fix It) Wanted Swing
Funfairs
Abroad

Phone Home - Weather
Family From Bradford / Keep in Touch
London Pubs
Nikata
Watchdog - Beans On Wall
Arcades / Track n' Field / Money Grabber

Slippos / Chippy
Don't Dirty Any Plates
Rola Cola / Hit Me / You Fuckin Drink It Bitch
Lord forgiveness / Crucify his own Son   NUNS
Jesus Of Nazareth a then / Sister Sledge
Dreams / Martin Luther
Valentines / Dress Up Jesus

Treacly Teacake
Detson / School trips
Lollies / Rola Cola Lollies - Why Don't You !
                        Say Ude Goodbye!   Club Tropicana

Then I'd run across Morrisons' car park over to the station and jump on a train to Manchester. If it was after half six I could get an Evening Ranger ticket, which meant I could travel anywhere between Rochdale and Buxton for a quid. But being a tight-arse I used to try and fake being asleep when the guard came to check the tickets. I'd even have my mouth open just to make it look as if I'd been travelling for a long time. Sometimes I'd even drool for believability. One time I heard the guard coming, 'Tickets please,' he said, and like a travelling narcoleptic I immediately fell into my fake slumber. Unfortunately I couldn't gauge where he was in the compartment. I waited for what seemed like ages, surely he must have gone by now. Slowly I squinted one eye open and there he was, crouched down, face to face with me. 'Tickets please,' he said in a deliberately slow voice. I tried acting all disorientated, with a 'How did I get here?' kind of look, glancing around shocked. Oh the shame, a bloody pound, was it worth it? After that debacle I just took to hiding in the toilets on future journeys.

Twenty-two minutes later I'd arrive at Manchester Piccadilly and walk across town to the Frog & Bucket, 'Manchester's Only Alternative Comedy Club' it used to say over the door (although the first thing you saw when you walked in was a huge framed picture of the manager Dave Perkin shaking hands with Stan 'The German Focker' Boardman).

After the stand-up was over they would always have a 'cheesy disco' where they used to play a lot of seventies music until 2 a.m. I'd have to hang around because the last train from Piccadilly wasn't until half one. I'd arrive back in Bolton and, too lazy and tight to queue for a black cab, I'd start walking back up the hill towards home and I'd always be starving. I'd only managed a handful of curly fries (with or without cheese) since my decadent Kiev eight hours earlier. But nothing would be open. Occasionally my hopes would be raised by the flickering of a distant neon sign but deep down I knew it was just the dry cleaner's or the tanning centre. Anyway, who was I trying to kid? I travelled up and down this road every day, it's not as if a shop could just pop up out of nowhere without me noticing, but then I saw it. An oasis of colour amidst the drizzle, shining out like a beacon of hope to every hungry straggler venturing home in the middle of the night. Three simple words shone out for all to see: 'The Complete Takeaway', and it certainly was.

It had everything: chips, fish, pies, kebabs, hot dogs, quarter-pounders, half-pounders, chicken burgers, chicken in a satay sauce, spring rolls, chow mein, ravioli, lasagne, kormas, bhunas, madras and a large industrial microwave. I pinched myself. Surely I was dreaming? That hadn't been there when I'd cycled home from the cinema earlier, or had it?

I opened the door and was instantly greeted by a Greek-looking gentleman with an enormous smile. He seemed delighted to see me, actually the way he greeted me he seemed delighted to see anyone at this hour of the morning. 'Welcome, my friend, I hope you are hungry,' he said in a deep booming voice followed by a laugh so loud it shook the Spastics Society box on the counter.

My God, I'd never seen so much food, it was like the banquet scene in Walt Disney's *Beauty and the Beast*. Piled high on every surface and crammed into every possible orifice, was just about every type of cuisine you could conceivably imagine, and all completely smothered in cling film. They must have been preparing this for days, weeks.

There was a girl behind the counter attempting to bang the debris out of the Insect-O-Cutor on the wall with a yard brush. She smiled politely but looked tired and weary, probably weary from being strong-armed into opening The Complete Takeaway by this Greek-looking fella.

Taking up his position, he proudly began rhyming off the menu. It seemed to take for ever and with a risk of passing out from malnutrition I had to intervene. 'I'll just have chips and gravy please.'

He looked at me confused. 'Chips and gravy?'

'Yes,' I nodded.

'Nothing else? A pie perhaps? Home-made?' he elbowed the girl, and she quickly grabbed a manky-looking pie off the side and started peeling back the cling film as if it was the star prize on a quiz show.

'Tempting,' I said, well I actually shouted it to be honest as it's what my dad used to do when he encountered anyone with a foreign accent. And it appeared to have been genetically passed on to me. 'JUST CHIPS AND GRAVY WILL DO, BUDDY!'

'No fish?' he said, looking dejected.

Fish with gravy? This man clearly was foreign.

'NO THANKS, PAL,' I said.

'Are you sure?'

Oh just give me the bloody food, I thought, but instead I just nodded again.

'No peas, beans, prawns?'

Prawns? Christ, where was I? By now I was wishing this *was* the tanning centre.

'NO PRAWNS, MY OLD SON,' I shouted.

'PEAS OR BEANS THEN?' he shouted back.

'NO, JUST CHIPS AND HER MAJESTY'S GRAVY, BROTHER.'

Reluctantly, he accepted defeat and as the penny dropped, so too did his smile. The happy façade was over, he clapped his hands and the girl lethargically started to make up my order as the Greek-looking fella just glared at me. All this food and all I wanted was chips and gravy? His stare was unnerving. The girl scooped the chips into a Styrofoam tray and then pulled a red thermos flask out from under the counter, unscrewed the lid and poured what looked like liquid cow shit all over my chips.

He leaned in. 'Hmmmmmm, home-made,' he said in a crap American accent.

He elbowed the girl again. This time she pulled out a huge, dodgy-looking pink cake covered in chocolate sprinkles and strawberries with what looked like blue mould on them.

'And for dessert?'

I paid him and left.

'Tell your friends,' he shouted after me as the door closed.

I looked down at my food, smelled it and chucked it in the nearest bin.

Four weeks later The Complete Takeaway was shut down after reports of salmonella.

Chapter Two

Dumbo's Feather

Across the road from the Northern Ballet School and Greggs is the BBC. I was sat in the reception area one night, waiting to appear on a regional phone-in, the subject being 'What Makes Us Laugh?'. Behind the reception desk was an elderly security guard who was becoming increasingly flustered by the sudden influx of telephone calls he was receiving. 'Hello . . . no, I'm sorry, I don't know. No, I've no idea . . . try this number: 0171 743 8000, OK, tara,' he said in a strong Mancunian accent. No sooner had he picked up his copy of *Puzzler* than the phone rang again. 'Hello . . . no, I'm sorry, I haven't got a clue love, no it's not, try this one: 0171 743 8000, OK, tara.'

This bombardment continued but each time he was unable to offer any assistance and was only able to redirect the callers. 'Hello . . . no, I'm sorry, I haven't got a clue madam.' By now I could tell that he'd really had enough. 'You shouldn't be ringing this number, try 0171 743 8000,' he shouted, slammed down the phone and turning to me said, 'How would I know why *The* fucking *Terminator*'s not on?'

Angry that the classic Arnold Schwarzenegger movie had fallen victim to a programme change and had been removed from their screens, irate viewers from across the North West of England were calling the BBC in Manchester and they wanted answers. All the poor sod that was on security could do was redirect the calls to Television Centre in London. In the radio studio fifteen minutes later, when asked by John Goodfellow, presenter at the Cosmic Comedy Club, 'What makes us laugh?' I launched into the story of the security guard and the mysterious case of the missing *Terminator*.

When the phone-in was over, myself and John chatted. He was a decent bloke who occasionally gigged himself, usually taking the role of MC. I performed on a bill with him and quite a few local comedians in aid of Amnesty International once and still cringe with embarrassment when I think of John struggling to remember the name of the headline act. What made it worse was that he went on for ages about how long they'd known each other and what good friends they were. 'So please would you welcome not only one of the finest acts on the comedy circuit, but also a close personal friend of mine . . . here he is . . . without further ado . . . I can see him in the wings . . . I'm sure you're gonna love him and . . . and . . . I can't remember his fucking name.' The comedian (who shall remain nameless, just because I think it's funny not to name him after all that) walked on stage, snatched the mic off John, and snapped, 'Some close personal friend you are!', leaving poor John to exit the stage, his head hung in shame.

Forgetting names was a common occurrence when I was compèring. Hundreds of comedians travel and work the comedy circuit, so trying to remember all of their names could sometimes prove difficult. I'd often find myself resorting to the stock line

'. . . and now please welcome on stage a guy who needs no intro-duction', only then to find a female comedian would walk out, swiftly elbowing me in the groin as we passed on stage.*

After I'd appeared as a guest on the Cosmic Comedy Club, John Goodfellow invited me to play a gig – he ran a comedy night, the last Saturday of every month in the back room of a Labour Club in Glossop. Well, how could I resist the bright lights of downtown Glossop? I said 'Yes' and then realising I was about to miss my last train, I ran out skidding past the BBC security guard who was now in the process of dialling 0171 743 8000 himself, in an effort to discover just why *Terminator* hadn't been on. As I leapt the station stairs like a gazelle† and reached the platform with a stitch I suddenly realised that I had no way of getting to Glossop for John's gig. And so once again I'd have to perform my Jedi mind trick on one of my car-owning driver friends. The having-a-licence-and-yet-no-car situation was really starting to bug me. My showbiz career was confined to venues falling within the radius of my £1 Evening Ranger ticket. At this rate the likelihood of anyone ever seeing me beyond Rochdale and Buxton was looking very slim. And as I heard the familiar holler of 'Tickets please' I locked myself in the toilet.

We pulled up at the Labour Club in Glossop and immediately I was filled with dread.

'Surely this can't be it,' I said, staring at my faxed photocopied directions.

'It says Glossop Labour Club, non members *not* welcome,' said my driver for the evening.

---

* If you ever hear a compère say 'Now an act that needs no introduction' you'll know they've probably forgotten their name.
† Well!

He was right; it did, in red felt-tip.

On the door was a sour-faced pensioner in an eye-patch. After trying to convince him that I didn't have any membership details, as I was an act, I managed to make it through to the main room. Well it was the only room, and judging by its size, it was possibly someone's front room with Real Ale pumps in the corner. When we walked in everybody turned round; well I say 'everybody', there was twenty-three of them but the room was full. I felt like one of the backpackers in *An American Werewolf in London*,* you know the scene where they walk into the Slaughtered Lamb pub and ask Brian Glover, 'What's that star on the wall for?'

John Goodfellow was on stage, padding (funny how things turn out), and looked relieved to see me, well he could hardly miss me, I was less then eight foot away from the pallet he was stood on. It still tickles me that he even bothered to have a microphone and speakers in a room that size. In fact that was the first thing I commented on once I was on stage, the second was the fact that I had to sign up for two years' membership and leave some DNA just to get past the one-eyed Scrooge on the door, it was like *CSI Glossop*. Well I never actually said *CSI Glossop* at the time as it hadn't been invented but I'm saying it now, to you, on reflection. I'm allowed to cheat time sometimes to get laughs.

The gig actually turned out to be a belter and I ended up doing my longest set yet, forty-five minutes (well it may have been longer but my TDK-90 cassette only recorded forty-five minutes a side).

---

* I know every scene in that film. Especially the one where they play 'Moondance' – Van Morrison, that got me through many a dark night, in fact I couldn't ever watch Jenny Agutter again in *The Railway Children* after that shower scene.

Performing at the Labour Club in Glossop confirmed something to me that I'd suspected for a long time. That alternative comedy clubs were really just a relabelling of the old and that comedy is and always will be the same. Either the audience laugh or they don't, it's as simple as that. And as far as I've seen, the only thing that's ever been alternative about alternative comedy is that it's an alternative to laughing. Funny is funny – end of story.

Having a comedy night at a Labour Club in Glossop made me realise just how wide the trend for these nights had spread. The alternative comedy scene had become big business in the mid-nineties and luckily for me I had arrived on the scene in the thick of it. Every pub that had a spare cupboard or back room suddenly found it had a weekly comedy night. Usually they were run by failed comedians (desperate to keep their hand in, they usually insisted on being resident compère) who'd managed to negotiate a room down the local Dog & Duck pub. And they always gave them 'comedy' names like 'The Ha-Ha Lounge', 'The Laff Café' or 'The Rubber Chicken'. I know because I played almost every one of them, at least four times. Repackaging comedy as 'alternative' may have suddenly made it fashionable but the punters still had the same basic need and that was to have a good time at the weekend. I think all they really wanted was an 'alternative' to the pubs and clubs frequented by the generation before them.

On the whole, comedy clubs offered the perfect ingredients for a good night out. Drink, laughter, chat, food and a bit of dancing at the end of the evening, all under one roof and all for under a tenner. (When it's put like that it's no wonder they were such a goldmine.) They were also the ideal place for couples, especially if it was a first date. No worries about painful small talk, you just talked about the act you'd just watched.

The only downside was when a comedian decided to pick on a random couple as part of their act. Sometimes they'd grill them about their past relationship and sexual habits. Warning: if you're taking a date to a comedy show, don't be tempted to sit at the front. Your relationship may not survive the night.

Sex is a popular topic for a lot of comedians, along with drink and drugs. I never felt comfortable talking about sex, knowing there was a minuscule chance my mum might find out and batter me. I didn't drink so couldn't really talk about getting drunk. And I can't remember talking about drugs but then again I was smacked off my tits most of the time and can't remember half of what I said.*

A lot of comedians at the time were influenced by Bill Hicks and Denis Leary, who were both brutal and shockingly funny stand-ups. I could hear their style and rhythm echoed in a lot of comedians' delivery around that time. But as much as they made me laugh, that style just didn't work for me.

It did take me a while to settle down and find my voice. I think you struggle at first to find who you are. I wanted to be satirical and political but I never felt clever enough. Occasionally I could be topical but usually it'd be about the state of play on *Coronation Street*, as opposed to war-torn Rwanda or Iraq. Listening back to a lot of my early performances again, I'm surprised at just how much I used to swear. A lot of the time swearing was a safe way of successfully punctuating a gag. You could tell a joke and get a laugh, but tell the same joke and stick a 'fuck' in the punchline and it knocks it up a gear. You can hear the difference. Bernard Manning was a master of this. He could stick a 'fuck' in a knock-knock joke and

---

* That is clearly a joke. Though I do admit to having a puff of a joint once and then burning my arse trying to do the *Tales of the Unexpected* dance in front of a campfire.

make it hilarious. I also found swearing to be a great ally on those rough and rowdy Saturday nights. It could calm a room and get people's attention very quickly. But sometimes too much swearing can almost undermine itself, the benefits can become diluted. So over time I began to ration the swearing, realising the benefits a strategically placed swear word could bring. If you built up to it correctly, it could bring the fucking* house down.

Comedians like Billy Connolly, Dave Allen, Jasper Carrott and Mike Harding were huge influences on me. I loved their anecdotal style. They had the ability to paint a picture and make scenes come to life on stage. When Billy Connolly talks about going to a church dance at school, I can actually see the dance, the windows, the people in the room. He paints the whole picture; that's what I wanted to be able to do.

I also saw the benefits of aggression in comedy. Audiences love to hear a comedian getting angry about something, a car breaking down, a bad flight, a relationship breaking up. If it's told with enough passion and rage you can lift an audience off their seats.

One of my early routines was about my mum's inability to work a video recorder:

My mum can't work a video. It drives me mad because she can't tape things. I'll come home and find I've only got half an episode of ER and she'll say, 'I never touched it. It just stopped and started rewinding itself in the middle of the programme. One of your friends will have taped it.' Or sometimes she'll say, 'I'll cut the adverts out for you.' I say, 'No you won't, you'll pause it, then forget about it and miss the last half of the show.'

* See.

I realised my strength was in talking about my real life, things that happen every day. Going to work, using public transport, standing on a plug with nothing on your feet. I realised that comedy could be like a mirror and that audiences liked to see their own lives reflected. Talking about ordinary things and making the mundane funny came naturally to me and the audience seemed to lap it up. I had found my voice.

Mornings, I can never get up at 8.03 or 8.07, I've always got to round it up to 8.10. Why? What difference will it make if I get up on a stray minute? Then I lie there and start wondering how long it's been since I last had a sick day. Then before I know it the clock says 8.13, so now I've got to wait till quarter past. Oh, sod it, I'll wait for this song to finish.

I also liked to tell jokes. Pointless throw-away jokes just to warm the audience up and make them feel at ease. I like to call these 'ticklers'.*

What do you call a judge with no thumbs? Justice fingers!
What's black and white and eats like a horse? A zebra.
How do you kill a circus? Go for the juggler.

My peers would often frown upon me telling jokes. I can remember one comedian having a strong word with me about how it was wrong to do gags. 'But they laugh when I tell them,' I said. He had no response to that. Funny is funny – end of story. I had no time for snobbery or the comedy police. The audience had been working all week, they'd paid good money to come and

* As if.

watch a comedy show. As far as I was concerned it was my job to give them a good time.

As a result I started to get a reputation for being more of a mainstream comedian on the comedy circuit. But I never had a problem with that. As long as the audience were laughing and I was getting bookings I was more than happy. It just felt natural for me to travel in a more traditional direction. After all, I had spent my life studying great comedians like Morecambe and Wise, Tommy Cooper, Les Dawson and Jeremy Irons.*

As a child I'd travel to Blackpool each summer with my family to watch variety shows built around comedians like Cannon and Ball, Little and Large, Russ Abbot and Mike Yarwood. Those shows had a huge impact on me. When I compèred I always felt obliged to end the night with a song, it just gave the show closure. Nine out of ten times it would be '(Is This The Way To) Amarillo'. I knew the song from my childhood and thought the 'sha-la-la' bit would make for a good sing-along and it always did. I dug out the Tony Christie LP that my mum used to play and I actually wrote the words down on a piece of A4 and sellotaped it to the back. I didn't even have any backing, I just sang it 'Acapulco' (as Brian Potter would say). Obviously this was years before I had any notion of doing a Comic Relief video. I never imagined that ten years later I'd be ruining people's karaoke for ever.

I also enjoyed trying out different things with an audience. I once found a wig down the side of a seat in the cinema. A wig? I mean you'd know if you lost your hair, wouldn't you. It couldn't have belonged to one of the customers. I knew some kids would have probably stolen it from Dimples, the wig shop next door, while Greta the owner was using our toilet. Dimples was a tiny

* Just checking you were paying attention.

shop, situated in what used to be the kiosk section of the cinema during the war, hence having no toilet or sink. As goodwill, Mrs Hayworth let Greta use our amenities twice a day and fill up her empty bottle of Lilt in the ladies' bogs. But Greta was too trusting and wouldn't lock her door. That's when one of the thieving kids will have whipped the wig out of her shop. Anyway, possession is nine tenths of the law and now it was mine, all mine.

The audience giggled at the sight of me wearing it when I walked on stage but I never referred to it. Then the laughter subsided and crossed over into embarrassment. For all they knew it was my real hair. I wore the wig all night and then took it off at the end. Funny thing was at that point I don't think anybody noticed.

I also used to like dressing up as a lion. I had a costume left over from when I'd performed *The Wizard Of Oz* at school with the nuns (well the nuns weren't actually in it . . . oh, just read the first book, that'll explain everything, it's only £2.99 as it's just been Whoops! in Asda). I'd compère the first two halves of the show in my normal stage attire, then get changed into my lion costume during the interval.

I put full make-up on as well, whiskers, false nose, the lot. I also bought a pack of pretend cigarettes from a joke shop, that looked real and blew out talcum powder when you gave them a puff. I'd go back on dressed as a lion with a fag in my mouth, do a bit of material, introduce the next act and leave. Never referring to my costume once. Then I'd go straight back up to the dressing room and take the whole lot off as quick as I could, ready to go back on. It got laughs and I really enjoyed the surrealness of it all. Unfortunately Graham Norton didn't find it quite so amusing when he performed at the Frog & Bucket one night when I introduced him dressed as a lion and he made some sarcastic quip as I left the stage.

Not one to hold a grudge, the next night we got talking in the dressing room and he happened to ask me what the gay area in Manchester was called. This was a common occurrence with comedians travelling the circuit and we'd often ask each other the names of some of the local hot spots, the rough areas, posh areas and areas most popular for doggin'. So we could then weave them seamlessly into our material.

It's common knowledge that the gay area in Manchester is Canal Street, but when Graham Norton asked me that night I said something that I'm still not proud of, in fact I'd like to take this opportunity to publicly apologise. When Graham asked me the name of the gay area in Manchester I told him it was Bury. If you're not familiar with Bury, it's a small factory town about ten miles out of Manchester with a good bus terminus and an award-winning thrice-weekly market. Forty minutes later Graham was closing the show and, hushing the audience, he said, 'Well it's time for me to go now, ladies and gentlemen, I've got to get down to Bury.' (Suggestive wink.) Silence, then mutters of confusion and murmurs of 'Bury? Why the fuck is he going to Bury at ten to midnight?' Bewildered, Graham quickly left the stage. Shame on me.

I have to admit that was a rarity because usually the camaraderie between comedians was quite strong (well at least it was to your face anyway). I used to love it when other comedians watched out for each other, they'd tell each other the lay of the land so you'd stand a chance of knowing what you were dealing with. Sometimes they'd tag each other information as they passed on the stage: 'Lady in blue, stage left is a mouthy piss-head' or 'There's an arsehole at the bar throwing peanuts, it's gonna kick off.'

The other type of comic camaraderie was listening to each other's woes and fears in the dressing room. It'd be like a comic

Samaritans backstage at the Frog & Bucket. We'd be helping each other out all the time. Going through material, bucking each other up before we went on stage. Then slagging each other off as soon as we left the room. It was standard practice. 'Useless prick, he's about as funny as trapped wind.' They say your enemies come with smiles but I never realised they were referring to comedians until I started doing stand-up. And I used to think the women at Top Rank Bingo were two-faced . . .

And if a comedian died on stage they'd be straight back up to the dressing room with a chip on both shoulders, blaming everything but themselves. 'The audience is shit tonight', 'The sound's dreadful, that microphone's crap' or 'It's too hot for them to laugh'. You'd never hear them blaming their material. I remember one comedian coming back to the dressing room in tears after losing it with a heckler. A voice in the darkness shouted, 'Get off, you're shit' (as you're aware from the first chapter, one of the worst things you can say to a comedian). The comedian decided to calmly throw it back to the heckler: 'Why? What are you into?' There was a silent pause and the voice said, 'Your mother.' Another pause, then the comedian said, 'My mother's dead' to which the voice replied, 'I know.' The comedian left the stage in tears and was inconsolable by the time he reached the dressing room. I was so impressed with the heckle I used the scene in *Phoenix Nights*.

If only dressing room walls could talk. I used to enjoy congregating in the dressing room at the Frog & Bucket, putting the comedy world to rights. The toilet was permanently occupied and for some reason there was always a full-size coffin stood up in the corner of the room. Apparently it'd been left over from some amateur dramatics performance. But nobody ever mentioned it. In fact when it was eventually removed the comedians kicked off so much the manager had to get it back, as it was now considered a strange source of good luck.

Comedians have weird superstitions and rituals. From lucky shoes, to lucky foam microphone covers, to getting rat-arsed on a certain type of imported vodka before they go on. I knew one comedian who had to have a tuna fish sandwich on triangular-cut brown bread and two red plastic buckets in his dressing room before he went on stage or he wouldn't go on. Christ knows why. He never divulged his secret but I went round to his house once and we couldn't move for red plastic buckets, they were everywhere.

When I first started performing I developed a superstition for wearing a lucky black waistcoat. I eventually downscaled it to just a lucky belt after I saw a photo of myself and realised I looked like a fat Art Garfunkel. But I genuinely felt that I wouldn't be funny without it. And then one night when my belt snapped, I completely freaked – without me realising it, my belt had turned into Dumbo's feather. 'How can I go on without my belt? We've been through everything together, I've never done a gig without it.' I remember ringing my friend Paddy from a payphone in a right state. 'Calm down, son, it's just a fucking belt.' He was right and I just went out and bought another one from Debenhams the next day as there was a Blue Cross sale on.

Over the next few months I gigged every week and was thriving on the opportunity to learn. I saw this time as my apprenticeship. I was becoming more confident and was still recording my perform-ances, slowly building up a huge backlog of cassette tapes. I was also now keeping my crib sheets/set lists from each gig. One night I devised a clever method of colour-coding my material. I wrote down my set list as usual but then circled the different topics in a variety of colours. For example, holidays would be coloured in yellow felt-tip, working in a video shop in red, my mum and the video recorder green, and so on in a variety of colours. Then, and here's the clever bit, I colour-coded them in the same order on the back of my hand, so now I had six coloured stripes that corresponded with my set list. I thought this was revolutionary and nobody would even suspect that the small rainbow on the back of my hand was my encoded crib sheet. That night I confidently bounded on stage, stared down at my hand and thought, What the hell does red stand for? I couldn't remember what any of the colours meant. Suffice to say I never used that method again.

Another experience that taught me a lesson was the first time I played my hometown. A club called Sub Zero (used to be Sparrows) had started a comedy night on Thursdays, yes the trend was that popular it had finally reached Bolton, 'where the M61 is cobbled and the people still point at aeroplanes' as my old friend Dave Spikey used to say.

How could I refuse such an opportunity? Quite gladly in hindsight. As it turned out, I never even contemplated the situation. Nobody knew me when I played around Manchester but as I stood backstage in Bolton, my head peeping through a slash in the curtains, I began to see my whole life arrive. There were past pupils from school, mates from college that I hadn't seen in years, co-workers from almost every job I'd ever had, it was like an episode of *This Is Your Life* but without the big red book. I was overwhelmed by the gesture of support but absolutely terrified. This was going to be hard.

The place was packed to the rafters, I got a fantastic response when I came on stage and then it all went downhill, well it did as far as I was concerned. I started telling a story about the time I was in an armed raid when I worked at the Cash and Carry. Then I was heckled with the truth. 'No it didn't happen like

that and it didn't happen to you anyway, it was Kevin Broughton.'
I could have died. They were right. Who was I to argue? I certainly
couldn't as it was Kevin Broughton who heckled me. Panic ensuing,
I quickly moved on, I talked about school but it happened again.
'No, no, no, he didn't draw a dick on Jesus, it was the Pope,' came
a voice from the darkness. I shielded my eyes from the spotlight
to see who it was; thankfully it wasn't a nun but one of my old
school friends, well ex-friends. It was a nightmare. Hadn't they
ever heard of comedic licence? If comedians told the whole truth
and nothing but the truth they wouldn't be funny. Exaggeration
is the basis of all comedy. That's why comedians say things like
'You wouldn't believe what happened to me on the way here
tonight' and then lie. If they don't it's boring. They have got to
have bumped into a talking giraffe or an Englishman, an Irishman
and Scotsman at the very least.

I'd like to tell you the night got better but it didn't. I wearily
reached the end of my set, and to my complete surprise I got my
first standing ovation. I was absolutely ecstatic – it mustn't have
been as bad as I thought – but it did teach me an invaluable lesson.
Never lie, or at least not when you perform in your hometown.

Things were going great, the gigs were flooding in. And then I
broke my arm. It happened whilst I was ice-skating. I thought it
would be novel to take my girlfriend there on our second date.
After about four minutes I slipped on my arse, whilst my arm
was underneath it. Ouch! Well it was a disgrace, there was ice
everywhere. Somebody should have put some salt down.

I was devastated; things were going so well, I didn't want to
have time off work with a broken arm. I had a booking that
Saturday for a works Christmas party at a hotel in Cheshire. I

told the guy who'd booked me what had happened but it was too late to cancel. So with a pocket full of painkillers and my arm in plaster I headed to the train station to buy my Evening Ranger.

Sitting backstage at the Cresta Hotel in Sale I noticed I wasn't nervous. Mind you I'm not surprised, I was too high to be nervous, drugged up to my eyeballs on Dextropropoxyphene and Carbamazepine (try saying that when you're stoned). I remember I kept scratching and couldn't feel my back teeth. Oh and the DJ, how could I forget him. He sauntered over to me with a back perm.

'OK, I'll be introducing you in a few minutes . . . are you all right?'

'Champion,' I said, itching my leg.

'What should I say about you?'

'I don't know, just tell them my name?'

'What's your name?'

'Peter Kay.'

'Yeah, very funny, go on, what's your name?'

'Eh? It's Peter Kay,' I said, confused.

'Is it? OK, whatever you say . . . smartarse comedians,' he said, wandering off.

What was *his* problem? Ah, well, bollocks to him, I thought, flicking my back teeth with my fingers.

I couldn't believe the way he introduced me.

'Ladies and gentlemen, please welcome your comedian.'

After all that the arsehole never even said my name. Then as I staggered out onto the dance floor, I turned round in an attempt to give him the 'V's (with my good hand) and saw his name emblazoned across the front of his disco lights! It said 'Peter Kaye – Mobile Disco'. No wonder he'd been funny with me, we had the same name. Well almost, he was Kaye with an 'e' – mind you, the way I was behaving you would have thought I'd had one too. What are the odds of that? Same name? Completely flabbergasted, I tried to convey my astonishment to the audience of haulage contractors and their wives. But it just came out in a sort of high-pitched jumble of slurred words and laughter. They stared at me in silence. Then someone shouted, 'Go on!'

'Go on? Go on what?' I said, groping for a bit of balance on the DJ's lights.

'Do it!' shouted another voice from the opposite side of the Pennine Suite.

Do what? I hadn't a clue what they were on about.

'How does Bob Marley like his jammin'?' I said. 'With dough-nuts,' I slurred all cocky, then realised I'd messed it up '. . . with jammy doughnuts.'

It wasn't going very well. I knew I should have stopped at home with *Kavanagh QC*.

'Show us your trick!' This time it was a lady.

I was completely lost. 'Trick? What trick, love?' I slurred.

'With your arm for fuck's sake,' snapped her husband.

But there was no trick. It was a real broken arm, not a prop. I tried explaining it to them, about how I fell on the ice, but they were having none of it. They wanted the flags of all nations out the end of it or a bunch of pretty flowers. Next thing I knew 'Stop the Cavalry' was playing and Peter Kaye was calling me off the dance floor. 'Here, feel it,' I said, staggering round the room with my arm outstretched.

The next six weeks were a nightmare. Every gig I did I had to start by telling the audience not to get their hopes up, it was just a broken arm.

Chapter Three

Goodbye Crack-den, Hello Mini-bar

The first time I ever found myself in Edinburgh was when I was changing trains on my way back from a school trip to the Isle of Rhum. I was battered and bruised – a week traipsing through mud to and from a derelict youth hostel with no telly was not my idea of a holiday. As far as I was concerned the Duke of Edinburgh could stick his award scheme right up his (blank or blanks).*

That was the trip where I was forced to borrow an all-weather coat off my dad's mate at the last minute. I'll never forget the shock I got when I discovered it was luminous orange and had 'Motorway Maintenance' inscribed on the back of it.

We had an hour between trains, so I followed the rest of the group past a long ramp of waiting taxis and up on to Waverley

---

* I used to love *Blankety Blank* – well I did until they put Geoff Capes in the comedy box, bottom row, centre. How dare they? That used to be Kenny Everett's box for Christ's sake, sacrilege.

Bridge. The view of the city at night was breathtaking. I sat down on a bench, reclining as best I could with a five-foot rucksack strapped to my back. I had never seen anything so beautiful in my life. The castle and city all lit up, I could have sat there for ever, admiring the skyline and eating Toffos.

It was 1987.

Ten years later I was on my way back. The memory of that moment had stayed with me ever since. I thought about it a lot and had built Edinburgh up to be my utopian dream of paradise. It was a stunning August day, with the kind of blue cloudless sky you could dive into. I sat reading the Preston evening paper as my train gently weaved its way through the green, lush valleys of the Lake District. With the afternoon sunlight streaming through the discoloured Virgin windows I read the sad news that Frank Sinatra had died.* My nana was upset, I'd rung her as soon as I found out, from an overheated payphone on Preston train station. She's always been a huge Frank Sinatra fan and used to have all his original albums and singles, I say 'used to' because eventually she gave them to Oxfam because they were 'cluttering' the place up.

'Well I've got them all on tape,' she said when I found out.

'You've got to get them back, Nan, they'll be worth a fortune.'

We went down to Oxfam the next day but they'd gone. I've managed to download most of them for her now and am in the process of transferring them to cassette, because the chances of her mastering an iPod at eighty-seven years of age are roughly nil. I'm talking about a woman who has had Sky+ for two years and only just realised you can record. When I told her she could

* Quite enjoyed that little bit of descriptive prose. Perhaps I could be a proper writer one day.

pause it if she wanted to make a brew she looked at me like I was mad.

'Pause it . . . but what about everybody else who's watching?'

'You don't control Britain, Nan, you just control your own TV.'

I had to laugh, I had a vision of a couple in Crawley sat tapping their fingers in the middle of *Holby City* while my nan toasts a crumpet two hundred and fifty miles away.

I was on my way to Edinburgh to compete in a couple of comedy competitions. I'd managed to make it through to the finals of both the BBC New Comedy Awards and Channel 4's 'So You Think You're Funny?' competition.

Heats had taken place across Britain for both competitions during the months prior to the Edinburgh Festival. I'd had both of mine in Manchester and they weren't easy, as each comedian was only given six minutes to perform. I found it very difficult trying to squeeze a variety of material into such a small amount of time. You were also penalised by the judges if you went over, something I wasn't used to as I'd never had to do an open spot in the past and usually had twenty or thirty minutes to fill. You wanted to show your versatility as a stand-up comedian, talk about something topical, throw in a bit of nostalgia, perhaps a joke or an observation, maybe even end on a bit of music. All that in six minutes was a tall order but I had to do it twice, with a different set for each competition. I slaved away at my material, honing it at every possible opportunity in the weeks leading up to the heats.

The BBC heat was held at the Frog & Bucket and, with family and friends offering their support, the place was soon packed out. I'm sure Dave Perkin the manager did his usual trick of turning up the heating, because the place was absolutely boiling. Ten local comedians had a chance to shine that night, some I knew well, and some I didn't. Without a doubt one of the best on the night was a comedian from Liverpool called Neil Anthony.* It was the first time I'd seen him perform and I thought he was a brilliant stand-up comedian, he had a very polished set, concise, sharp and very funny. He was also great at doing voices too. Reluctantly I laughed a lot as the knot in my stomach grew tighter. And I recalled the familiar pain of entering a competition. It's hard to be objective and I'd be a liar if I told you that somebody else doing well when you're in a competitive frame of mind doesn't hurt; it does. Don't get me wrong, it's not that you want them to fail or that you don't find them funny. It's just that you have this irrational fear that each laugh they get is one less for you. Like they're using them all up and the audience will be all laughed out by the time you get on.

I eventually got to perform my shortened set and, even though my material went down a storm with the audience, Neil was victorious on the night. Unbeknownst to me, Dave Perkin was allowed the final vote on a second act, a comedy wild card or something, and fair play to him, he chose me, so although I didn't win I was officially in the final and so off to Edinburgh.

Two weeks later I had to go through the same rigmarole all over again for the regional heats for Channel 4's 'So You Think You're Funny?' competition. These took place across town at The Buzz Club. Unlike the Frog & Bucket, The Buzz Club wasn't an independent comedy club but it was Manchester's longest-running comedy night. Held every Thursday in a cabaret room above the

---

* Neil later dropped his name of Anthony and reverted to his real name of Fitzmaurice. He also went on to co-write several series with me including *That Peter Kay Thing* and *Phoenix Nights* where he played the part of the Romany DJ Ray Von.

Southern pub in Chorlton-Cum-Hardy, its sequinned stage had played host to almost every British stand-up comedian of the last twenty years. Lee Evans, Jack Dee, Eddie Izzard, Frank Skinner had all been introduced by Agraman (– The Human Anagram) at one time or another. I had a lot of affection for The Buzz Club, having done one of my very first stand-up performances there for the heats of the North West Comedian of the Year competition. Agraman (– The Human Anagram) was legendary throughout the comedy circuit for his deliberately bad jokes and poems that he insisted on performing. He actually seemed to enjoy dying a death before introducing each act. Then after the act was finished he would escort them to a smaller room behind the bar where he'd pay them. He'd pull open a large black briefcase that was always empty apart from a roll of twenty-pound notes and a single packet of Polo mints. Why Polos, I'll never know. He always used to say the same thing every time he paid me: 'Great show tonight,' he'd say, counting out my money. 'Here you go, I wish I could give you more,' then offered me a Polo.

I always wanted to say, 'Well if you want to give me some more money feel free, don't let me stop you' but I never did. I just thanked him and took the Polo. I later discovered that he did exactly the same with every stand-up: 'I wish I could give you more money' and then offered them a Polo. And I thought I was special. Ah well, maybe the Polos were there to cushion the blow.

Myself and several other local stand-ups performed our specially edited sets for the 'So You Think You're Funny?' panel; well I say 'panel', it was a seventeen-year-old researcher called Haley with a camcorder. It was her job to record the night and take it back down to London for judging. So nobody was victorious on the night. We were just told to sit tight and we'd receive word in time.

Four months later and two days before I left for Edinburgh I received word: I was through to the finals of that competition too.

I was slightly anxious on the train, what if my utopian ideal of Edinburgh wasn't the same? What if I'm crap in the competition? And what if somebody spikes my drink with Rohypnol and tries to rape me up a back alley? The last one was one of my mum's irrational fears about my trip to Edinburgh, but as long as I gave her three rings every two hours she'd be happy. I'd heard so much about the Edinburgh Festival, I'd seen the programmes every year on BBC2. It seemed like such an amazing thing to be part of. I was fast approaching Edinburgh station for the second time and I couldn't wait.

Walking up the ramp past the taxis again and out into the sunlight, the view was as breathtaking as I remembered. I asked directions to the old town and headed across Waverley Bridge. Although I wouldn't have thought it possible, Edinburgh looked even more beautiful in the daylight. I headed on to the Royal Mile, I'd never seen so many people, the place was packed and the atmosphere was fantastic, you could feel it straight away. People shouting, 'Come and see *my* show', performing in the streets, singers, break-dancers, fire-eaters, the whole city seemed to be alive, vibrating to a beat. It felt so good to be there. Then I turned the corner and saw a Greggs sign. It was too much for me to take in. I got to enjoy all this *and* have a Steak Bake? I'd not experienced this level of decadence since I'd urinated on a Spanish man riding a moped from the top floor of my hotel in 1989. I officially felt carefree.

I'd arranged to meet a good friend of mine called Smug Roberts in Edinburgh. He was a bit of a legend around the Manchester comedy circuit (in fact he still is) and he'd taken me under his wing ever since he'd started wearing this huge bird costume. Sorry, that was dreadful. He'd shown me the ropes and helped me out with advice on bookings etc and was at the festival performing stand-up. He was sat outside a comedy club called the Stand as I approached him covered in flaky pastry. We hugged. He invited me downstairs as there was a gig on. I couldn't believe it: stand-up? It was five o'clock in the evening! Comedy and daylight simply don't mix. Comedians are like vampires. But there I was sat watching comedy at teatime. I was falling in love with this place.

Smug told me all about the festival and that basically there were three main areas for comedy: the Assembly Rooms over in the new town (well new-ish, considering it was built in 1802. Well, I think it was 1802, my headphones were broken on the open-top bus tour and so everything I heard was in Japanese), the Gilded Balloon where I would be performing the Channel 4 competition, and the Pleasance where the BBC ruled the roost and I had to meet my contact and pick up my accommodation keys. Good old Auntie Beeb had seen fit to throw in some digs during my week at the festival. What would she have picked for me? Perhaps a stunning apartment overlooking Edinburgh Castle? Maybe a suite at the Balmoral, the finest hotel in the city, apparently Sean Connery won't stop anywhere else? Or possibly a decrepit basement flat, adjacent to a crack-den on the outskirts of Leith? Right third time, well what did I expect for free?

Trust the BBC to piss on my rainbow. To add insult to injury (and the eighteen quid taxi fare to get there. I've still got the receipt – if the producer in question is reading this, I did leave numerous voice messages that you plainly ignored), when I eventually arrived on the set of *Trainspotting*, the bloody key wouldn't fit the lock.

So I had to sit on a damp step for three hours developing haemorrhoids and flat batteries in my Walkman. It was half twelve before somebody arrived back with a key. By that time I was praying for some Rohypnol and a back alley, just to alleviate the boredom.

Thankfully my flatmates were two lovely and naturally funny comedians who were also in the final, Gareth Hughes and Justin Lee Collins (yes, the very same). They agreed that the place was a shithole, but they'd attempted to make it homely in the short time they'd been there. It's amazing what you can do with a few fire-lighters and the foam from an extinguisher. I had a well-deserved cup of tea and we sat putting the comedy world to rights until the sun came up.

With only the two finals to perform in I had a wonderful week soaking up the sights and scenes of the festival. There was so much to choose from, with shows at every hour of the day. I was knocked out by the bravery of some of these performers. Some of the after-noon shows had only four people in the audience. How could they go on and perform? While I was there I went to see a favourite comedian of mine: an Irish stand-up called Tommy Tiernan. He was very funny (still is) but unfortunately he's not very widely known in Britain. If you ever get the chance to see him or come across his DVDs I highly recommend him.

I also went to see a very lovely and naturally funny comedienne called Jo Enright, who was performing her own show at the festival. Stand-up comedy has always been a business dominated by blokes. I can honestly say that I've not really worked with or seen that many female stand-ups. There are very few on the circuit. Jo Enright in my opinion was, and is, certainly one of the best. The first time I met her backstage at the Frog & Bucket, she was so petite and gentle that I have to admit I was concerned for her – they could be a vicious crowd on a Saturday night – but I couldn't have been more wrong. She came on stage and, in her soft Birmingham accent, she succeeded in quietening the whole room. I'd never seen that done before. Normally comedians would charge on shouting and swearing at an audience in an effort to get their attention but Jo didn't have to raise her voice once. I've always held the belief that comedians can recognise the spark of true genius in each other. I saw it in Jo Enright instantly. Taking her time, she didn't waste a single line of her material, and even though I saw her act many times it never failed to make me laugh. Just by watching her perform I knew she had the makings of a fine comic actress and consequently I was chuffed to be able to cast her in almost everything I've ever made for television, including *Phoenix Nights*, where she did an incredible portrayal of Brian Potter's girlfriend, and most recently in *Britain's Got the Pop Factor*, where she played one quarter of Two Up, Two Down.

While at the festival I met up with quite a few of the local comedians from Manchester who were at the festival performing on a bill with other stand-ups. They had to do twenty minutes every day for the whole festival, a total of twenty-three consecutive shows. Twenty minutes a day wasn't difficult to do but I didn't envy the monotony of being tied to a daily show. The idea of performing for that number of nights didn't appeal. Appearing in the two finals was more than enough for me.

Before I knew it, it was Friday night and the final of the BBC New Comedy Awards. Myself and the other contestants gathered in the Pleasance courtyard. The show was to be filmed and we had to do a camera rehearsal. It was all very exciting and then suddenly the realisation began to hit me hard. I couldn't believe where I was and what I was about to do. It had all happened so fast. The previous year I had been at college in Salford, doing an HND in Media Performance, studying stand-up comedy as part of my curriculum, and now I was about to perform stand-up on television. It was too much to take in and I honestly didn't know if I could go through with it. I had to go to the toilet, and quick.

My girlfriend Susan had come to support me on the night with some family and friends, and peeping through the curtain I was so grateful to see them all. It was getting near to show time and the audience were taking their seats. The sound of their chattering echoed around the walls of the Pleasance theatre, which resembled more of a church with its high beamed ceilings and raked wooden seating.

The compère on the night was the comedian Ardal O'Hanlon, famous at the time for his appearance in *Father Ted* and for hosting *The Stand-up Show* on BBC1. He was a quiet, unassuming man who made all the contestants feel at ease as we nervously hung around the backstage area, chewing our nails and pumping.

The lights eventually went down and the magic began. After the magician had finished, the competition started. Neil Anthony was on second, he did a similar routine to one he'd done at the Frog & Bucket, but sadly one of his strongest jokes where the punchline involved a rapper from St Helens didn't transfer well to Scotland. It taught me a lesson about using parochial references in material. Neil went down very well but he wasn't pleased with the performance he gave and like almost all stand-up comedians he was little bit too hard on himself afterwards.

I'd like to tell you about the performances my flatmates, Justin and Gareth, gave but I can't honestly remember and my mum taped over the only recording that I had of the show with an episode of *Peak Practice*. Bless her.

I was on fourth and thankfully Dictaphoned my performance for posterity. I decided to hit them with my best stuff first so I opened with a tried and tested routine:

Why do mums buy crap pop? Why do they? She comes back from the supermarket every Friday with crap pop, Rola Cola or Top Star Cola, something like that. Seven litres of shit for 40p. She doesn't care as long as it's coloured and fizzy.

'I'm not drinking that, it tastes like floor cleaner.'

'Get it drunk,' she says.

'Look, it won't go in the fridge, it's too big, not only is it crap but it's warm.'

'Get it drunk, there's children starving.'

'They wouldn't drink it. It's warm crap pop.'

She threw the bottle at me, knocked me out. I woke up on a drip filled with Rola Cola.

I was getting laughs, good ones, big ones, it was going well but I hadn't got the time to analyse. I moved on to old people, always a winner:

Is it hot in here or is it me? Old people always say that: 'Is it hot in here or is it me?' Of course it's you, unless you're some kind of ventriloquist. They hate hot weather, old people. They're always moaning about it. 'Oh it's hot, oh it's too hot for me. I like it warm but I don't like it this warm. It's sticky weather, it's clammy, I can't get me breath.' Good! It's called summer, have a Solero and shut the fuck up.

I dropped the 'eff' out on the night. Swearing? On my first ever television appearance? My mum wouldn't have been able to hold her head high at her sewing class for months on the strength of that stray 'fuck'.

Ever the traditionalist, I chose to end my short set on a piece of music, Soft Cell's 'Say Hello, Wave Goodbye'. I said that when Marc Almond formed the band he didn't have much money so he got his dad to play keyboards. Then I basically mimed a bloke nervously playing two notes on the keyboards every time he gets the nod. Obviously it doesn't work in a book but if you want to see it, I sell copies of my DVDs most Sundays on various car boot sales around Lancashire. I also do Mach 3 razor blades and four litres of bleach.

The judges on the night were Rhona Cameron, Barry Cryer (who also had the cheek to sit in Kenny's box on *Blankety Blank*) and my dear friend-Graham Norton (who'd just got back from a midnight session in Bury). Their winner on the night was a comedian called Paul Foot. I'd like to say I agreed with the judge's decision but of course I couldn't. None of us could.

Competing has never been one of my strengths; no matter what it was, from five-a-side football to Connect Four, I am a sore loser. Mind you, show me the person who accepts defeat graciously and I'll show my arse in the Vatican.

But never down for long, I was back on form and back in competition mode the following night. I felt good about this one. No cameras to intimidate me this time, just good old-fashioned stand-up. I made my way to the Gilded Balloon for the final of 'So You Think You're Funny?' and, as it was Saturday night, I certainly did.

As the generous people in charge from Channel 4 wouldn't

allow me to have a guest, it looked as though Susan wouldn't be able to watch me in the final. Luckily I bumped into comedian Bob Mortimer in the gents' who had seen me performing in the BBC final the night before. 'You were robbed,' he said out of the blue as we both urinated. Glancing down at my penis, I replied, 'Was I?' He laughed (though we didn't shake hands) and over by the hand dryer I happened to mention that I couldn't get my girlfriend into the final. Thankfully for us, he pulled a few strings (well he was a judge) and managed to smuggle Susan in under his donkey jacket.

My overriding memory of the night is of being shoved into a poky little holding room with the other finalists. Strictly no eye contact and polite smiles was the backstage etiquette that night. It was torturous. Ten strangers united in fear. You could have cut the atmosphere with a special atmosphere cutter. All of us were incredibly nervous and you could smell it. I literally had to smash a window with the leg of a chair during the interval just so I could breathe.

Julian Clary was the compère; he did a few opening innuendos about bumming and then flippantly he introduced the first act. We'd drawn straws for the running order (I used one of those novelty curly straws so it gave me a big advantage) and luckily for me I was on last. Unluckily though it meant I had to be cooped up in this box of farts all night. The finalists pacing around, mumbling their acts to themselves, I didn't think I could take much more.

By the time my spot came round my head was wedged so far through the window I couldn't hear them calling my name. To say my performance went well would be putting it mildly. Maybe it was the final relief from boredom that did it, who knows? But

I was on fire that night. I ditched most of the material I'd rehearsed and instead talked about my week in Edinburgh. I decided to kick off with my train journey up and an old favourite:

I was on Preston train station and this announcement came over the tannoy. 'Warning for passengers on platform number five: the next train is an express to Carlisle. We advise passengers to move away from the yellow line at the edge of the platform as they may get sucked off.' I was hanging off the end of the plat-form shouting, 'Bring the train on, I'm ready.' [Thrusting my groin forward towards the front of the stage.]

Jokes aren't funny, you say? That one cleaned up. I swear I saw Julian Clary writing it down in the wings. I talked about the joy of arriving back in Scotland after the previous experience I had on the school trip to the Isle of Rhum and my luminous Motorway Maintenance coat. Deciding to change my material at the last minute was a great decision, it was going down a storm.

So I arrived at the festival and, joy of joys, what was the first thing I saw? Greggs. I felt at home already. I paid the lady with a twenty-pound note but as she was putting it into the till, she turned to the other woman serving and shouted, 'Twenty pound going in, Jean.' I said, 'Hey, mouth, what's all that about? There were two drug dealers eyeing me up for me change, love.' They're thinking, He's got seventeen pound change, this lad. I'm going to be lying on the main street in a minute covered in flaky pastry.

I ended by telling them about the BBC's accommodation in the crack-den outside Leith and then a red light came on to tell me my time was up and I was off. That was it, it all went by in a flash. The place erupted with cheers and I triumphantly returned to the room of farts. I'll never forget that smell as long as I live.

I think there was a musical act while the judges deliberated and then finally Julian Clary made the announcement we'd all been waiting for: '. . . and the winner is . . .' It was me! I walked back out on to the stage in shock. Deafened by the applause, I took hold of the mic and said, 'Thank you.' Somebody from Channel 4 handed me one of those giant cheques that you see on *Children In Need* for £1,500. I'd forgotten all about the prize money; this time last week I didn't even know I was in the final. I dedicated my perform-ance to my girlfriend Susan who was somewhere in the audience, possibly still under Bob Mortimer's donkey jacket, and I made an announcement of my own: 'I passed my driving test last year and ever since I've begged almost everyone I know with a car for lifts to gigs. So now I'm going to use this money to finally buy myself a car.'

Ten minutes later I was on a payphone to my Mum, holding the receiver away from my ear as she screamed her congratulations down the phone at me.

'I'm so proud,' she said. 'What are you going to do now?'

'I don't know, I think there's a party,' I said.

'Well be careful and keep your hand over your drink.'

There was a party downstairs in the Gilded Balloon but Susan and myself decided to bow out gracefully after a couple of drinks as the sight of Eddie Izzard gyrating across the dance floor in combats was too much for any man to take. We strolled down towards Grassmarket, my favourite part of Edinburgh. It sits directly beneath the castle and so did we, eating crepes from a van. It was two o'clock in the morning and the place was still full of life. What a fantastic night. Ah well, back to the shit digs.

I was woken the next morning by the payphone ringing in the hall. It was a producer from the BBC (unfortunately they weren't ringing for my taxi receipts) asking me if I'd like to perform on *Edinburgh Nights*; she said all I'd have to do was four minutes' stand-up. I'd get £300 and they could move my accommodation to the Balmoral. And if I hadn't just stood on an upturned plug as I ran for the phone, I would have sworn I was still dreaming.

I must have woken up everyone in the surrounding flats singing 'Things Can Only Get Better' by D:Ream at the top of my voice. I was now up £1,800, my second appearance doing stand-up on television in less than a week and a room in Sean Connery's favourite hotel. Goodbye crack-den, hello mini-bar. I will say at this point that I did do the decent thing and invited my flatmates, their girlfriends and anyone else we knew to join Susan and myself at the Balmoral for afternoon tea, courtesy of Auntie Beeb of course. Well why not? I'd paid enough of my mum's licence fee.

First things first (I love that saying), I called Mrs Hayworth to beg her for an extra day off from the cinema. God love her, she obliged and was just made up I had won the competition. 'Make sure you mention us on the telly,' she shouted as the pips went. There's a whole generation probably reading this right now wondering what the hell 'pips' are.

The Balmoral was amazing, I'd never stayed anywhere like that in my life before. I wasted a full roll of film just taking photographs of the room. Mints on the pillows, hairdryer in a drawer, trouser press, we even had an en suite with a Jacuzzi bath, and toilet paper with the ends folded over into a triangle! I'd made it now! It was a step up from the B&Bs in Blackpool that I was used to, where you could have a shower, a shave and a shit all at the same time, the en suite was that small. This en suite was as big as my front room at home.

I ran three baths and pulled the plug out each time I was that giddy.* I'd have to have the immersion heater on for a fortnight back home in order to do that.

A car came to pick us up and take us to the Usher Hall where I was performing that night in front of two thousand people. Wow! And to think the week before I'd been lying in bed watching *Edinburgh Nights*, wondering what the festival would be like.

Once again I ended my set with the Soft Cell routine (always a sucker for a bit of music). Leaving the stage to the sound of two thousand people applauding was the perfect end to a perfect week. But less than twenty-four hours later I was back to reality with a bump, compèring at the Frog & Bucket in front of an audience of six – four people with special needs and their care workers. And they all left in the interval having come on the wrong night. Ah well, that's showbiz.

* Of course I stole the toiletries.

Chapter Four

Show-business as Usual

Having worked part-time in a garage for five years, you'd think I'd know 1 thing or two about cars but I knew absolutely nothing. Anyway it wasn't like I was a mechanic or anything, I was just a humble cashier. It was my job to dish out the Tiger Tokens and tell gypsies it was illegal to fill up watering cans with Four Star.

Steve, who'd worked with me at the garage, agreed to scout round for a car with me. Having just returned from Edinburgh victorious, my giant cheque from Channel 4 was burning a hole in my pocket. I felt like one of The Borrowers when I went to cash it at the bank. Now suddenly I was a real man, buying copies of *AutoMart* from the newsagent and talking about engine sizes, when really all I wanted to know was if the cassette player worked.

Steve and I must have covered the whole of the North West that Sunday and we were almost suicidal. Not because we couldn't find a car but because Princess Diana had died the night before and all the radio kept playing was 'Everybody Hurts' – REM, 'She's Gone' – Hall & Oates and 'If You Leave Me Now' – Chicago, in rotation. It was bleak. One used-car salesman was even wearing a black armband out of respect.

I'll never forget where I was when I found out she'd died. I'd been working at the Frog & Bucket the night before and completely avoiding The Complete Takeaway on the walk back; I arrived home to find a note from my mum stuck on the front of the microwave: 'Princess Diana's been killed in a car crash and there's shepherd's pie in the fridge.'

Two months later, after kicking more tyres than I care to remember, I finally settled on a red Ford Fiesta, 1.5 Diesel, five doors with a sunroof and a cassette player that worked. However, the petrol gauge didn't, and so halfway home from Oldham I ran out of fuel. Ironically all I had in the boot was a watering can.

I hadn't driven for eighteen months so I was very rusty. My knuckles were blue clinging to the steering wheel and I forgot to breathe for the first few miles and almost blacked out on a round-about. Traumatised, I decided to save the motorway for another day and drove home on the A roads instead; it took me two hours. I contemplated getting a few refresher lessons from one of my instructors – after all I did have five to choose from, well four, one of them had died in the time it had taken me to pass. Anyway when I did call they were all mysteriously busy.

If you're reading this and you're a driver, try and remember that feeling of exhilaration when you bought your first car. Well that's exactly how it felt for me but times a hundred. Finally getting a car was a huge thing for me. No more buses, no more Evening Rangers and no more blagging my driver friends for a lift. Now I was officially a driver I could look forward to spending the rest of my life gaining weight and fighting for the closest parking space to the gym.

Mind you, after saying all that, when the time did come for me to drive to a gig I bottled it. Drive all the way to Harrogate and back? I was just about able to make it to the Red Lion on the outskirts of Bolton where I sat with my mate Warren contemplating what to do. Drive all the way to Harrogate in the dark or have a mixed grill? Decisions, decisions.

Fortunately the Red Lion in Bolton is situated on the side of the M61. So the sound of motorway traffic came in very handy when I went out into the car park and with Warren's mobile phoned the manager of Chuckles in Harrogate to tell her I'd broken down near Bradford and was waiting for the AA to come and tow me home.

'Get them to tow you here,' she said.

'To Harrogate? I can't do that,' I said, waving the noise of the motorway towards the phone with my cupped hand, 'I'm an hour from home.'

'That means you're an hour from Harrogate, so get them to tow you here.'

I'd heard she was a mentalist but this was ridiculous. She used to make comedians travel separately to Chuckles just in case they had a car crash and she was forced to cancel the show.

Comedians would often ring each other if they knew they had a gig together in order to share the journey and split the petrol, but this psycho had it written into the contract that it was forbidden for them to even travel together. But of course comedians would do it anyway. They'd just park down the road from Chuckles and walk the rest of the way, arriving separately.

I know I was booked to play her club but surely she could see sense. I'd never cancelled a gig in my life but I wasn't confident enough to drive to Harrogate and, besides, Warren was tapping on the window, telling me my fried egg was congealing. I told her how sorry I was again but she just completely lost it and said she would 'personally see to it that I never perform in Harrogate again'. Anyway, I ended up playing it a few years later and was tempted to knock on the front door of Chuckles and say 'TA DA! Guess who's just played Harrogate!' but I didn't. I wasn't in the mood. I'd been hosting a staff pancake race for Tesco (don't ask) and was feeling a bit sorry for myself.

My mixed grill was stone-cold when I got back, I knew I should have paged her. Paged her! Jesus, do you remember pagers? What was all that about? I had a navy one and it was like a house brick. I got it out of my mum's catalogue, 20p a week for three hundred weeks. Everyone had a mobile by the time I'd paid for it.

I used to page people all the time. When you think about it, it was just a primitive and expensive way to text. 56p it used to cost me to ring up an operator, give her a message, then she'd forward it on in the form of a text and your mate would get your message on his pager and ring you. Christ it was quicker to get a bus round to his house. It all sounds so archaic now.

Hey I've still got my pager upstairs in my drawer, I'm going to get it out later and send someone a message. I wonder if there's anybody still answering? I can imagine some old woman sat on her own, phones all around her covered in cobwebs: 'Hello, you'd like to page someone?'

I'll tell you something I've never told anybody. I used to shove my pager down the front of my pants when I was doing stand-up and set the alarm to vibrate, so it would let me know when I'd done my time. Twenty minutes, no bother. Except with all the adrenalin and excitement I'd completely forget it was down there and twenty minutes into my set I'd think I was having a stroke or something. I couldn't switch it off, so I'd discreetly try to knock it on to snooze with my penis. Now you know why I've never told anybody.

Any apprehensions I may have had about driving long distances soon disappeared as I found myself driving all the time. I quickly realised that stand-up comedy is basically 20% performing, and 80% travelling. Looking back I really don't know how I survived for so long gigging without a car. Now I was on the road all the time, it could be a gruelling and lonely existence; that's why I always took a friend with me. Having company always made the journey more bearable, it also meant I had somebody to change CDs on the portable player I had wired through the cigarette lighter. (It saved me having to weave all over the road trying to do it myself in the dark.)

Just like a having a pager I find it mad when I think back to when I used to have cassettes everywhere too. I'd turn a corner and they'd fly all the over the place. Yes, gone are the days of hurtling down the fast lane trying to reach for a TDK D-90 stuck under the driver's seat or having the remains of shattered CD boxes jammed into the side of my door. Now I have an iPod as big as a cassette box hidden in my glove compartment,* with all the music I could ever want at the touch of a button and you know what: I still can't find anything decent to listen to.

Having a friend also meant they could test me on my set on the way to the gig, running through my material with me, editing and adding bits. They'd also have to suffer my post-gig adrenalin-rush

---

* Smack-heads, please note: I remove said iPod from my car every time I leave my vehicle and there's fuck-all in the centre console, apart from a few Euros on a good day and perhaps a couple of Werther's.

during the drive home. Listening to me jabbering on incessantly as I came down from my performance.

One of the other drawbacks of the adrenalin is hunger; that's why you'll always find stand-up comedians in motorway services in the middle of the night. It's still hard to resist the temptation, the lure of that blue sign with a knife and fork on it. The excitement of calling at motorway services was instilled in me as a child. Travelling on coach trips with my family to Butlins each year, we'd always call in to services, the driver warning us over his mic that 'this is a toilet stop and leg stretch so don't go getting a meal'. But there would always be a rebellious couple that'd do just that. The other passengers couldn't wait to grass them up to the driver when he attempted his routine head count. 'We saw them, they were queuing with a tray,' came an anonymous voice from the back. We'd all wait impatiently for the condemned couple to return, the driver over-revving his engine every few seconds in disgust. The couple would eventually get back on board acting all innocent, wiping their mouths as if nothing had happened. And nobody said a thing, it was all very British. Maybe the driver would mumble or cough the words 'leg stretch' into the mic as we drove off but that was as far as it went.

We always got off and had a browse but my dad would always tell us that we wouldn't be getting anything. It's common knowledge that motorway services are ludicrously expensive. And besides, my mum had been up since half six making sandwiches and putting a flask up for the journey. I'd already had four Blue Ribands, three whist pies (two turtle doves . . .) but my dad would always succumb to our pleas and I'd get a *Beano* Holiday Special, my sister would get *Smash Hits* and we'd all share a tin of boiled sweets covered in what I can only imagine was cocaine, with a picture of the Queen on the lid.

After all those years of excitement how could I possibly drive past any services again? My usual post-gig order would consist of a cold Ginsters pasty, some Dairylea Dippers and a king-size Twix (sharing a finger with a friend). I never got a meal, except for once.* On the way back from Birmingham I threw caution to the wind and, filled with bravado, I marched straight up to the 'Granary' and, lo and behold, found the shutters down. I was informed by a lethargic cleaner with an unfathomable Brummie/ Jamaican accent that if I 'wonted furred ad 'ave turgo o'er to da udderside,' she said pointing east. Still full of bravado, I marched over the bridge to the Granary where I bought myself a steak and kidney pie, chips and beans. Manna from heaven. I took a seat, licked my lips and then I shook a full sachet of sugar all over it. What a tit. Without any bravado whatsoever I walked back over to the Granary, with pleading eyes like the cat from *Shrek 2*, and told the lady serving all about the 'easy' mistake I'd just made.

'You did wha?' she said in between chews.

'I poured a sachet of sugar on my food.'

'Why did you do that?'

'I thought it was salt.'

'Oh,' she said laughing. I lingered for a few seconds in hope but she just stared at me. It was checkmate. Crushed, I walked back over to my meal and attempted to pick the sugar grains out of my food with a fork.

The first time I played darn sarth was at a club called the Comedy Box in Bristol. I was booked for three nights and asked my mate

* Occasionally when I did interviews and they asked me what my ambition was I used to say 'to afford a meal at motorway services'.

Paddy if he fancied coming with me. We booked into a B&B down the road from the club and it was a dump. En suites were just a dream in this place, it had a communal bathroom. Gross. I remember Paddy had brought a towel from home and some gear for showering and he took it into the communal bathroom to get ready before the show. He nipped back to our room for his razor and when he got back the door was locked. Whoever it was, was in there ages. Spying from our room we watched as the door finally opened and a comedian from Liverpool called Billy Flynn came out with Paddy's towel wrapped round his crotch. Paddy was furious 'the dirty Scouse bastard used me towel'. On further investigation we discovered he'd not only used Paddy's towel but also his shampoo, shower gel and he'd even had a roll of his deodorant. He must have assumed they were compliments of the B&B. Not bad for £15 a night.

I met up with a comedian called Gareth Hughes, he was in the BBC New Comedy Awards final and we'd been flatmates in the crack-den. He was resident compère at the Comedy Box and introduced me that night. I was nervous playing darn sarth for the first time and self-conscious that they might not understand my material or me for that matter. So in my insecurity I tried to soften my accent a little. The set went well but I thought it could have gone better.

Gareth noticed what I'd done and said, 'Why was your accent different when you were on stage?' I admitted that I'd toned it down slightly because I thought they might not understand me. Gareth said that I should just be myself and that my accent was one of my best allies. The next night I went on, and don't get me wrong I wasn't all 'ee by eck, tha knows', I was just myself and Gareth was right. I've never been self-conscious of my accent again as I realised it was part of who I am and that it's also one of my comedic strengths.

They don't do peas darn sarth, why is that? I went into a chippie last night and said, 'Chips and peas please.'

The bloke behind the counter said, 'We don't do peas.' [Best Bristol accent.]

I said, 'You what?'

He said, 'We don't do peas.'

My mate was outside, I shouted through the glass, 'They don't do peas', well I didn't shout I did that talking-through-glass-voice, I just exaggerated everything I said and kept opening my mouth really widely every time I spoke. 'They don't do peas,' I said.

'Do you do curry sauce?'

'No we don't do curry sauce.'

I said to my friend, 'They don't do curry sauce.' [Mouthing the words again.]

'Do you do gravy?'

'No we don't do gravy.'

I said to my friend, 'They don't do gravy.' [Mouthing the words again.]

My friend came in, he said to the man behind the counter, 'Has tha nowt moist?'

While I was on stage Paddy would stand at the back and occasionally he'd hear the other comedians slagging me off. This happened one night at the Comedy Box but to make matters worse it was Billy Flynn who was doing it. I came off stage and walked over to Paddy. Billy Flynn's face was a picture, as he realised

Paddy had heard every word. When we were leaving I went over and said, 'You'd better watch what you say in future,' and, leaning over, Paddy added, 'And I'll have my towel back an' all you cheeky bastard.' Billy hadn't got a clue what he was going on about, but he must have realised later as the next morning we found it outside the bedroom door, washed, dried and folded sitting next to a brand new roll-on deodorant.

With nowhere to go we just headed back to the B&B after the gig and tried to get a picture on the portable. It was *Mrs Merton* and she had Bernard Manning on. He did himself no favours, controversial and racist as ever, but I had to admit his comic timing was perfect. I went to visit him at his house one day when I was writing *Phoenix Nights*. There was a character called Den Perry in the series and I thought it would be great if he could play him. I knew he'd never acted before but that didn't bother me. I like to use stand-ups as well as actors anyway as I think they always bring something fresh to a performance. And basically all stand-ups are actors anyway as they're acting every time they go on stage. Bernard was funny, sometimes without even realising it. He sat in his armchair in just his underpants and we chatted for hours about club land and all the different performers he'd known over the years. I found it fascinating. I also wanted him to play the part because I thought he might be redeemed by the public when they saw his unique comic ability and not just what he was perceived as being, a comedian who was famous for doing racist material. Unfortunately Bernard was far too ill to do it. 'I'm injecting myself with this shit every ninety minutes,' he said, holding up his syringe filled with insulin. 'Ah well, it'll not stop me laughing. I'm on in Suffolk tonight, five hours' drive, do an hour and get home to bed. Lovely.' He was one on his own.

Driving home from Bristol we spent a lot of time talking about ideas for a new Channel 4 series I'd been offered called *Comedy Lab*. Since I'd won 'So You Think You're Funny?' in Edinburgh the powers that be at the channel had taken an interest and had offered me my own half hour to do whatever I wanted. That was hard as I didn't know what to do or rather which to do, I had so many ideas. The producer suggested I do a stand-up show which basically consisted of my stage act, but I wasn't so sure. It felt too easy; I knew inside I had something else to offer. I thought long and hard about what made me laugh and what I'd like to see.

I'd always loved the spoof fly-on-the-wall documentaries each week on *Victoria Wood – As Seen On TV*. The next day at school we'd spend the whole of English reciting them. 'Swim the Channel' where Victoria Wood played a schoolgirl left to swim the English Channel while her parents go off to London to watch a show was brilliant. I loved the uncomfortable looks the actors would give when the camera lingered too long on them. I decided it should be something along the lines of a spoof documentary. They were very popular at the time with programmes like *The Cruise*, *Hotel*, *Lakesiders* and *Paddington Green* all being very successful, so it felt right to send it up. I also fancied the opportunity to do a bit of acting. There wasn't much money to make the show so surely it would be cheaper if I played most of the characters. I was hugely influenced by Ronnie Barker – he was an amazing comic actor, and the characters he portrayed in *Porridge* and *Open All Hours* were both funny and believable. So why not try it myself? Surely the whole point of doing something like this was to experiment, hence the title *Comedy Lab*. After all, I had gone into stand-up as a way into comic acting, now I would be writing for myself. At least this way I knew I'd be happy with the script.

The only thing left to decide was what the subject matter would be. I knew it had to be something original and then as Paddy and me pulled into the services for a Ginsters and a Twix on our way home I had my second comedy epiphany, that was it: motorway services. It was perfect and at least I knew my subject matter well, having spent enough time in them. I could get a wealth of comedy out of a place like this. Everybody has to stop there, young, old, rich, poor – it's a classless place.

There could be some great characters. Perhaps I could play a lethargic cleaner or a coach driver just like the one we used to have taking us to Butlins. Maybe a manager who's constantly stressed about which side of the road is more successful and spends most of their time running back and forth across the footbridge. All the ingredients were there, all I had to do was write it.

Driving to gigs was now a weekly occurrence and my trusty Fiesta was quickly racking up the miles. Funny to think only a few months earlier I had cried off driving to Chuckles in Harrogate. Driving so much also gave me knowledge of the roads and I got to know almost every inner-city ring road and roundabout in Britain. And there was no such thing as satellite navigation in those days, my friend, all I had was a photocopied map or the text of an address on my pager and off I went. In fact I once drove all the way to Nottingham with just the name of a pub on a scrap of paper. I followed the signs on the motorway, turned off at Nottingham and headed for the city centre. Eventually I'd pull into a garage and buy an *A–Z* for a few quid. I've still got drawers full of them.

The gig in Nottingham was at a place called the Malt Cross Music Hall; it was a weird venue and not really right for comedy. The audience were in front but they were also towering above me on a series of balconies that went right round the stage. I was a bit disconcerted, as I had to look straight up most of the time and felt like I was performing on an operating table with people looking down on me. But that was the downside of everybody jumping on the comedy club bandwagon. They didn't think it through, they thought they could just throw some sort of stage in the corner and expect it to work. Sometimes you could turn up to anything. At the Barracuda Club in Lincoln the stage was made up of those blue pallets you see outside factories. I daren't move as I was swaying all over the place. Sometimes you didn't even get that, you just had to stand in the corner. The Banana Club in Grimsby was in a cellar: if you got too excited you could end up with a concussion as the ceiling was that low. I once played a doorway in Crewe, I kid you not. The stage was in the corridor between two rooms so I had to keep leaning round the partitioning wall. I practically had to tell every joke twice just so both sets of people could see me.

The night I played the Malt Cross Music Hall the compère and guy who ran the gig had a big chip on his shoulder. He'd already been ranting to me backstage about Jongleurs opening down the road. Jongleurs was a comedy club that had originated in London and, due to its success, they'd decided to branch out, opening clubs all over Britain. Still angry, he went on to introduce me and then he completely lost it. He started shouting and swearing, slagging off Jongleurs, saying things like 'they're a bunch of corporate arseholes that couldn't care less about comedy', and that basically everybody should support their home-grown comedy clubs instead. Then without missing a beat he said, 'And now here's Peter Kay.' Shell-shocked, I walked on, took the mic off him and said, 'Thanks for warming them up, mate, it's always good to perform in front of an angry mob.'

So I then started doing my act and the mic kept cutting out like Norman Collier. It was embarrassing. I was blowing into it and tapping but it kept cutting out. Finally the compère ran on with another mic and plugged it in. Then *I* lost it: 'I'll tell you something, there's none of this down at Jongleurs, they're a proper comedy club. *They've* spent some money on their sound equipment, they're not sponsored by Tandy. In fact we should all go down there right now and have a look!'

When the corporate comedy clubs started branching out I knew that stand-up was at its zenith. I never played Jongleurs after they told me I'd have to do a total of ten unpaid open spots at various Jongleurs around the country before they'd consider booking me, so I gave them a wide berth. The Comedy Store was another and together with Jongleurs they led the way with this new corporate style of comedy, or McComedy as it was affectionately nicknamed due to its fast-food approach to the business. Very successfully they both had early and late shows to accommodate the demand. In order to keep things to time, these clubs operated a light system, which meant a comedian would be flashed off after twenty minutes in order to keep things moving. For me it felt a bit clinical and more like a factory than a comedy club; anyway I was still doing jokes and ending on a song so they'd have fired me off straight away.

Dave Perkin, the manager of the Frog & Bucket, soon got wind of this new corporate-style comedy and, not one to miss out on a business opportunity, quickly revamped the structure of the club. We too started having an early and a late show on a Saturday night but the social structure of London just didn't transfer to Manchester. And there were teething troubles. For a kick-off the doormen couldn't get the audience to leave after the early show.

They just weren't having any of it and couldn't comprehend what all the rush was about. As a result the late show now started even later and by the time the headline act came on half the audience had either left or nodded off.

Having two audiences was confusing for the comedians too and half seven till two in the morning was a long night. You'd lose track of what jokes you'd told and to whom. I'd get halfway through my set and suddenly stop and think, I'm sure I've just told this already. The only good side was the money, or so we all thought. We imagined we'd all be on double bubble but of course Dave Perkin had other ideas: a sliding scale based on audience numbers. We got our normal wages plus whatever the late show's audience capacity was. If there were a hundred and fifty people in or more we got an extra twenty quid, over a hundred and sixty we got some more and so on. The only problem was how were we to know how many people were in the club? And so in an effort not to get shafted the comedians started to count the audience themselves in between the laughs. I'd come on and say 'Good evening, ladies and gentleman, is everybody alright?' (and count 1, 2, 3, 4, 5, 6, 7, 8, 9, 10, 11, 12). 'Everything OK, had a good week?' (and count 13, 14, 15, 16, 17, 18). Then after I'd introduce the act and as we passed I'd whisper, 'Lady at the bottom of the stairs, buck teeth, 48' and then the next comedian would continue the count. I'd pass them as they were going off, 'Bloke at the bar looks like Shipman, 97.' It was like something out of *The Great Escape*. At the end of the show we'd go up to Dave and say, 'One hundred and eighty-two in tonight.' I'm happy to say that McComedy didn't last long at the Frog & Bucket and within a few weeks it was back to show-business as usual.

By now my life was pretty hectic. I was writing the *Comedy*

Lab special during the day, mid-week I was working part-time at the cinema and the Manchester Arena, and at weekends I was performing stand-up. I knew something had to give and it had to be my part-time jobs but I was scared to leave them. Doing that meant I would be taking the plunge and admitting I was a professional comedian. And even though things had been going well and I had a regular income, I was worried about the future and whether I could sustain it. Keeping my hand in part-time meant I didn't have to burn that bridge.

But fate made the decision for me when the multiplex finally came to Bolton (well two of them to be precise). Suddenly the town went from having three screens to twenty-four. It was David and Goliath and our three screens just couldn't compete. Inevitably we were forced to close. Walking out with Mrs Hayworth that final night, I think we all had tears in our eyes. After seventy-six years and six *Police Academies* the Lido closed its doors for the final time. So in the end I didn't jump, I was pushed – something I considered ironic as I looked up at the front canopy and read a word that seemed to sum everything up: 'Titanic'.

Chapter Five

My First Comedy Epiphany

Stand-ups can sometimes get work as warm-ups if they're lucky, (or unlucky, depending what type of show you get). Living locally to Granada Television, I occasionally went to watch the recordings of shows as part of the studio audience. Peter Simon, who was a presenter on the Saturday morning children's show *Going Live*, was the first comedian I ever saw do warm-up, on a quiz show called *Runway* with Richard Madeley. He was outrageously funny (I am referring to Peter Simon now and not Richard Madeley) and I definitely could see the need for having somebody like that in the studio, keeping the audience warmed-up. You need a court jester to alleviate the boredom because television can be deceptive, even a simple half-hour show can take up to three hours to record. Or six hours in the case of *You've Been Framed* – mind you, we did spend most of that night watching security guards try to remove a gang of unruly sixth-formers from Eccles College out of the studio for taking the piss out of Jeremy Beadle's hand. The police were called in the end and the audience each got a carton of Just Juice as compensation.

Fast-forward six years and I was back in the studios at Granada Television once again, only this time it was my turn to warm up the audience. The show was called *Conspiracy Theory*, presented by the then Radio 1 DJs Mark Radcliffe and Lard (Marc Riley in real life, well I say 'real life' . . . can we define it?). I can only describe the show as a sort of cross between *Celebrity Squares* and *The X Files*. It was themed around events like the alien invasion at Roswell, the Loch Ness monster, who killed JFK, that kind of thing. As usual I was very nervous. Just watching the audience coming in sent me over the edge of insanity. How could I make this work? I decided to treat it just like a bit of compèring. I welcomed everybody, then explained the concept of the show and introduced Mark and Lard. Then I sat round the back of the set and waited until I was needed to fill the gaps. And that's what a warm-up basically does, fills the gaps whenever there's a technical hiccup. I had to be on the ball the whole time and couldn't let my guard down in case something happened, which meant I spent the night poised, with a huge list of jokes and stories. The floor manager would give me a nod when I was needed and I sprung into action. The only thing that threw me was having to stop halfway through a gag or a story when they were ready to record, but I was there to facilitate and go with the flow. I even managed to turn this constant stopping and starting into a gag itself by continuing with my story each time. I was on a mission to get to the end of it even if it took all night.

I also found that shifting focus from myself to the audience helped enormously and soaked up a lot of time. This was a skill that I'd also honed compèring. I asked them what they did and where they were from. I also got them to grass up who'd smuggled in sweets, then as punishment made them share them with everybody, even the cast and crew. Four hours later, stuffed with fudge and mint imperials, my first warm-up ended. I was shattered but I thought I'd taken to it well and considered it a success. Something that unfortunately can't be said about *Conspiracy Theory* – well did you ever see it on television, let's put it that way? Mark and Lard later admitted that I was the best thing on the show and I wasn't even on it. Which I took as a backhanded compliment.

I took quite naturally to it, and an additional bonus was I got £250 for warming up *Conspiracy Theory*, I'd usually get the same amount for gigging all weekend and so I decided I fancied trying a bit more of this warm-up lark. Eventually after ringing round I got the number of a producer who worked at the BBC in London. She invited me down for an interview – an interview to do warm-up? Seemed a bit over the top. Still, if it meant extra work I was on my way. I remember the first time I ever arrived at BBC Television Centre, I was in complete awe of the place. I'd seen it in programmes like Noel Edmonds' *Multi-Coloured Swap Shop*, *The Goodies* and *EBC 1 – Emu's Broadcasting Company*. This building was an iconic part of my childhood. The first thing I saw was the huge fountain in the centre of the circular reception area. The producer put her hand out to greet me but all I could say was, 'That's where Roy Castle did that tap dance on *Record Breakers*.' Luckily she found my enthusiasm refreshing, she liked me and I was soon to be seeing a lot more of the place, as she offered me a job doing warm-up on *Rolf's Amazing World of Animals*. And the Rolf in question was of course Sir Rolf Harris. Is he a Sir? Hold on while I google him . . . yes he is.

A week later I found myself back at the BBC deliberately circling the corridors, past the studios. Outside of one of them '*Top of the*

Pops' was written on a blackboard in white chalk, '*Tomorrow's World*' on another. I so wanted to sneak inside for a look but daren't. Ah, this was mine – '*Rolf's Amazing World of Animals*'. I pulled open the fire door and strolled in. The set was designed like a jungle and there he was, the man himself. He looked just like Rolf Harris. It was a moment to behold and was right up there with the time I urinated next to Johnny Briggs (Mike Baldwin) in the Press Club in Manchester.

Sitting in the empty audience seats, I watched the end of his camera rehearsal, then the producer called me over and I was introduced to Rolf. I was giddy being that close to him, why on earth? We chatted, small talk. The weather, train journeys down and then he said, 'I recognise your accent. Is it Lancashire?'

'Yes,' I said, 'Bolton.'

Rolf said, 'Listen there was this fucking guy . . .' and launched into a joke about a Lancastrian. Well I can only think it was a joke but I honestly can't say because after he said the f-word I completely zoned out. I just stood there shell-shocked with a smile frozen on my face. 'Rolf Harris just effed', that's all I could say to myself. He carried on, his voice muffled under my chants. 'Rolf Harris just said the f-word', 'Rolf Harris just said the f-word'. I was just getting a rhythm going when he got to the end of the joke. Well I presumed it was the end because he stopped talking and I laughed. Oh how I laughed, false and hard. Rolf 'Two Little Boys, Stylophone, Learn to Swim' Harris had just said the f-word. Still laughing, he patted me on the shoulder, winked and walked off, leaving me gobsmacked in the jungle. Honestly, I don't know what shocked me the most. The fact that he swore or that he only had two legs.

Having a warm-up on a Rolf Harris show was a mistake because every time the floor manager gave me the nod Rolf was already on it, singing, dancing, ripping off a piece of the set and turning it into a makeshift wobbly board. The man *was* a walking warm-up, he didn't need me. By the third chorus of 'The Court of King Caractacus' I admitted defeat. Completely redundant, I sat down in the audience and joined in with the sing-along. Ah well, it was an experience I'll treasure and I even got paid for the privilege too.

I did quite a few warm-ups on various shows at the BBC but my least favourite was *They Think It's All Over*. My sister was a fan of the show so I got her a seat in the audience and she came down with me on the train. It was the first panel game show that I'd been to, let alone warmed up, and what a disappointment it was. Maybe I was naive but I'd always been under the assumption that these comedy panel game shows weren't rehearsed. I was shocked to discover that on most of them they're given the questions in advance. All that quick-witted stuff is a load of bollocks. But considering they already had the answers they really dragged it out. They each spent ages answering every question, squeezing almost every possible bit of humour out of it and by the time they'd finished the recording four hours later, I was glad it was all over (see what I did?). When R Julie and I watched the show the following week we were shocked at how different it was. Edited down to practically nothing with big audience laughs added on to the jokes that definitely didn't get any. It was a huge eye-opener for me into how those programmes are put together.

Hanging around the BBC a lot, I struck up a friendship with a producer from Manchester called Danny Dignan.* We both shared

* Factoid: In *Phoenix Nights* the character Jerry's full name is Jerry 'the saint' St Clair Dignan, named after Mr Danny Dignan. I feel like I'm on Steve Wright's show.

an enormous love of television and at the time Danny was working on a compilation show that consisted of classic *Parkinson* interviews. Occasionally if I was doing warm-up and missed the last train I'd stop over at his flat in North London – he lived over an estate agent with his fiancée Rachel, they're married now and have two lovely children. We'd sit up for hours watching episodes of *Parkinson* that Danny had got out of the BBC library. Hearing people like Mohammed Ali, Orson Welles, Morecambe and Wise, Tommy Cooper, Dustin Hoffman, to name but a few, talking about their careers in such detail was fascinating. I'd been too young to appreciate them first time round. My grandad used to insist on watching *Parkinson* every Saturday night while he babysat R Julie and me. I found it dull, just grown-ups talking about grown-up stuff. I didn't see the appeal. I wanted Bo and Luke Duke tear-arsing around Hazzard County in the General Lee, but they'd long since disappeared over the horizon by the time *Parkinson* came on. Over the years I'd begun to appreciate its value, its worth, and subsequently I longed to see the interviews again.

The compilation series of forgotten *Parkinson* interviews was screened to great acclaim and it wasn't long before the powers that be managed to coax the man himself out of retirement (well semi-retirement, as he was presenting a lunchtime quiz show about antiques called *Going for a Song*). Widely regarded as the best interviewer British television has ever seen, Parkinson was back. And you'll never guess who managed to bag the warm-up?

Danny, who was associate producer, had put a good word in for me. This was a prestigious gig. Everybody was talking about *Parkinson*, it was a big event and quite a remarkable return after an absence of fifteen years. Suddenly I was in the warm-up premier league. I got £350 a week, my travel paid and a driver to pick me up from Euston station. It felt very weird at first having a driver; they used to wait at the end of the platform for me holding a piece of cardboard with my name in felt-tip.

The first time I ever met Caroline Aherne she was stood with my driver after reading his piece of cardboard with my name on. She confessed that she'd actually been stood there for about ten minutes as she wanted to say hello. I was a huge fan of *The Royle Family* and knew Craig Cash but had never met Caroline. We hugged and chatted for a few minutes before she went off to get her train back up to Manchester and I went off to *Parkinson*. That was a lovely thing to do.

Hating formalities, I always used to insist on getting in the front with the drivers, which is unheard of in the world of chauffeuring. They'd quickly have to swipe their empty sandwich box or porn mag off the passenger seat, mumbling an apology. I had a few different drivers and they always used to make me laugh because they were always so professional when they first met me at Euston. It was very much 'Could I take your bag for you, Mr Kay?' and 'Pleasant journey down, Mr Kay?' but by the time we got to Television Centre the façade had slipped and they'd be telling me the arse end of some filthy joke that usually involved midgets and prostitution and in that order. 'Ere, you can use that in your act, mate.' By the end of the series not only did I know all the drivers very well but I also knew enough dirty jokes to rival Chubby Brown.

Seeing the word '*Parkinson*' scrawled on the blackboard outside the studio sent shivers down my spine. Then I saw that iconic set and the childhood memories of Saturday-night babysitting came flooding back. That staircase, the band just to the right of it at the bottom and those chairs, those empty chairs where the guests sit. How lucky was I to be there?

The floor manager Quentin Mann ran through what I had to do. He said the audience would arrive around 7 p.m. and he would go through the fire and safety regulations with them. Then he'd introduce me and all I had to do was about ten minutes tops, that was it. I couldn't believe that was it. Just ten minutes. I was expecting to be there for hours. At this rate I would be able to make my last train home, the infamous 22.10 to Manchester Piccadilly.

The reason the warm-up was so short was because the show was recorded 'as live', just like it had been in the old days. Parky (like I knew him) ran the show to time leaving very little to edit out before the final broadcast. So my job was to just briefly warm them up.

Then Quentin casually added, 'And after you've done ten minutes or so all you have to do is introduce Michael and you're done.'

'Me?' I said.

'Yes, you.'

'I introduce Michael?' I said, confused.

'Yes, then Michael will come down the stairs, chat to the audience about what guests are on, then he'll go back up and we start the show.'

It was as simple as that: five months in the warm-up game and I was introducing Michael Parkinson.

Only having to do ten minutes, the pressure was off and I was able to have a ball. I did a few jokes, chatted to the audience, most of whom were a mixture of Michael Parkinson's family and friends and pensioners who'd come down on a coach from Bristol (although I honestly couldn't tell the difference). I have to say I had it easy. The time flew by and then I introduced the man himself. 'Ladies and gentlemen, please will you welcome back Mr

Michael Parkinson.' The studio erupted in applause as Parkinson walked down the staircase. It was an honour to be there that night.

Those next eight weeks were magical. Sitting on the front row watching interviews with legends like Sir Anthony Hopkins, Sir Richard Attenborough, Peter O'Toole, Morgan Freeman, to name but a few, and musical performances from Sir Elton John, Sir Paul McCartney, Phil Collins. I think my favourite was Robbie Williams, who sang an acoustic version of his song 'Angels', which was beautiful.

After the show everybody would congregate in the Green Room, the guests with their agents, Parky with his family and friends. I used to just stand in the corner smiling and helping myself to tea and biscuits. I knew my place and never approached anybody, although bizarrely Robbie Williams recognised me and came over for a chat; he was lovely. Oh, and I did offer Neil Diamond a chocolate digestive once; he practically had the packet. I had him pinned as more of a Bourbon man.

One of the highlights of working on *Parkinson* was getting to meet Billy Connolly. Well I say 'meet', I just hovered in the corner of the Green Room after the show, scoffing custard creams, trying to pluck up the courage to say hello. You want your heroes to realise just how much they mean to you without coming across as just another fan jumping on the celebrity bandwagon or, worse still, a stalker. I wanted him to be able to see inside my head and realise just how much he meant to me. Actually that does make me sound like a stalker and a psycho.

Eventually I saw he was leaving and went over. We shook hands and he recognised me from doing my warm-up before the show.

'You were very funny and that's a tough gig. I couldn't do anything like that,' he said.

I was so overawed at meeting him my mind went blank and the only compliment I could respond with was 'I like your suit', it was maroon, crushed velvet. 'I've got one like that myself from Topman.'

'Is that right,' he said politely and left looking bemused.

'I've got one like that myself from Topman'? What a thing to say, I'm sure he didn't get his from Topman. What an idiot!

It was a pleasure meeting him though. He's had a huge influence on me as a comedian; in fact he has probably influenced every British comedian of the last thirty years. I fell in love with his anecdotal style and his observations at an early age. My dad used to get his live shows through his record club at work and copy them on to cassette.* I wasn't supposed to listen to them, so would smuggle the tape player under the duvet. I loved to hear him talking about his life, growing up, getting a job, his family. The impact of his style on me is immeasurable. He's a rare thing in this world, a naturally funny man, and he still never fails to make me laugh.

His finest hour for me was *An Audience With Billy Connolly*, that's a very fond memory of mine. The whole family sat round the television, howling with laughter. My dad laughed so much at his routine about a man wearing incontinence pants chatting up a girl in a disco that he actually slid off the armchair and on to the floor. How could something like that not leave an impression on me? You know when you hear musicians saying when they first saw The Beatles on *The Ed Sullivan Show* they knew exactly what they wanted to be. Well *An Audience With Billy Connolly* was my first comedy epiphany. And to think all I could say when I met him was 'I've just bought a suit like that from Topman'.

* Home taping is killing music. Think on.

Every Thursday I made the round trip to London to warm up the *Parky* audience. Not that they needed that much warming, it was the hottest show in town. Everything was going great, Danny had received reports from the powers that be that Michael was happy with me and gradually over the weeks I began to get acquainted with Parky (like I now knew him). He took quite a shine to me. I think it was a northern thing, him from Barnsley and me from Bolton, we just got on. We'd talk about comedy, we both shared an admiration for the old style of front-of-cloth comics like Rob Wilton, Jimmy James, Les Dawson. I'd watched these comedians over the years, studied their styles and techniques. He once said to me, 'Comedy can't be taught or learnt, you have to be born with it in your soul.' That's exactly how I'd always felt. It is part of me whether I like it or not. I'd spent years denying myself any opportunity to perform, working in part-time jobs when I knew deep down it was what I had to do. It would have been such a shame if I'd never had a go, I know I would have regretted it for ever. You wouldn't be reading this.

The return of *Parkinson* was an enormous success and the series was recommissioned in the New Year; thankfully so was I. Still making my round trip every Thursday, I was now practically part of the furniture. With my dad's fiftieth birthday approaching I thought it would be nice to bring him down to the show. I squared it with Parky and the producers and booked an extra train ticket. My dad was delighted. I also booked a hotel for the night in Piccadilly, the Regent Palace (which it certainly wasn't, but at least it meant we didn't have to dash off after the show).

My dad was over the moon when I told him where we were going. A trip to the *Parkinson* show and the chance to do a bit of trainspotting on the way down, I don't think I'd ever seen him so happy. I even brought a double adaptor for my Walkman and we listened to a compilation tape I'd made especially for him featuring the Eagles, Lionel Richie, Sam Cooke and Neil Diamond (it's a pity he hadn't come the week Neil was on, my dad could have handed him the digestives). I'll never forget the look on my dad's face when the driver met me at the end of the platform. He didn't bother with the cardboard any more, as we were now good friends. My dad said he felt like a king driving to the BBC. That made the whole thing worthwhile. The driver was even taking it easy on the blue jokes until my dad piped up with, 'Have you heard the one about the two dwarves in a brothel?' I'd forgotten how much my dad loved telling jokes when he was in a good mood. And once he started he couldn't stop, he was still at it when we drove into Television Centre, '. . . I said ping pong balls, not King Kong's balls.' Then I'll never forget it, the first thing he said as he got out of the car was, 'Hey look, that's where Roy Castle did that tap dance.' The similarities between us were now starting to frighten me.

My warm-up went very well that night; I was on cloud nine with my dad being there. It was the first time he'd ever seen me perform. He'd never been to any of my stand-up gigs – no real reason, I suppose like most things in life the opportunity had never arisen before. I did my ten minutes' warm-up, introduced Michael Parkinson and took my seat on the front row next to my dad. Without saying a word he just put his hand on mine and gave my fingers a little squeeze. That said everything to me.

Phil Collins and John Prescott were the guests but it wouldn't have mattered who it'd been, my dad was made up just to be there. We went back to the Green Room after the show and both hovered in the corner. Then Michael Parkinson came over to my dad and shook his hand hello and said, 'I believe it's your fiftieth birthday, many happy returns Mr Kay, you must be very proud of your son, he's a funny lad.' That moved me, in fact I've got tears running down my cheeks now as I'm typing this. Michael Parkinson didn't have to do that, it was such a lovely thing to do and my dad was just completely overwhelmed, he just kept shaking his hand and calling him sir: 'Pleasure, Mr Parkinson, sir.'

Laurie Holloway had been the musical director on *Parkinson* for ever and his wife, who was a jazz singer called Marion Montgomery, was also in the Green Room that night. She overheard that it was my dad's fiftieth and decided to serenade him. Hushing the entire room she sang happy birthday and then gave him a kiss. My dad was floating on air.

He was still smiling two hours later when he got into bed at the Regent Palace. 'Do you know who that was? That was Marion Montgomery, do you know who it was?', that's all he kept saying as he drifted off to sleep.

The next morning my dad was up at the crack of dawn, slamming drawers and running water.

'Peter? Are you asleep?' he said over and over, each time a little louder, so I had no chance of escape.

'No,' I said.

'Well I'm up, I'm going for a walk and a paper.'

'What time is it?'

'Quarter past seven.'

Our train wasn't until eleven. He always used to do that on holiday. Get up first thing and wake everybody else just to tell us he was 'up and going for a walk'. Then he'd return an hour later and wake us all up again, gloating about where he'd been: 'Come on, you're missing it, there's not a cloud in the sky out there, I've already had a walk down the beach and a coffee.' My dad's idea of a family holiday was that we all did what he wanted or else.

We left the hotel and I headed towards the Tube.

'Woah, woah, woah, what are you doing? We can walk it,' he said, 'it's only up here', and with that he was off.

'Only up here? It's miles away,' I said, pleading after him, but he was like a machine, marching towards Oxford Street, with a flat bottle of lemonade under his arm that he's bought from a newsagents in Piccadilly Circus the night before.

I followed him into a huge HMV megastore and straight to the jazz section.

'See, this is her,' he said, holding up a CD of Marion Montgomery. Now I understood why he was so eager to walk, he was still on a high from his serenade the night before.

'Aren't you buying it?' I said as he put the CD back.

'What, at that price? Am I bloody hell.'

We made it to Euston in time for my dad to do a bit of spotting. It was a relief to be getting a train home during the day for a change. I was getting tired of having to catch the dreaded 22.10 home to Piccadilly each week. I never felt safe and it was always full of weirdos like the night we were just about to leave Euston and this big bruiser of a bloke with tattoos got on with a lovely little blond-haired boy who looked like Little Lord Fauntleroy and who couldn't have been more than five or six. It was a bizarre combination for that time of night. They sat opposite each other a bit further down the carriage from me. After a while the little boy started yawning; the bloke (who may have been the boy's dad but was only ever referred to as Duggy) said, 'Are you tired?' in a deep Scottish growl.

'Yes, Duggy,' the boy said, nodding wearily.

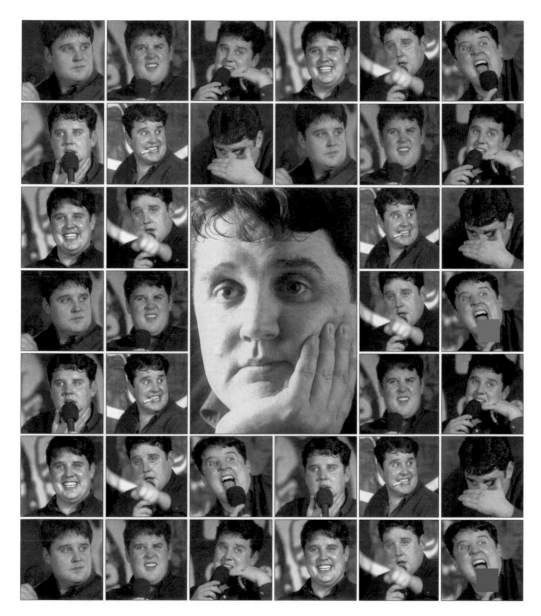

The many faces of Peter Kay, most of them all the same. This was taken
at the Frog & Bucket on one of those rowdy and raucous Saturday nights.
It sums up all the frantic energy of those early performances and if you stare
at it long enough it's also a magic eye picture of the Taj Mahal.

Here's an historic flyer from the night that started it all. I'm particularly fond of the travel advice in the right-hand corner; well what more do you want for £6?

My very first publicity photo. Wanting it to be different, I managed to catch this moment just as the lady was walking past and looking straight into the camera. Sadly it backfired when stand-up promoters saw this and assumed we were a double act. They weren't too thrilled when I'd turn up on my own without the old girl and the wheelie bin.

The Moon Landings of '84.
This photo should have been in
the first book, *The Sound Of
Laughter* (next one along on
the shelf if you don't mind).
I searched high and low and
then found it inside a hardback
copy of *The Thorn Birds*.
I'm the astronaut with high
blood pressure in the middle.

My bus pass and my lifeline,
which got me from A to B
to A – and if you think I
look happy on this you
want to see my passport.

'Top of the world, ma'; well top of the World Trade Center to be precise.
Freezing cold and ironically looking a bit like a terrorist.

This is Agraman –
The Human Anagram
from The Buzz Club.
He's hard of hearing.

The Buzz

AGRAMAN:
Buzzing on
Thursday

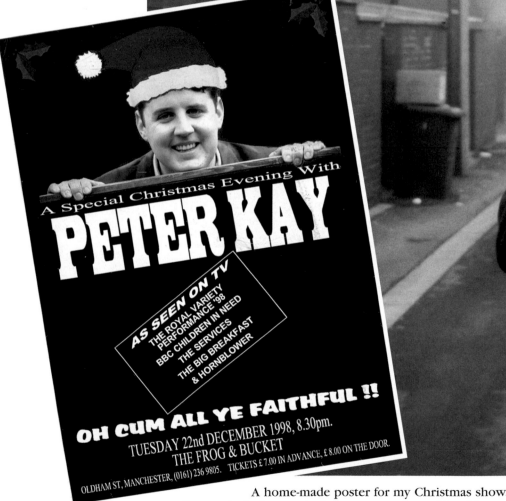

A souvenir from my
first time at the BBC –
you know the place
where Roy Castle
did that tap dance.

A Special Christmas Evening With

PETER KAY

AS SEEN ON TV
THE ROYAL VARIETY
PERFORMANCE '98
BBC CHILDREN IN NEED
THE SERVICES
THE BIG BREAKFAST
& HORNBLOWER

OH CUM ALL YE FAITHFUL !!

TUESDAY 22nd DECEMBER 1998, 8.30pm.
THE FROG & BUCKET

OLDHAM ST, MANCHESTER, (0161) 236 9805.   TICKETS £7.00 IN ADVANCE, £8.00 ON THE DOOR.

A home-made poster for my Christmas show.
I'm particularly proud of my appearance on *Hornblower.*

Acting like a comedian in the backstreet behind our house.
Please take note: fashion is a circle.

384 • 7 - 22 JULY 1999 • £1.60

CITY LIFE
WHAT'S ON IN
manchester

TRICKY
The return of the Bristol maverick

ADAM COLE
Galaxy 102's morning glory

GROOVE ARMADA
Housing up Counter Culture

Star Wars Special
THE PHANTOM COMIC
Peter Kay remembers the first time

+ George Lucas - mythmaker or menace?
The merchandise - the good, the bad &
the downright ugly

Plus **WIGAN JAZZ FESTIVAL JANE ROGERS CANTEENA BILLY MAHONIE CARLOS SAURA**

A rare cover from *City Life* magazine around the time of *Star Wars:
The Phantom Menace.* It actually fuelled a rumour that I was to be the
new Obi-Wan but unfortunately the part went to Ewan McGregor.

And that's it for this first photo section, now please carry on reading the book or,
if you're just having a nosey in the shop, there's some more photos further on.

Duggy stood up. 'Right, I'd better make you a bed,' and with just one hand Duggy proceeded to rip the individual seat cushions from the chairs opposite him. He then placed them in the aisle in between the seats – you know, where you can put your luggage.

Myself and everybody else in the carriage simultaneously shifted in our seats and glanced out of the window as if to say 'Did we really just see that happen? I don't think we did' in typical British fashion. But we still carried on watching Duggy's reflection in the window.

'There, I've made you a bed,' said Duggy.

He scooped the little lad up in his mitts and gently placed him on the newly made bed. Then he took out a pack of pornographic playing cards and started playing Patience. About thirty minutes later everybody simultaneously shifted in their seats a second time when the carriage doors opened and the guard shouted, 'Tickets please.'

Eventually he reached the vandalised seats and Duggy.

'Who's done this?' he said in a voice that I can only describe as Brian Potter.

Duggy shrugged his shoulders.

'Dizgrace. Tickets please,' the guard said, but Duggy just carried on playing. 'Have you got your tickets?'

'No,' said Duggy.

'Where are you going?'

'Home.'

'Not without a ticket you're not,' said the guard defiantly.

'Watch me,' said Duggy without looking up.

With that, the guard charged off shaking his head and everybody simultaneously shifted in their seats for a third and final time. Now what? I expected there to be lockdown at the next station. Police swarming all over the platform, a SWAT team on the bridge. But nothing happened. Duggy and the boy got off at Crewe and as for that guard, he never even came back! He must have shit himself in the buffet car.

Sadly my time working as warm-up on *Parkinson* came to end. But I never really got to the bottom of why. I just got a call from Danny Dignan saying that the producers had decided that it wasn't cost-effective to keep shipping me down from Manchester each week and I was being replaced by one of Michael's golfing buddies who used to warm-up for him on *Give Us a Clue*. But I had my doubts about the whole cost-effectiveness thing. I think the truth lay in the fact that I'd started to get a bit edgier with my intro-ductions to Michael at the beginning of the show. One week I said, 'Ladies and gentlemen, it gives me enormous pleasure to sit on bath taps and welcome Mr Michael Parkinson', then the week prior to me leaving I'd told the audience that my uncle had suddenly been struck down with Parkinson's and kept going around the house interviewing people. I'll let you be the judge. Anyway it was great while it lasted but *Parkinson* was the end of my warm-up career and even though I had offers I never went back after that, well how could I top it? I'd definitely peaked too soon (story of my life).

Chapter Six

Self-mutilation in a Fez

My warm-up stint on Mark and Lard's doomed quiz show *Conspiracy Theory* must have made a good impression because they invited me to support them when they embarked on a short university tour in the guise of fictional rock alter egos The Shirehorses (they were sort of a cross between Spinal Tap and The Barron Knights). They performed pastiches of popular songs of the time like 'You're Gormless' (as opposed to 'You're Gorgeous') and 'Why Is It Always Dairylea?' (I shouldn't have to explain that one). With that kind of tomfoolery on the menu how could I refuse?

It was still a bit like doing warm-up; I had to do twenty minutes each night at various universities around Britain before The Shirehorses took to the stage. With a gruelling five-nights schedule in front of us we hit the road. It felt very rock'n'roll screeching out of the gates of the BBC in Manchester, past the beefy ballerinas queuing outside Greggs* straight up Oxford Road and off into the horizon.

* I never intended this pattern to evolve but now that it has, some Greggs meal deal vouchers wouldn't go amiss.

Our first stop was Newcastle, with the friendliest people in Britain. If you ask somebody a question up there you don't get an answer, you get a conversation. I'd played there many times, in particular the Hyena Comedy Club. That night myself and The Shirehorses stayed at a hotel beside the Tyne Theatre and after the gig it was straight to bed and lights out as Mark and Lard had to be up each morning at the crack of dawn to present the Radio 1 breakfast show from their tour bus, which literally was a double-decker bus.

In the middle of the night there was a fire alarm and I sleepily staggered out onto the corridor to see if it was real and not a practice. To my surprise the rest of the guests were taking it seriously and as I turned to go back to my room I saw the last few inches of my door close shut. There I was, in just my underpants, locked out in the middle of an evacuation, much to the amusement of Mark, Lard and the rest of their entourage. Luckily one of their assistants gave me her denim jacket to wear as we gathered on the front street. I was mortified. The denim jacket was four sizes too small, I looked like The Incredible Hulk, hugging myself for warmth on the pavement, trying to act nonchalant, the only half-naked person amongst eighty guests. Mark and Lard had much merriment the following morning, informing their listeners all about my midnight exposure in the centre of Newcastle.

Revenge is a dish best served cold and I got mine a few months later when I appeared as a guest on their Radio 1 show plugging my new Channel 4 *Comedy Lab – The Services*. It had turned out a treat, and sticking to my vision of multiple characters I took on several comic roles including one as the services manager, Pearl Hardman.

'You play a woman in your new show, is that right?' Mark said enthusiastically.

'I do but it's a proper woman, it's not like in *The Crying Game* when you discover she's a man.'

'You can't reveal that,' said Mark.

'Is that what happens in the end of *The Services*?' said Lard, fumbling for a question.

'I can't reveal what happens in the end, that would ruin it, it'd be like telling you Bruce Willis is a ghost at the end of *The Sixth Sense*.'*

Well *The Sixth Sense* had only just come out the weekend before and the phone lines went crazy with listeners ringing up to complain about my revelations. The backlash was so severe Mark and Lard were forced to apologise on air.

'Er . . . moving on,' said Mark, 'where do you get your ideas from?'

'Oh I just get them from whatever's around me, a bit like Kevin Spacey at the end of *The Usual Suspects*, when you find out *he's* Keyser Söze.'

Horrified, they apologised again as I tried to crowbar in the ending of every film with a twist there's ever been. Quickly fading me into the next song as I shouted, 'IT'S GWYNETH PALTROW'S HEAD IN A BOX AT THE END OF SEVEN!' Suffice to say I was never invited back.

We headed towards Leeds for the second night of our short tour. Another city I'd played many times doing stand-up. Sundays were usually my designated comedy night in Leeds at a surreal-looking establishment called the Dry Dock, which was basically

* I apologise if you didn't know the end of *The Sixth Sense*. You clearly mustn't watch ITV2 because they show it twice a week.

a pub in the shape of a boat. Looking like it'd fallen out of the sky, it sat landlocked and slightly askew in the middle of a bypass in the city centre. The whole thing was constructed out of wood and this often led to interesting variations in the acoustics. The whole room rattled when the microphone peaked, and the cymbals on the drum kit would vibrate so loudly, acts would often be reduced to a whisper. I remember meeting a lovely group of lads there who would later become a group themselves called the Kaiser Chiefs. Funny how life works out.

Playing universities with the Shirehorses was something I was more than familiar with as I'd already had experience playing the student circuit having worked on the Comedy Network. This was a network of gigs run by a comedy promoter called Avalon, which consisted of almost every student campus across Britain. It could be good work, if it was local, but if you weren't careful you could end up out-of-pocket at the other end of nowhere. The first year I did them I got £125 a night supporting a headline comedian whose stage name was Duncan D'Sorderly (see what he'd done). We travelled everywhere on those gigs from Belfast to Basingstoke, Torquay to Tobermory, thankfully in separate cars, as he was a bugger for giving my act a post mortem as soon as I left the stage each night, analysing every line and giving me tips on my delivery. Then he'd go on stage and die on his arse. Should have called himself Pot Kettle.

The second year, I became the headline act and got £350 a night but I never enjoyed the gigs as I found them to be too easy. All I had to do was sing kids' TV themes and talk about serial killers. They couldn't relate to my stories about working in Top Rank Bingo and Netto because most of them had never worked themselves. I was playing to eighteen-year-olds on freshers' week, who were quite happy lying face down in their own vomit while I sang the theme tune to *Button Moon*, and talked about Fred West. The money was good but it never felt like real comedy.

Meanwhile back on tour with The Shirehorses we found ourselves in Portsmouth, which was a hell of a drive to a hell of a gig. And I mean hell. It felt wrong as soon as I walked on stage to find a group of pissed-up lads in rugby shirts spinning in a circle chanting, 'We are the lads, we are the lads, we are, we are, we are the lads', the audience around them scattered in all directions.

'Hello and welcome to The Shirehorses . . .' I hadn't even said the word 'tour' when a pint of beer hit me on the arm and smashed on the floor followed by a cheer from the lads.

'Who threw that?' I said like a schoolteacher, my shirtsleeve dripping with beer.

'Me,' said a cocky one at the front of the stage, so I stepped forward and booted him in the head. As he went down, a cheer went up as I quickly introduced 'The Shirehorses'.

This of course came as a complete shock to Mark, Lard and the rest of the band who were expecting my usual twenty minutes as opposed to two.

Hurrying on stage, Mark had no sooner sat down behind his drum kit when a second pint of beer whistled past his head and smashed to the floor.

'Fuck you, Plymouth,' he said angrily, which was completely justified, if unfortunately the wrong town. This did very little to calm the crowd.

The same thing happened to Kiss when they played the Manchester Arena. After numerous pyrotechnic explosions, the band eventually bounded on stage, Gene Simmons grabbed the mic and shouted, 'We are here to rock you, Birmingham.'

Ace Frehley the lead guitarist leant over to Gene Simmons and subtly shouted something into his ear.

'Er . . . I mean Manchester,' said Gene, correcting himself. By the way, just for your information, I was stewarding that night, in case you had visions of me being a closet Kiss fan.

The worst gigs I ever did for pissed-up students were in the summer when the Comedy Network was quite literally a load of balls, graduation balls, which would usually take place in grand hotels on the outskirts of town, as opposed to the dingy Student Unions I was used to playing. They'd go all out for one night at the end of the year, the lads in their bow ties and dinner jackets, the girls in their fabulous ball gowns, but they all still had the same thing in mind: getting completely rat-arsed. Graduation balls would take drinking to a completely new level. They'd be so paralytic by the time I came on they couldn't see each other, let alone the stage.

The most bizarre graduation I ever played was in a marquee at Stafford Uni, which was ludicrously situated by the side of a second marquee containing the American rapper, Coolio. That noise was unbearable. How I was supposed to compete with it I'll never know. I resorted to singing a mashed-up version of the theme from *The Littlest Hobo* to 'Gangsta's Paradise' next door. Those that can remember it had a great time.

A similar thing happened to me when I played the Leeds festival. In the wake of its success, stand-up quite literally became the new rock'n'roll when comedy began to appear on the bill at music festivals. Like most stand-ups I got several bookings to appear at these mud fests. On the plus side the money was good and you had access to semi-clean Portaloos backstage, but invariably the gigs weren't.

It was a bad juxtaposition, in particular in Leeds when some tit decided to put the stand-up marquee next to the rave tent. It was probably the same gobshite who'd organised the graduation ball at Stafford Uni. The drum and bass was so powerful it virtu-ally made it impossible to resist performing to the beat. As a result I went through forty minutes of material in quarter of an hour. Every comedian similarly suffered that day, the only exception was The Bastard Son Of Tommy Cooper, who was so far removed from reality I don't think he even noticed there was a rave next door.

His act basically consisted of self-mutilation in a fez. If he wasn't hammering nails up his nose or into his eyes he'd be cutting his arms with an enormous kitchen knife. Hence our insistence on him topping the bill, as we knew we couldn't possibly top that. Plus we also knew from previous experience how difficult it was to perform on a stage covered with blood. I had no intention of slopping through my material, even if I was wearing wellies.

I encountered quite a few peculiar acts during my stand-up days. Martin Bigpig was another one, an extremely funny Irish comedian whose finale usually involved a member of the audience reluctantly holding a handgun at arm's length, while Martin pulled the trigger using a piece of string clamped to one of his nipples. It never failed to bring the house down and tears to my eyes every time.

Another bizarre act I once had the misfortune of sharing a stage with was Mr Methane, the ex-British Rail train driver who had managed to turn a personal affliction into a successful stage career. You may have come across him (though hopefully not in a confined space) on TV, most recently on *Britain's Got Talent* (or *Britain's Got Tired* as my nan prefers to call it). His act consists of him farting to music. The professional farter, or stage flatulist as he prefers, was appearing at the Pleasuredome, which at the time was Doncaster's newest and finest entertainment complex (or so the manager kept telling me).

I watched from the wings with a mixture of shock and nausea as Mr Methane lay on a trestle table, legs akimbo with a hand-held microphone jammed up his rectum, the audience applauding loudly, as he fired out his arsenal of toxic missiles in perfect time to Strauss's 'Blue Danube'. When his 'act' was over I had the undesirable task of having to wade through his poisonous fog to get centre stage. I'd managed to get halfway with my jacket over my nose when the dirty, cheeky bastard tried to hand me his soiled mic. I declined and had to resort to shouting his name from under my jacket.

Without a doubt the strangest gig I ever played was a private party at Tankersley Manor in Barnsley. I knew little if anything about the gig except I was booked to be the MC for the evening for about three hundred people attending a four-course meal with a variety of entertainment. It sounded like a typical bog-standard Saturday night or so I thought. On arrival I was given a room to freshen up in and was told by the manager that one of the acts had already arrived and was next door to my room. Not knowing who was on the bill, I decided to pop next door and say hello. The door was opened by a six-foot lizard and I shit myself, well more or less. Well you would have probably have done the same. It looked like something from *Doctor Who*, all scaly and green with big yellow eyes; it truly was a terrifying sight.

'Ullo,' it said in a deep Brummie accent.

'Hi, I'm the compère tonight, thought I'd come and say hello,' I said casually, looking over its shoulder to find two other men dressed as full-size lizards sat on the bed watching *Baywatch*. It was a whole lizard family.

'Kiss my axe,' he said.

'What?'

'Kiss My Axe, we're on first tonight, come in and say hello to the lads.' (Or rather lizards.)

I crept into the room as casually as I could muster, given the circumstances. On closer inspection the two lizards on the bed watching *Baywatch* were taking turns painting each other's scales. I heard a toilet flush and then a voice say, 'Would you like a beer?' I spun round to find a fourth lizard emerging from the en suite holding up a can of Stella. Jesus, where did he come from? This was getting more surreal by the second.

'No thanks,' I said nervously. Although I knew I had nothing to really be nervous about, standing in a tiny hotel room with four grown men in lizard costumes didn't half put the wind up me.

'What would you like me to say in your introduction?'

'Er . . . er . . . I don't know,' said the Brummie lizard who had answered the door.

'Mention the full lunar eclipse next week and tell them the end of the world is nigh,' said lizard number four with the Stella.

'That'll get them warmed up . . . by the way, what exactly do you do, if you don't mind me asking?' I said.

'Oh, that'd be telling,' said lizard number four as he put down his Stella and pulled out a chainsaw from the wardrobe. He fired it up, the noise was deafening. That's when I think I really did shit myself. I backed off to the door.

'Turn it off, Roy, I'm trying to watch this,' said one of the lizards on the bed. I quickly left them to it. Shell-shocked, I wandered back to my room for a lie-down. If they were on first then I didn't know if I wanted to meet the rest of the line-up.

The structure of the night was an act per course, I was to top the bill doing twenty minutes' stand-up. That was no bother; Kiss My Axe had just given me twenty minutes alone. With the audience gathered in the Sutcliffe Suite I began, 'Good evening and welcome to Tankersley Manor, we've got a great show for you tonight and without further ado, ladies and gentlemen, please Kiss My Axe.' (Well how could I resist, it was on a big fat comedy plate.)

The Sutcliffe Suite immediately plunged into darkness, the applause severed by the sound of revving chainsaws, then into the spotlight they crawled, like giant Velociraptors wielding their chainsaws over their heads. A few of the women screamed at the sight of them and a few of the men almost passed out from the smell of petrol fumes. Then with cutlery shaking to the opening of 'Bring Your Daughter to the Slaughter' by Iron Maiden, Kiss My Axe began a violently choreographed chainsaw battle against each other. Sparks were literally flying, as chainsaws clashed. They were chasing each other around tables, throwing bread rolls, the place was in uproar. After what I can only describe as ten minutes of unbridled carnage, Kiss My Axe crawled back out of the room silhouetted against a blinding stream of pyrotechnics and the big light came back on.

'Kiss My Axe, ladies and gentlemen . . . what about that? Now if you can enjoy your soup through the smell of Four Star please do so and I'll see you in a bit.'

Next up was 'Gerard Naprous & Smokey Joe'. I know, me neither. It's what was written on the back of the running order

I'd been given and after the Kiss My Axe debacle, I didn't know what to expect.

'Ladies and gentlemen, would you please welcome your next act this evening, Mr Gerard Naprous and Smokey Joe.'

It had sounded a bit like a ventriloquist act to me, but how wrong I was when the doors to the Sutcliffe Suite burst open and in rode a man on a full-size horse.

'Fuck me,' I said. I thought I'd inhaled too much Unleaded myself at that point. 'There is a horse in the Sutcliffe Suite'.*

With the room once again in uproar, Smokey Joe proceeded to perform a number of horsey-type tricks like dancing, drinking a bloke's pint at table twelve and taking a shit in the middle of the dance floor. Though I don't think that was part of the act. The management weren't too happy either after their three-million-pound refurb. 'What kind of a nutter booked this nutter?' I said to myself as I stood open-mouthed in the wings. The act came to an abrupt end when Smokey Joe bolted through the fire doors and into the car park dragging Gerard Naprous behind him. Well I hope it was part of the act, as nobody went to check if he was all right. Completely gobsmacked, I begged the audience to show their appreciation for Gerard Naprous & Smokey Joe and asked a passing waiter if he had a dustpan and shovel handy. The room now stunk of horse shit and Four Star.

And for dessert what could be better than a professional regurgitator, Mr Stevie Starr, surely the perfect accompaniment for any meal. I was at the end of my tether by now, some clown was seriously having a laugh with those bookings.

I'd seen this fella before on *The Last Resort* with Jonathan Ross

* A line I would repeat a few years later when I would re-create that very moment in an episode of *Phoenix Nights*.

and had almost spewed up then. I couldn't believe some moron had booked him to perform at the end of a three-course meal. Don't get me wrong, I'm not knocking the bloke's act, he's clearly a gifted man, but watching somebody sicking up live goldfish when you're tucking into your profiteroles is not my idea of entertainment. He swallowed everything that night, from people's car keys to snooker balls, and then brought it all straight back again. How does he do it? Why does he do it? And more importantly when did he realise he could do it? There's bad planning and then there's taking the piss. It was almost as bad as the time I once performed on a variety charity show where the Falklands war hero Simon Weston was scheduled to appear directly after a fire-eater. I kid you not. Walking on to a stage still reeking of paraffin, Simon bravely accepted a cheque on behalf of his charity Weston Spirit. Somebody was having a giggle that night too.

It turned out to be a right old week for weird and wonderful gigs as the following night I found myself in a Trusthouse Forte just outside Blackburn performing at a taxi drivers' Christmas party, the odd thing though was that it was the middle of July. After the previous night's fiasco in Barnsley I was beginning to suspect that there was some kind of vendetta forming against me. Nevertheless I drove towards Blackburn with a boot full of suspicion.

Sure enough it was exactly that, a Christmas party complete with a thirty-foot decorated Christmas tree with presents underneath, and a DJ dressed as Santa playing Slade as I walked in. Sadly, though, the huge room was only a third full. Typical taxi drivers, I thought to myself, they're probably still on their way or trying to find it. Apparently the reason they were having a Christmas party in July was because it was the quietest time of the year for them as Christmas is normally choc-a-clock when they're out ripping people off, charging them triple fare and then some on New Year's Eve.

Thankfully I had quite a lot of material about taxi drivers to go at but in a moment of inspiration I decided to kick off my performance by getting them all to turn their chairs around so that they had their backs to me. They were quite reluctant at first but eventually they conceded just in time for me to say, 'So have you been busy? What time are you on till?' It was a glorious moment and thankfully it was one they all recognised, having been bombarded with those same two questions every time they got behind the wheel.

People say it because they can't help it. I always say it to taxi drivers every time I get in. I try not to but I don't know what else to say. My mind goes completely blank every time. We'll be driving for about half a mile and the silence will be unbearable. I can't stand it, I have to say something and it just comes out: 'Have you been busy?', 'What time are you on till?', 'What time did you start?' . . . I honestly couldn't give a shit, it just comes out like Tourette's. I've got taxi Tourette's.

But I have a bone to pick with taxi drivers: why are they all liars? I'll order a taxi and nothing comes. Ten minutes, twenty minutes, nothing comes so I call back and they tell me, 'Oh he's coming now' but still nothing arrives. We have a taxi firm in Bolton, you phone up to book a taxi and they answer the phone by saying, 'He's just turning your corner now.' I'm like can I order it first before you start lying to me? Talk about jumping the gun.

Blackpool Opera House was the setting for a variety show in aid of the North West Air Ambulance, which I was asked to compère.

With the usual last-minute pandemonium ensuing backstage before the show, I came on stage to find the enormous red curtains that were behind me were closed. 'These should be open,' I said waving to the crew in the wings. I walked to the centre of the stage, hoisted up a huge swatch of red curtain and, slinging it over my shoulder, I walked towards the wings, the curtains separating behind me. 'That's more like it,' I said and started the show.

For some reason I arrived back on stage in the second half to find the curtains closed once again. 'What's going on?' I said, shaking my head as I hoisted up another swatch of curtain and headed toward the wings. Immediately I heard a shriek. I turned to see a magician squashing his female assistant into a box. Whoops! The audience cheered and I quickly closed the curtains.

Next we've got a magic act, as if you didn't know. They're called Sapphire and I hope they're good because I've never been keen on magic acts, especially the ones that gesture all the time and insist on holding up every piece of their stage equipment for the audience to see, like it's not a trick. We know it's a bloody trick, it's magic. And they always play 'It's a Kind of Magic', too.

Then I introduced Sapphire, who jogged on stage to the opening bars of 'It's a Kind of Magic' and proceeded to gesture every piece of stage equipment they had. For their big finish the magician's assistant mysteriously disappeared into a box, well there was very little mystery left after me exposing their trickery to the world. All I can say is, it was an accident.

After piercing numerous swords into the box, the female assistant miraculously reappeared to a very weak applause. And I thought they'd finished. 'Ladies and gentlemen, Sapphire,' I said, walking back on stage, desperate to raise a better response from the audience by way of an apology for ruining their big finish. Well (and this was the excruciating bit) I assumed it was their big finish but no. The magician wheeled out another trick, leaving me standing a third of the way across the front of the stage with my hand outstretched, looking, may I add, like a complete cock. I had two choices: do an embarrassing retreat into the wings or stand there and pray it was a short trick. I stayed and it wasn't. Jesus, it went on for what seemed like an age, my outstretched hand slowly returned to my side, an embarrassed smile glued to my face. Finally they finished to even weaker applause from a now confused audience.

'Sapphire, ladies and gentlemen, how do they do it? . . . Why do they do it? And why did that last bit take so bloody long?'

I seemed to be plagued with unlucky magicians. Like the time I shared a bill with Welsh magician The Great Ddewin. Some local yobs set fire to the bins round the back of the theatre. The smoke slowly found its way to the stage in the middle of Ddewin's act, where the audience simply assumed it was part of his stage theatrics, well they did until he collapsed from smoke inhalation in the middle of an elaborate rope trick and had to be rushed to Llandudno General.

The most unfortunate magician I ever had the pleasure of working with was Sheikra! The Bird Lady Of Barrow. The transsexual ex-army cook who hailed from Carlisle may have had the forearms of Popeye and Noel Gallagher's unibrow but 'it' could quite literally charm the birds down from the trees and, on that particular night, straight back up into an extractor fan. Nobody saw it coming, least of all the dove. It happened in an instant. With the audience in uproar and the backing band covered in bird's innards, a traumatised Sheikra fled the stage to the strains of 'Every Little Thing She Does Is Magic'.

Chapter Seven

Comedy Prostitute

The corporate circuit was one area I was keen to work in. I'd heard comedians talk of doing private gigs for big companies for even bigger money, but how did I get booked for one of these gigs? What did I have to do?

'About half an hour, that's all I did last night,' said comedian Smug Roberts in the dressing room at the Frog & Bucket.

'But what material did you have to do?'

'Just the same stuff you're doing tonight except at a corporate you get a shit load of money for it.'

'But don't you have to tailor your gags to the client?'

'Nah, I never do, the last thing a load of accountants want to hear are accounting jokes. They just want to get hammered and cop off, corporates are basically the same as works dos,' he said.

He wasn't wrong.

Surely there must have been more to this exciting secret other world but there wasn't. Management may see these dos as a team-building opportunity, a chance to discuss sales figures and appraise each other's pie charts. But most workers saw them as a bit of a jolly. It's generally the law that on the last night they have some entertainment and a bit of piss-up and that's when our two worlds collided.

Having fun is a serious business and money is no object when it comes to corporate events. Usually a PR company is hired to do the organising. They oversee everything from the fold of a table napkin to picking up VIPs from the airport. They're also responsible for booking the entertainment: comedian, DJ, cat-juggler – whatever the client wants, they'll find it, at any price.

Anyway, after years of waiting I'd finally booked to go to New York for the weekend with my girlfriend, Susan. I had a friend who worked at the airport and he sorted us out some discounted tickets; he also said if the ground crew saw me wearing a suit we'd get bumped up into first class. So I did and we didn't. I even lingered slightly longer than usual when handing my ticket over at the gate, nodding down at my suit expectantly. Nothing, just seven hours squashed up in economy wearing a shirt and tie. We arrived in the middle of a blizzard, it was February, but I'd never felt cold like it. I sound like my nana when I say that. Every winter she says she's 'never known cold like it' – she's eighty-seven, I'm sure she must have.

We left the hotel for a wander around New York and my face was burning with the cold. I stopped to buy gloves and a balaclava, which Susan found very amusing until two blocks later she ended up buying the same. I'd never felt cold like it (there I go again). When I returned to the hotel I noticed the light was flashing on the phone in my room. I had a message from a PR company back in the UK requesting me for a corporate booking at Euro Disney. They said they'd cover the cost of flights for both of us and my fee was to be five hundred pounds. The only downside was I'd have to cut my dream trip to New York short by a day. What a dilemma! What was I to do?

Out of Sight starring George Clooney and J.Lo was the in-flight movie on our Air France flight to Paris. It had been on nearly twenty minutes and I couldn't make head nor tale of it. My French at school never got beyond *Je m'appelle Peter, j'habite Bolton* but Susan seemed to be enjoying it.

'I didn't know you spoke French,' I whispered.

'What are you on about? It's in English,' she said.

She was right, it was. I had it on the wrong audio channel. Le Dickhead.

So now I finally had my foot in the door on the corporate circuit. Five hundred quid, mind you I didn't know quite what they wanted me to do for that, but you know what: I didn't care. It was an adventure and maybe I'd be able to blag a couple of free passes for Euro Disney so it wouldn't be all that bad. What I didn't take into consideration was the time difference. Leaving New York and arriving in France meant we skipped a night's sleep so I was practically nodding off as we stood waiting at the baggage carousel in Charles de Gaulle airport.

Why do people fight to get in line at the baggage carousel? You see them running with their trolleys trying to shoehorn themselves in near the front. Like a few seconds of time is really going to make a difference. You still have to wait for the bags. 'Come on suitcase, come on suitcase, where are you?' Then when the carousel starts moving, nothing comes, no bags. It's the baggage staff, they're just teasing us. You can see them spying at the passengers through those black flaps on the end.

'Are they all waiting?'

'Yeah, they look well pissed off.'
'Good. Give it another five minutes.'
'Here, stick this broken pram on, that'll wind them up.'
So the pram comes round and nobody claims it.
'Here, stick this cuddly toy on.'
It's like The Generation Game.

A combination of fear and adrenalin kept me going as I performed for thirty minutes in two marquees to over a thousand people. I wondered why my stories of crap pop and baggage carousels weren't hitting the high notes. What the PR company had failed to point out was that a large percentage of the audience were international delegates. Luckily I had a trick up my sleeve, up my M&S Blue Harbour extra-large short-sleeve-shirt-sleeve that is. There was a routine that I occasionally performed in the clubs that involved music. In particular misheard song lyrics that I'd discovered listening to and loving music over the years. Fortunately I had some CDs with me so I gave them to the sound man who played the sections I required, right on cue.

Songs such as 'Drive' by The Cars where at 57 seconds into the track the lead singer throws in an obscure reference to a 'pork pie', in pretty poor taste when you consider that song was played over harrowing footage from Ethiopia at the Live Aid concert. Another was K.D. Lang's 'Constant Craving' (or 'Can't Stand Gravy') where she sings about 'arseholes' at 1 minute and 22 seconds. Check it out if you don't believe me. Hey, I didn't waste my teenage years.

The music routine saved my tired bacon that day as it went down a storm with the international delegates. Both the client and the PR company were very impressed and assured me that they'd be booking me again, and true to their word I found myself on a plane to Geneva two weeks later. But not before I'd blagged two Euro Disney passes for Susan and myself. And why not?

'I had no idea Easyjet flew to Geneva,' said Paddy as we stood in the queue for check-in at Liverpool airport.

'Oh yeah, they get where water can't these days,' I said.

Low-budget flights were really taking off at the time (if you'll forgive the pun). Flying had always been an upper-class sport but now you could suddenly fly to places like Madrid for a fiver or Amsterdam for a quid, and nobody questioned it. If somebody offered you a car for a fiver or a turkey for a quid you'd probably tell them to feck off. Yet fly to another country for under a tenner and we're all straight to the front of the queue. Myself and Paddy included.

This was a highbrow affair, we were checked into a suite at an extremely lavish hotel in the centre of Geneva. Bill Clinton had stopped the previous week, though I doubt he stole as many toiletries as Paddy. I had to physically restrain him in the end – if it wasn't nailed down it was straight in his holdall.

Most of the stuff he took he later wrapped up and gave out as presents to family and friends. Imagine my disgust when I received a set of shampoo, conditioner and shower gels from our trip to Geneva the following Christmas.

I'll never forget when he rang room service just before we left, to complain that there were no towels anywhere in the room and that it was an absolute disgrace. Two minutes later there was a knock at the door; it was a young maid, she was slightly out of breath and balancing a big pile of neatly folded towels. 'Thank you,' said Paddy, as he took the towels off her, and just as the door closed placed them straight in his holdall.

The corporate in Geneva wasn't to be the usual bog-standard thirty minutes stand-up and get off. This was to be a four-day no-expense-spared conference for a major computer consortium (I'll refrain from revealing any more details just in case there are any legal repercussions, oh go on then it was Microsoft).

I'd been booked by the same PR company on the proviso I specifically did my misheard lyrics routine again for the international delegates. But that wasn't all I was required to do, they also wanted me to be master of ceremonies for the full four days of the conference and I was fine with that until they told me exactly what they had in mind.

The event was to take place inside a huge amphitheatre, and as we were in Geneva some bright spark had come up with the idea of having a skiing theme. The stage had been done up to look like a ski lodge. This was no-expense-spared, remember, and I couldn't believe my eyes when I saw the set they'd constructed. It was incredible, like something straight out of the West End. The detail was amazing, right down to the fake snow falling outside the window. In keeping with the skiing theme, the PR company insisted I dress as a skier, bobble hat, ski suit, moon boots, the lot. I felt like a dick. I looked like a dick. Paddy almost fractured a rib from laughing when he saw my ski wear: 'You look like a dick! Now that is *piss* funny.'

Whichever bright spark came up with the idea of the ski outfit hadn't taken into consideration the heat. The snow outside the lodge may have been fake but unfortunately the temperature in the amphitheatre wasn't – it was roasting in there and in that godawful outfit, I almost fainted twice from dehydration. Plus I had to read this bloody awful corporate script from a clipboard.

LINK 1

[Ski lodge door opens – Peter enters/blast of snow behind him]

Ladies and gentlemen, welcome to Geneva and welcome to our base camp. Here we sit at the foot of the Alps, the most awe-inspiring and technically challenging mountains in Europe. My name's Peter Kay and I'll be your guide over the next four days as we scale the heights of success. Let us make a pledge now to reach higher summits and build stronger partnerships as we move onward and upward. Please will you welcome your expedition leader and Director of Logistics, Mr Bob Taylor.

[Music: 'The Only Way Is Up' – Yazz & The Plastic Population]

Mr Bob Taylor – forty-minute seminar.

[Music: 'Moving On Up' – M People]

LINK 2

[Peter entering through ski lodge door again – another blast of snow]

Thanks, Bob, for mapping the terrain and showing us the bigger picture. Well we've been climbing for the best part of an hour now *[Peter looks at clock on the wall of the ski lodge]* and if your metabolism is anything like mine you're probably in need of some refreshment, so please help yourself to tea and biscuits and we'll continue our climb in twenty minutes.

[Peter exits – another blast of snow as he opens door]

[Music: 'Climb Ev'ry Mountain' – Peggy Wood]

I felt like a comedy prostitute. My performance was so wooden you could have built another ski lodge with it. It was truly shocking, my only consolation being that I got to redeem myself on the last night doing some real stand-up, minus the ski suit, and my music routine went down a storm once again.

Meanwhile back at the hotel Paddy was still in bed. As I toiled, he slept, drank and wandered around the centre of Geneva looking for porn. Bizarrely he found some in a tobacconist's but then felt compelled to buy four ounces of shag in order to justify his purchase. 'I didn't want him thinking I was a pervert,' he explained, walking out with six copies of *Shaved Asians* under his arm.

Without a doubt the most memorable moment of our excursion to Geneva was the flight home. 'We may experience some slight turbulence,' said the captain, who was obviously drawing on his experience of flying 'copters in Nam. Then the whole cabin began to violently shake as we bounced round the clouds like a deflating balloon. Paddy and myself just casually chatted throughout the whole incident and, apart from a few obvious beads of sweat on Paddy's forehead, we never once flinched.

Later, as we began our descent into Liverpool, we both glanced out of the window and suddenly we saw the tops of the trees appearing through the clouds. Abruptly and violently the plane pulled vertically up, throwing our heads back and pinning us to our seats. I heard a scream over the roar of the engines as the pilot fought mercilessly to pull up. Once again Paddy and I casually continued our conversation as if none of this was happening, only this time when I glanced over Paddy was completely drenched in perspiration.

'Apologies for that, ladies and gentlemen, it appears quite a bit of fog has rolled on to the runway here in Liverpool but not to worry, we'll just circle this old bird round and then we'll have you back on the ground in no time.'

You get what you pay for with flights for under a tenner.

Shell-shocked, we got off the plane in silence and collected our bags in silence. Neither of us spoke a word until we got on to the

M62 and then Paddy screamed, 'WHAT THE FUCK JUST HAPPENED THEN?!'

Paddy remains mentally scarred from that flight home from Geneva. To this day he won't even contemplate boarding a plane without the two 'V's: Valium and vodka.

Word spread about my misheard lyrics routine and the corporate bookings started to come thick and fast. I found myself all over the place, from Newport to Dublin, from Southend to Canvey Island, working for everybody from Millie's Cookies to Coloplast – one of the world's leading manufacturers of colostomy bags and penal sheaths.

After much trepidation on my part, the Coloplast gig actually turned out to be quite a pleasant one. It wasn't the colostomy angle that had bothered me, it was being asked to perform in the after-noon – as I've said before, comedians are like vampires when it comes to performing in daylight. I had to have a conference call with the client, to be briefed before the gig. It was very bizarre, I'd never done one before. The PR company were on the line and they put me through to the chairman of Coloplast. She spent the next twenty minutes telling me how the company was founded, when it was founded, how closely it works with NHS nursing staff, providing penal sheaths, colostomy bags and drainage pouches. God love her but all I wanted to know was did they have a CD player.

She also asked me to pass on a sincere heartfelt thank you from Coloplast to all of the nurses present at the corporate. So at the end of my set I honoured her request:

Before I leave you, Coloplast have asked me to pass on their sincerest gratitude for all the hard work that you do. They want to thank you for being angels, for being the unsung heroes of the medical profession. And while we're on the subject, I'd personally like to pass on my own gratitude to Coloplast because thanks to their products I've been able to go to the toilet twice in the last half hour . . . hang on . . . make that three times.

Slowly I began to understand the protocol surrounding corporate events. A pattern evolved that was quite clandestine. I'd be sent directions and given a phone number to ring when I arrived. I'd then be guided round to the back of the hotel or conference centre to the tradesman's entrance, where I'd normally park next to a skip usually containing old mattresses. I'd then be led through a fire door and the kitchens to the backstage area. I've done so many corporates over the years, I now like to consider myself something of an expert when it comes to the rear entrances and kitchens of British hotels and conference centres. I could even have it as my specialist subject and go on *Mastermind*.

Normally the client would request I arrive early for an informal briefing. I always obliged, it *was* their money after all. Most of the time the clients were lovely people, down-to-earth and modest. Occasionally I got the odd arsehole, whose sole reason for meeting was to try and get me to crowbar obscure references to work colleagues into my material. I realised I was being paid to fulfil the client's wishes but there were limits.

Sometimes I think they saw the comedian as a means to airing their grievances, as some of their requests could be extremely cruel. 'Listen, can you get a joke in about Steve Rogers, he works in accounts and he's on table twelve, he got caught with his pants down in Loughborough last week and his wife's just left him', or

'Can you point out our regional sales manager, he looks like a fat Ian Botham with a hair-lip'. I'm not joking.

'I'll do my best,' I said, but I could never bring myself to say anything like that. They weren't using me as a spleen venter.

There was one corporate I did for a company that shall remain nameless (It was Primark. Shit! How did you get me to say that? I can't believe you did it to me again) where I was badgered by a managing director to 'weave in some funnies' regarding a certain store manager whose wife had just been paralysed from the neck down after performing a parachute jump for Cystic Fibrosis. Of course I never said any of those things. I just nodded, winked and pretended to write it all down until they left me in peace.

The majority of the time all I had to do was just act sincere about a world I knew nothing about. Like when I hosted the regional supermarket awards in Scarborough (OK, it was Aldi, now bugger off) and had to announce the winners of categories like 'best regional produce manager' and 'grocer of the year'. It was all completely alien to me but it was like the Oscars to them. They'd travelled the length of Britain to be there, all dolled up in their Sunday best, sitting nervously as I read out the nominees.

'Winner of the deputy sales manager of the year, South West region is . . . Steve Vickers.'

Huge cheer from a table at the back of the room and up he came, high-fiving as he approached the stage to strains of Mariah Carey's 'Hero'. He hugged me, said he loved me in those tea bag adverts with 'Monkey' and before I had a chance to correct him he was sobbing into the mic like Gwyneth.

'This isn't just for me, this is for all my team at Aldi Shepton Mallet [*another cheer from the back*], there they are [*pointing*], they've had a drink and quite rightly so, 'cause they deserve this award just as much as I do.'

The only drawbacks I've ever experienced doing corporates was when a company spent seventy or eighty grand on an event and you'd turn up to discover it was badly organised or the sound system was crap. Like the time I did a corporate for British Aerospace at The Belfry in the West Midlands. There was some money spent on that – they had a Scalextric in one room, a mechanical bull in the other and a full-size funfair in the car park. And yet some dickhead had wired my microphone through the disc jockey's PA, which was fine until I raised my voice and the whole of his light display revolved. I was reduced to whispering, and when occasionally I forgot my technical constraints I was left either blinded or in total darkness as the DJ's lights rotated straight into my eyes.

Another corporate I did was for a computer programming company in Kent. After driving for what felt like a week through Friday traffic, I turned up to find the disco already in full swing. Then I can't believe what the DJ said: 'OK, right, everyone's got to sit down now as it's time for your comedian.' I was raging as I nervously made my way across the dance floor to the sound of boos and jeers. I remember standing in the middle of the dance floor watching the last of the stragglers reluctantly returning to their seats. They hated me before I'd even started. I didn't blame them really, I mean one minute they're dancing to the Vengaboys and then up I tip with my jokes, ruining their fun.

Completely unnerved and desperate for an exit, I suddenly had an idea. By discreetly slipping my thumb underneath my hand-held microphone I was able to flick it off. It felt like I was committing suicide but what did I have to lose? They didn't want me there anyway. I began doing my material but they obviously couldn't hear me. Feigning alarm at my lack of sound, I scoured the room for my contact from the PR company and managed to catch her eye, which wasn't hard, as she was standing in the corner of the room with a look of sheer panic on her face. Gesturing helplessly to her, I shrugged my shoulders and waved my hands as she beckoned me off the dance floor. As I was walking towards her I carefully turned the microphone back on.

An anxious sound man waiting with her took my microphone: 'Two, one, two', it was fine (of course it was, I'd just flicked it back on). 'It must be the radio waves,' he said, clutching at technical straws. I thanked him, rolled my eyes and wearily walked back to the dance floor and casually flicked the microphone off again. I began again, still there was no sound. By now the audience were on their feet shouting obscenities. The sound man waved me back over to him. With bread rolls whistling past my ears, I walked off the dance floor and flicked the microphone back on. The sound man changed the batteries so I walked back out, turned it off, gestured and he called me back again. I was eventually advised by my PR contact to 'just forget it'. She hastily gave the DJ the thumbs-up to resume playing, and I headed for the car park, leaving a completely stumped sound man behind me and three hundred computer programmers doing the Macarena. I just hope they never read this, otherwise they'll probably want their money back.

Chapter Eight

The Untold Dangers of Genital Piercing

Sometimes it's difficult knowing how to pitch the entertainment at corporate events and my comedian friend was correct in his description, corporates are just like works dos. You really don't know what you are dealing with until you arrive, and you have to live off your wits. Like the corporate I did in a castle in Wales. It was extravagance to the max, a private party for a wealthy family who were celebrating their youngest son's retirement at the age of thirty-one. I think you can gauge the level of wealth I was dealing with.

Paddy and myself travelled down on the train and had to catch a later one than planned, as 'Paddy time', (like Chico's) appears to be completely out of sync with the rest of Britain. Arriving late at the castle, we were whisked up to a room in the east wing to freshen up, which in Paddy's language means seeing how much you can stick on the client's tab. He was a bugger for doing this and with his tendency to enjoy the perks of *my* job a lot more than me I'd been forced to keep *his* corporate invites to a minimum. I just couldn't cope with the stress. He saw every corporate as a freebie, and I know there was plenty of money floating about but you've got to show some respect. It was like sharing a room with Led Zeppelin. I'd not even have the chance to take my coat off and he'd be on the phone to room service, placing his order whilst simultaneously raiding the mini-bar. 'Come on, chill, its on't tab,' he'd say. He'd order everything on the menu: 'Oh this looks good, Paddy's never had lobster before.' I did a corporate at the Grosvenor House Hotel on Park Lane once and he ran up a £280 bill; we were only there one night. I was downstairs grafting for some Arabs, he was upstairs in a Jacuzzi bath supping Champagne & Red Bull and watching *Charlie's Anals*. Then he drunkenly ordered two breakfasts at fifty quid a pop. He basically ticked everything on the menu card, stuck 'x2' on it and hung it on the door.

When the five waiters wheeled in breakfast at half eight the next morning I almost shat the bed. Paddy'd ordered waffles, omelettes, pancakes, cereal, kippers, yoghurt and a full English for both of us with a side order of baked beans and twelve rounds of toast. For a second I thought I was back in The Complete Take-away and I wasn't even hungry.

They had a facility that enabled you to bring your bill up on the telly by keying in your room number.

'TWO HUNDRED AND EIGHTY QUID?'

'Chill, it's on't tab.'

'They'll never book me again.'

'Course they will, that kind of money's feck all to an Arab, son.'

Coming out of the lift, we went our separate ways. Paddy inconspicuously whistled his way through a revolving door with a copy of *The Times* under his arm, while I checked out at reception.

'Excuse me, there seems to have been a bit of a mix-up, I think room service brought me the wrong breakfast this morning, I only ordered a continental.'

There was a lot of mumbling and pointing at the computer screen, then the Chinese receptionist said, 'You are Mr McGuinness?'

'Who? Never heard of him, flower.'

Mind you they still charged me for *Charlie's Anals*, as the Arabs wouldn't pay for Paddy's smut.

Meanwhile back at the Welsh castle my contact from the PR company and the main client (and head of the family, he sold yachts) decided to call in to my room for a brief pre-gig chat. Catching us unawares with four courses of room service scattered across the room, he didn't appear that impressed.

'I believe you missed your train?'

'Bastard taxi never turned up, I rang him twice,' said Paddy with a mouth full of Szechuan pork.

'Yes we did miss our train, apologies for that,' I said, quickly trying to gloss over Paddy's outburst.

The client then gave me a scenario: 'OK, say I've got three comedians . . . er . . . Billy Connolly, Ben Elton and Mike Reid. Which one are you most like?' he said.

'Mike Reid? I thought you said you had comedians,' said Paddy butting in.

'Er . . . Billy Connolly I suppose,' I said, hoping it was the correct answer.

'Oh, right,' he said in a tone suggesting it wasn't.

'Hey, by the way, cheers for this food, mate, really enjoying it, you don't mind if we order some more drinky droos, do ya?' said Paddy.

'What time do you want me?' I said, glossing again.

'Well they're just starting the meal and then they're watching the football so you've plenty of time,' said my contact from the PR company.

'Hey, Paddy forgot about that, stick the telly on.'

The client could hardly conceal his look of disdain as he left the room.

This is the last time I'm bringing him, I thought as I searched for the remote.

It was gone eleven by the time England had been kicked out of the World Cup by Argentina, so let's just say the clients weren't exactly in party mood. Paddy was inconsolable, suggesting that the death penalty wasn't good enough for Beckham after the stunt he'd just pulled. I was at my wits' end – if there was ever a bad time for comedy, it was tonight.

I'll never forget the girl from the PR company chatting to Paddy as I stood waiting to go on. She asked him how he would rate me as a comedian.

'I'll put it this way, flower: I've never seen him die.'

That was all about to change.

The silence was unbearable. I felt like a court jester standing in the corner of this gargantuan dining hall draped in Union Jacks. The few remaining family members, eight to be precise, sat round an enormous wooden table, drunk and devastated. I didn't stand a chance nor did I have a microphone, which was apparently an oversight on the PR company's part, as well as any lights or a stage. But I did have candles, the floor and a fair pair of lungs, so a bad workman couldn't really blame his tools that night. To be honest I did get a few titters, well a couple of coughs at least. The only person who did laugh was Paddy, squatted in the opposite corner; he almost cracked a rib watching me suffer and was forced to leave the room he was laughing so loud.

It was a horrible experience but I did my time, thirty of the longest, most uncomfortable minutes I have ever spent.*

The pisser came a week later when I found out that the client was refusing to pay me on the grounds that I wasn't funny. What a bloody cheek! It wasn't my fault Beckham got the red card and England lost on penalties, I'm sure if they'd have won things would have been different. I could have chased them through the courts and got the money but didn't want the hassle. In the end I just put the whole thing down to experience and was relieved for once that Paddy had ordered all that room service.

It's been quite a while since I last shared a hotel room with Paddy but coincidentally we ended up in the same hotel together just last week, and even more bizarrely he was next door. He phoned me for a chat and mentioned the name of the hotel where he was staying in London.

'I'm staying there,' I said.

'You're kidding, what room are you in?'

'210.'

'Bollocks, I'm in 211.'

'Bollocks, are you?'

'I am, 211, right on the main road.'

'I'm walking up the road now.'

'Where?'

---

* That's not counting an episode of *Tonight With Trevor* I once watched about the untold dangers of genital piercing.

I looked up to the second floor and saw the curtains open in one of the rooms followed by a vision of Paddy standing at the window.

'I'm here . . . wey hey! I can see you!'

It was a funny moment, two grown men on mobiles, waving to each other hardly able to contain their excitement.

We met up that night for something to eat and ended up back in my room for a drink. As usual Paddy helped himself to the mini-bar; some things never change. He was down filming something for TV and said they were picking up *his* tab. I thought, Heaven help them, they'll be filing for bankruptcy by the time he's checked out. It got late, we said goodnight and he went back to his room and then I noticed that we had connecting doors. Excited, I called him. I could hear his phone ringing next door.

'Hey, we've got adjoining doors.'

'Oh aye, so we have, hang on, I'll see if I can open it,' he said. I heard a bit of fumbling and banging.

'It's locked,' he said. 'I'll ring down and get them to open it.'

After numerous attempts by various members of staff and several keys, forty-five minutes later the door was finally opened.

I walked into Paddy's room and had a look around, while Paddy walked into my room and had a look around.

'OK, right, I'll see you in the morning, goodnight,' and with that we went back to our separate rooms.

Six hours later I awoke to the sound of knocking. Fumbling for a glance at the bedside clock, it was 7.03 (stray number, now I'd have to wait till five past).

'Are you up, son? I've got an omelette going spare here if you fancy it?' shouted Paddy through the adjoining door.

'No ta, you're alright.'

It's on't tab,' came his muffled response.

Then I had a revelation. If all of Paddy's extras are being paid for by the TV company, why couldn't they pay for mine? It was about time the tables were turned, and now the shoe was on the other foot Paddy was about to get a taste of his own medicine* after all those years of frivolous corporate spending.

With revenge in mind I strode completely naked through the adjoining door and straight over to his mini-bar.

'Wow! What are you doing, you dirty bastard? I'm eating a full English.'

'I'm restocking my mini-bar and why not, yours is on't tab,' I said, removing three bottles of Budweiser from his fridge.

'You tight-fisted . . .' and before Paddy could finish his sentence I heard the sound of the adjoining door slamming shut.

'Shit!' we both said simultaneously.

Five minutes later Paddy opened the door to a concierge and some other bloke who resembled a young Derek Griffiths and who was holding what looked like some kind of ice-cream scoop. Lord knows what he was planning to do.

'Could you open the adjoining door please, bud,' said Paddy.

'Er . . . you know who is in there?' said the concierge in some accent. I couldn't hear properly as I was hiding in the bathroom.

'Yeah . . . er . . . it's my mate, he's in there,' said Paddy.

'What is your friend's name please?'

'Mr Kay,' said Paddy.

The concierge then started knocking at the door.

'Mr Kay, Mr Kay . . .'

---

* I lost my proverbial mind.

This seemed to go on for what felt like an eternity. It was painful. I was so desperate for Mr Kay to answer the door that at one point I even tutted with impatience and shook my head.

It was excruciating but I had no choice but to come clean. With zero options and the same amount of dignity, I silently strolled out of Paddy's en suite wearing a robe I'd found on the back of the door, three sizes too small for me. Still holding my Budweiser, I gave a gentle, if slightly effeminate, cough. All three of them turned.

'Yes, I'm Mr Kay,' I said, as if it was a normal situation.

'Um . . . you are Mr Kay?' said the concierge, pointing at the door.

'I am indeed and I need to get back into my room,' I said quite forcefully, acting all masculine, if indeed I didn't look it.

'Mr Kay, do you know who the person is next door?'

'It's me.'

'You are next door?'

'Well no, not right now, I'm here but I'm locked out of next door.'

'I'm confused,' he said.

'Join the fucking club,' said Paddy, who by now was sat on the bed with his head in his hands. Whichever way you looked at it, things looked queer. And you can take that how you like.

'OK, I will need to use my master key and try the other door.'

'What other door?' I said, looking round.

'The room door, next door,' he said.

Christ, this was shaping up like I was in an episode of '*Allo, 'Allo*.

'Just open this one,' I said.

'I do not know who is occupying next door, I would prefer to try the main door.'

'I'm in next door!' I said, getting all high-pitched and defensive.

But he was having none of it and left with the young Derek Griffiths, scoop in hand.

Paddy and me, we didn't speak. He glared at me. I shrugged my barely covered shoulders. I could hear some muffled knocking and the odd 'Mr Kay' then they returned.

'There seems to be somebody behind the door,' said the concierge with concern in his voice, the young Derek Griffiths raising his scoop to elbow height. That's when I remembered the duvet. Second confession of the book: I hate light in my bedroom, any kind of light from the red TV light to streetlight shining over the curtains. I am aware that simply shutting my eyes will solve the problem but even with my eyes shut I know it's shining and as you've probably surmised by now the cheese slid off my cracker a very long time ago. As a result of my OCD I'd put a spare duvet behind the bedroom door in an effort to block out the light.

'You've put the covers behind the door, haven't ya?' said Paddy, obviously aware of my disorder, having shared many a hotel room over the years.

I nodded sheepishly. The concierge turned away as if eavesdropping on a domestic. Whereas I don't think TYDG* even spoke the Queen's.

Without a word Paddy marched out of his room, into the corridor and booted my bedroom door open. 'Stick that on't tab,' he said as he grabbed his coat and left the building. A joiner was called to patch up the lock and as for the cost, well like Paddy

* The Young Derek Griffiths.

said it went 'on't tab'. One hundred and thirty two pounds, which turned out to be a lot more expensive than three Budweisers.

Ten minutes later I got a text from Paddy en route to the TV studios: 'You need mental help, my friend.'

Occasionally I've stood in for other comedians on corporate events – a last-minute cancellation or illness can often lead to a lucrative opportunity. One occurrence was standing in for the comedian Al Murray – the Pub Landlord – at the eleventh hour in Manchester. I literally got the call that afternoon and luckily for all parties I happened to be free that evening (well I could tape *Casualty* and watch it when I got back, as the gig was only down the road).

On arrival I was immediately whisked into an office to speak to the client, the managing director who himself had booked Al Murray and wanted to explain what had happened:

'I had Al Murray booked, very funny man, love his shows but I saw him a few weeks ago on tour and he used one or two eff words, nothing too strong and I mean I'm a man of the world, I've been in sewage thirty-six years next May, but I can't have it, I won't have it, we're a family company, I've got delegates out there tonight from Kenya and beyond. I can't be held responsible for lowering standards. I wanted to speak to Al Murray to get some assurance from the man that his expletives could be quashed in light of this being a family performance but he's a busy man is Mr Murray and I could not get hold of him, oh I got reassurances from his *people* but I wanted to hear it straight from the horse's mouth. I waited and I waited but with the clock ticking I was left with no choice but to pull the plug. I was out of the frying pan and into the fire.' (This man was worse than me for speaking in proverbs.)

I was drained when he finally left and then before I went on he took to the stage and told the whole story again, about how he'd had to cancel Al Murray because he didn't want them being subjected to the possibility of foul language. They weren't happy, and if that wasn't bad enough I peeked round the side of the curtain only to see the entire stage decked out for the old Pub Landlord. Beer pumps, barrels and Union Jacks. Christ, this was going to be tricky.

'Once again I apologise, ladies and gentlemen, but I didn't want to run the risk of subjecting you to any obscenities, so please would you welcome your replacement entertainment for tonight, he's a local lad, all the way from Bolton, Mr Peter Kay.'

I walked on stage to 'Rule Britannia', grabbed the mic and said, 'Fuck me, I thought he'd never shut up.' Well I couldn't resist. Luckily it brought the house down and the next half hour went like a dream, without, may I add, any more expletives.

Have you ever been to Wick? Hang on, let me rephrase that question. Have you ever seen where it is? On a map of Britain it's right at the top of Scotland, just twenty miles from John O'Groats. It was to be my destination for a far-flung corporate for Vodafone. I assumed the journey would be a piece of piss: a flight from Manchester to Aberdeen then a connecting flight to Wick, easy. Well the first half of the journey was.

I have a fear of flying, well not so much the flying as the actual checking in/boarding bit. I hate it. Manchester was traumatic enough but at least I roughly knew where I was going, what queue to get in etc. On arriving in Aberdeen I was immediately thrust into the rush-hour chaos. Looking at monitors, trying to clock where I should be headed for a connecting flight. I mean Aberdeen airport isn't exactly JFK but still I get so worked up and stressed with it all. I have no real idea where this comes from. I've been tracing it back to my youth and the closest travelling incident I can attribute it to is the time my whole family caught the train to Great Yarmouth and I decided to get off at Sheffield. Don't ask me why I thought it would be funny. I was nine, almost ten, and when we pulled into Sheffield midway through our eight-hour journey I decided to get off the train and walk down the platform, casually waving through the window as I passed by my family who sat in the compartment. I'd never seen my dad do a double-take like it. He almost choked on his Bovril. Then the train started to move. The look of terror that came over my face was reflected in the glass along with my mum's and R Julie's and her friend Sharon, who always came with us. My impromptu humour thwarted by a British Rail timetable. As I ran along the side of the train I could see my dad doing the same on the inside. This was in the days before train doors locked and I'll never forget the feeling of relief as my dad thrust open the train door and yanked me back on board with one hand. He then proceeded to clip me round the ear as I did a huge walk of shame back to my seat, the other passengers shaking their heads and tutting in disgust. My dad didn't speak to me again until we changed trains in King's Lynn.

Who knows, perhaps it was that one incident that instilled in me a fear of travelling, of being left behind, of missing my flight. Funny then that that was exactly what I did in Aberdeen. I asked a man in a luminous jacket, 'Where do I queue for a connecting flight to Wick?' He pointed and I began queuing. It was a long queue, a very long queue. I thought they'd call me or better still ask for 'all remaining passengers to Wick to make their way to the front'. They probably would have done if I'd been in the correct queue.

'The connecting flight to Wick is over there,' said the lady at the front pointing towards a Servsair desk.

'What?' With that I ran, shouting 'Knobhead' as I passed the bloke in the luminous jacket who had duped me with false information. On reflection, the mop was a bit of a giveaway.

When I reached a closed shutter that read 'Servisair', I realised things weren't looking good. A member of staff was padlocking the door as I handed her my crumpled ticket.

'I'm afraid the flight is closed.' I just made a short high-pitched whining noise. 'You'll have to catch the next flight.'

'When is that?' I said.

'Tomorrow morning.'

A second high-pitched whining sound, this one slightly longer and louder. I felt sick, I felt lost, I felt like one of those passengers you see on *Airline*. I tried pleading my case about the man in the luminous jacket but it was pointless. I could already hear Tony Robinson narrating my scenario as I trudged over to some plastic seating: 'Having missed his connecting flight to Wick, Peter is left stranded till morning in Aberdeen.'

In shock and gutted, I weighed up my options, of which there were few. I chose to make the call to the PR company and try to explain my predicament to them. Standing in the payphone, I almost burst into tears as I rambled on about the man in the luminous jacket and how he'd betrayed me in my hour of need, just like Peter in the Bible. In fact I could have sworn I heard his cock crow three times but maybe it was his mop scraping along the plastic seating.

Surprisingly calm, she told me to 'just get a taxi and get up here as soon as you can'. Clearly she had no concept of the distance involved. Surely it couldn't be that easy? It wasn't. Wick to Aberdeen is like Manchester to Somerset, it's a long haul, made even longer by the fact that motorways are just a dream in that part of the world.

Spying a bank of taxis, I headed over.

'Hello son, where are you headed?'

'Could you take me to Wick please?'

He just laughed, 'Oh aye, where are they?' he said, looking round.

'Where are who?'

'The camera crew, son, this has got to be a wind-up.'

I explained my predicament to him, all about the **** in the luminous jacket, as he was now known, the corporate for Voda-fone and how he would be rewarded with payment and hot soup. I had no idea where the soup came (or would come) from. But God love him, like some ye olde Scottish fairytale, he smiled, said 'Nae bother' and told me to hop in. It was a quarter to five. We arrived in Wick six hours later.

It was a journey from hell and one hell of a journey. No matter how far we drove the place seemed unreachable. I felt like the mother in *Poltergeist* in the scene where she's trying to get to the children's bedroom and no matter how hard she tries it just keeps getting further away. I was worked up and frantic when I got into the taxi; imagine how I felt six hours later. I'd been in fifth gear the whole journey. To make things worse the radio 'didnee work' and all the taxi driver had was a singles compilation tape, *Seventies Gold*, which was on a constant loop until I snapped it in a Texaco garage when he went for a piss in Loch Brora. I had to, for the sake of my sanity – if I'd been forced to endure 'Angelo' by the Brotherhood of Man one more time I'd have opened the passenger door and jumped down a mountain.

We eventually arrived at our destination, which was a huge stately home on the outskirts of Wick. My contact from the PR company was anxiously hovering in the drive, fortunately with some hot soup. With no time to waste I thanked the taxi driver once again and legged it inside before my contact had a chance to read the meter: a grand total of £456.78 – funny how a price like that stays imbedded in your mind for ever. And as much as I wasn't in the mood for performing stand-up, I didn't envy the taxi driver's return journey home.

I'd had plenty of time to run over my material and was keen to just get on stage and use up what little adrenalin I had left. One thing that did tickle me was while I was waiting outside to be introduced I could hear harp music. It eventually stopped and then a few seconds later a young girl staggered out through a doorway dragging an enormous harp behind her. I thought it had been on a CD.

'Please would you welcome your entertainment for this evening – Peter Kay,' said the MC followed by a surprisingly enthusiastic round of applause. With my trusty Dictaphone in hand I leapt on stage (OK, I climbed).

'Good evening, ladies and gentlemen, you wouldn't believe what happened to me on the way here tonight . . .'

Chapter Nine

Jill Dando's Cat

'You've got to go to London,' that's what everybody kept saying to me, but it just never appealed. I like working near home; I like my own bed, it's as simple as that. The whole Dick Whittington scenario wasn't for me and besides, whenever I went to London the streets always seemed to be paved with urine and litter – I never once saw any gold.

Occasionally I read the comedy listings in *Time Out* and as far as I could see the comedy circuit was more of a treadmill, with comedians endlessly doing the rounds week in, week out. Sure there was plenty of work but nobody appeared to be getting anywhere. Plus if I did work down there, by the time I'd deducted the costs of my train fare and digs I made less than I did working back home.

My only incentive to go there was to play somewhere prestigious like The Comedy Store. Almost every comedian had performed there, including one of my heroes, Robin Williams. I'd kept in touch with my old friend Dave Spikey since we'd met during the final of the North West Comedian of the Year. He travelled down to London all the time to do gigs including The Comedy Store, and put in a good word for me with the owner, Don Ward, who offered me a booking.

As I mentioned earlier, The Comedy Store was one of the first clubs to have an early and a late show. And with a long gap in between shows I was able to squeeze in a third gig at The Laugh Resort somewhere in South London. Triple gigs on a Saturday night: I could now see the financial sense in working in London. And fortunately I managed to save some money on digs as my friend Danny Dignan, who you'll remember from my warm-up days on *Parkinson*, kindly put me up at his house in Kensal Rise.

Finally getting to play The Comedy Store was a big deal for me and so I was a bag of nerves going down on the train, repeatedly sifting through my set lists, trying to determine which material was the best and worrying whether or not they would get it darn sarth. I'd alrcady played Bristol, but this was different, this was the smoke, the capital, L-O-N-D-O-N, and I was bricking it. I caught the Tube across to Piccadilly Circus. I tried having a sing-along but the rest of the passengers weren't having any of it, funny how they'll only sing when there's a war on or when Doc Cox dressed up as an aubergine on *That's Life*. I then made my way up to The Comedy Store and there it was: my name. I'd love to say 'in lights' at this point but it wasn't. It was in tiny white individual letters stuck on a black notice board. Nevertheless I'd made it to The Comedy Store and that was good enough for me.

My nerves increased as the audience took their seats. I hadn't been as bad as this in a long time. I mentioned earlier The Comedy Store was one of the clubs that operated a coloured-light system to let you know when your time was up. I'd never worked like that before. But it was a tight ship at The Comedy Store with two shows to do; I'm surprised they didn't just send the comics out on a conveyor belt. I was so worked up about timing my set right I came off stage before the red light had flashed. Don Ward came into the dressing room for a chat with me.

'Eighteen,' he said.

'Pardon?'

'You did eighteen minutes.'

I was supposed to do twenty. He wasn't aggressive about it or anything; it was just a firm reminder of what was required: twenty minutes, no more and no less. It was the complete opposite back home where the club owners practically cheered if you went over your time, as they saw it as getting more for their money.

The gig went well and any worries I'd had about the North/Sarth humour divide proved pointless. They got everything. In fact if I'm completely honest I'd say they actually laughed more than they did at home.

We'll end up like our parents, you know. It's inevitable, forty years from now I'll be telling my children that they don't know they're born and saying things like 'All me and your mam used to have in the evenings was Sky digital and a PlayStation, that was it, and we used to have to make do with a car each. Your mum used to use a thing called a dishwasher, you won't remember them, look at her face, she doesn't remember them. Your mum used to have to load all the plates in, by hand, on her own and turn it on. There was no such thing as androids back then. And you can turn this music off an' all, bloody rubbish, stick some decent music on, put a bit of Prodigy on for your Mum, she loves that 'Smack Your Bitch Up'.

Hurriedly leaving The Comedy Store, I headed out on to Piccadilly Circus to hail a taxi. What are the odds, twenty thousand taxi drivers in Central London and I got a nutter. Squashed behind the wheel, which he practically had to steer with his gut, he was that fat, he looked like a black Hagrid with dreadlocks. And without so much as a 'hello' he launched into an angry tirade of abuse. I almost jumped out of my skin.

'LET ME TELL YOU SOMETHING, *this* country has gone to rack and RUIN. Deprivation, degradation, people dying in the streets and who cares, NOBODY, my friend, NOBODY. It's kill or be killed, it's kill or be killed.'

This man clearly had more than a chip on his shoulder; he had a full bag of Maris Pipers.

'And let me tell YOU I've had enough, I'm getting OUT of here and I'm gonna take a FEW of these FUCKERS with me.'

Oh my God! I thought, What have I got here?

'Er . . . Have you been busy? What time are you on till?'

With a crumpled photocopied fax of a map in my hand, I stood in the rain outside what appeared to be a primary school. Bewildered, I paid Hagrid, minus a tip, which caused him to tear off up the road in search of some fucker to take with him. Thankfully as the roar of the taxi engines subsided I heard the sound of laughter* cascading from the building. Upon closer inspection I observed a tatty banner draped wearily across the school sign. This has got to be a joke, I thought to myself but no, this was indeed 'The Laugh Resort'.

Entering the school through the staff entrance, I followed the sound of laughter† down past the caretaker's room and into the

* Still available from all good stockists.
† And a variety of car boots.

gym/dining/assembly hall/comedy club. The place was packed, hot and rocking with laughter. I'd seen it all now: a comedy club in a primary school? What next, karaoke down the morgue?

Fortunately I was just in time and was on stage within a few minutes. As unexpected as it was to be playing a school, I quickly decided to adapt my material for the situation.

Most of you would have gone to school about the same time as me, about half eight quarter to nine? So we've got a comedy club in a school hall, well this is a first for me. I take it the school know? Oh, they're on holiday? Oh yeah, it's the big summer holidays, six weeks of light nights, water fights and sucking on Jubblies! What were they all about, Jubblies? You could take someone's eye out with a Jubbly if you threw it. Triangular blocks of supposedly flavoured ice and they last you for ever, I've still got half of one in the top of the fridge at home, left over from a street party in '77.

My mum used to force us to make our own mini Jubblies rather than buy them. She'd get the ice cube tray from the top of the fridge and fill it up with Rola Cola. They were horrible. I remember I made one out of bleach one year and almost killed my sister. Mind you, she had it coming. She tried selling my Magna Doodle in the front street when we had a sale outside our house. We did that every summer: put a blanket down and sell stuff – toys, annuals, you name it – and my sister and her mates used to make rose perfume. They'd get an empty bottle of Rola Cola, fill it up with tap water and then put rose petals in it and then sell it. I bet the Avon lady were shitting herself. Eight litres for 40p.

Then when the big summer holidays were over you'd go back to school in September and you find you couldn't write any more. 'What's the matter with me, I can't use a pen?' Six weeks of

Why Don't You? and your hand's frigged. Then the teacher
would come on stage in assembly: 'Come on now, quiet every-
body, simmer down, you're not on your holidays any more' and
there'd be one lad wearing trunks and a snorkel. 'Eh? What?
Nobody told me, quick rub that sun cream in for me, will you.'

My second gig of the night and thankfully not a red light in
sight – sounds like a limerick. With two down, one to go, I quickly
got my money and dashed back out into the rain, hopefully to
find a sane taxi driver who didn't have a death wish and make my
way back across town to gig number three. I felt like Anneka Rice
in *Treasure Hunt* but without the pink jumpsuit.

Shattered and stressed by the time I got back to The Comedy
Store, they'd just started the late show. This was madness. I admit
the money was good but it messed with my head. I didn't know
where I was or who I played to by the time I was introduced for
the third time that Saturday night. Bewildered, I completely veered
off my set list and found myself continuing with the school theme:

Have we any teachers in? Don't shout out, put your hands up,
you should know better. I used to love it when teachers went on
school trips and they used to turn up in their play clothes. They'd
ditch the suits and turn up in kagools and blue jeans, and I'm
talking the bluest of blue you can imagine, bright blue, sky blue,
with the biggest turn-ups you've ever seen, and bright white trainers,
really shit ones too, like your mum would get from the market.
We used to make them pay 10p 'cause they were wearing their
own clothes. We were always allowed to wear our own clothes on
the last day of term. I always wore my uniform, well it was my
own, I hadn't hired it. And you could bring a game in, like Ker-

plunk, Tank Command or My Dog Has Fleas. If you were clever
you brought in Mastermind with that Vietnamese lady on the lid
– who was she and where was Magnus Magnusson?

The gig went down a storm, and after I'd finished Don Ward
came back into the dressing room for another chat.

'Twenty-two,' he said.

'Pardon?'

'You did twenty-two minutes.'

'Well I owed you two from earlier so we're straight now, aren't
we?'

The Comedy Store was a joy to play because the venue had
been specifically designed for stand-up. It made a huge difference,
as normally I had to play to audiences at awkward angles, facing
pillars and people still queuing at the bar. The Comedy Store had
raked seating allowing the whole audience a decent view of the
stage, and a bar tucked away at the back (and closed during
performances) so I didn't have to vie for the audience's attention
whilst I was on. But London was a long way to travel for such
luxury and, to quote Dorothy Gale, 'there's no place like home'.

If playing London that night did anything, it reinforced my
desire to stay local and made me realise how fortunate I was to
have so much work near home. If I could survive in the North I
knew I'd never leave.

You know, it's only become apparent whilst I've been writing this
book just how much work I actually did during those five years
doing stand-up. I honestly never stopped, which I find funny on
reflection because at the time, work was all I seemed to worry
about, or rather the lack of it. I was a worrying workaholic. Could

I get enough stand-up gigs to justify it as a full-time job? And would I be able to sustain the work? Apart from the occasional night I was able to work stewarding at Manchester Evening News Arena, stand-up was now my main source of income and being self-employed caused me to worry even more. I had to get my head round things like tax and national insurance. I'd always had all those things done for me working for a boss. But now I was my own boss and not having somebody telling me what to do took a lot of getting used to. I had to motivate myself to *get* work. Luckily working on the comedy circuit meant bookings tended to generate themselves.

I was still regularly compèring at the Frog & Bucket and was loving my work, churning out new material at a rate even I couldn't keep up with. I also enjoyed the chance to work with some fantastic comedians, one of them being the inimitable Johnny Vegas, who was also a regular compère at the Frog & Bucket.

We'd first met each other in the final of the North West Comedian of the Year where he came runner-up. He was a rising star of stand-up and his appearances had since become legendary on the comedy circuit. His spontaneity could be captivating for an audience, as nobody ever knew what to expect, least of all Johnny. He was like a force of nature, charging around the stage in his maroon jacket with flares to match, causing pandemonium wherever he played. 'Comedy is a campfire, come and get warm,' he'd say in his husky St Helens accent and his legion of loyal fans would always gather.

Johnny never ceased to amaze me with his natural ability to be the clown and fortunately, even though we rarely worked together, as headline acts would only cross paths when they compèred for each other, we became very good friends. He was offered his own fortnightly show at the Frog & Bucket and I was delighted when he invited me along as co-writer and -performer. Still very keen to develop and perform characters at every opportunity, I jumped at the chance.

Every week I would travel over to Johnny's house in Thatto Heath, where after treating ourselves to a chippie dinner we'd endeavour to write *The Johnny Vegas Show*, well I'd attempt to write it while Johnny fumbled through his many cassette tapes in an effort to distract me. 'Listen to this, we could use this,' he'd say as he leapt around his front room singing along loudly to Barbra Streisand's 'Don't Rain On My Parade' as his elderly neighbours thumped the walls.

We had some great ideas for shows, each one with its own theme, like Vegasville, a fictitious holiday park in the style of Butlins. We treated the show like an investment seminar where the audience were invited to help fund Johnny's dream for a better family holiday. We worked really hard, hiring costumes and screens for the show, we even designed the plans for Vegasville, from funfair rides right down to the folding kitchen table/beds available in each time-sharcable chalet. We displayed them on an overhead projector while Johnny encouraged the audience to part with their money.

I appeared on stage as an archetypal Irish builder complete with fluorescent jacket and shovel, and when Johnny asked why we're behind schedule I said we were 'waiting for a skip'. Later I returned as the camp fitness instructor. Wearing a pink shell suit and headband, I attempted to get both Johnny and the audience to do a physical workout to 'Lifted' by The Lighthouse Family.

Two weeks later we were back again with an election special, the audience were given ballot papers and the chance to 'Vote for

Vegas'. We spent hours at Johnny's house making banners and flyers for the show. I remember sitting in the audience for most of that night wearing a false beard and moustache, waiting for the perfect opportunity to leap from my seat clutching a toy gun and assassinate Johnny during his inauguration speech. He died and went to heaven, while I quickly made my escape up to the lighting box where I took on the voice of God whilst frantically working the controls for the smoke machine on stage.

We had such a good time doing those shows. It felt great just getting away from stand-up and trying something different for a change. Such was their success, word spread and Steve Coogan came down one night to watch us. That blew me away: here I was on stage performing characters in an effort to follow in his footsteps and there he was, leaning against the bar and laughing, he was actually laughing at material I'd helped create.

After the show he came up to the dressing room to meet us both. Larger than life and slightly inebriated, he burst in, flung his arms around the pair of us and announced to the rest of the room, 'These two are gonna be the next Vic and Bob, you're gonna be huge.' I remember Johnny's manager's reaction of a lukewarm smile and I sensed that our seal of approval from Steve Coogan as a double act was not part of his comedy plan. 'I hope that's a prop?' said Steve as he clocked the coffin in the corner of the room.

Sure enough, the next day I got a gentle call from Johnny, saying he'd decided to do the next few shows on his own and hoped I'd understand. 'But we're booked till June,' I said, crushed, particularly for financial reasons as I was counting on the money. We didn't fall out and reading between the lines it sounded like he'd been put up to making the call. After all, any fool could see his

potential, there was a TV special in the pipeline and his own one-
man show in Edinburgh. I wished him good luck and we went
our separate ways.

Jesus, I've just got a text saying Michael Jackson is dead! Hold
on while I stick Sky on a minute . . . Bloody hell, CNN are saying
it's as yet unconfirmed. He'll not be dead, he can't be! I've got
tickets for his show at the O2 in a fortnight. He's probably just
trying to get out of it. Shit! Now they're saying he *is* dead. He
has got out of it.

I can't believe this, it's utter madness. Michael Jackson is dead.
I also can't believe I'm writing this down as it happens but I feel
compelled to, it feels historic. Hold on, I've got another text . . .
you're kidding, it's a joke: 'He's not going to be buried he's going
to be recycled.' Jesus, it's not even been five minutes and the jokes
have already started. They'll have a bloody field day with Jacko,
it's on a plate. I wonder what he's died of? He has been looking
a bit pale – See, even I can't help it.

You have to be careful when it comes to jokes in poor taste – and
I should know. I was once on the cover of a national newspaper
for telling a joke about Jill Dando. It was about four months after
she died and I was compèring at the Frog & Bucket. Opening
with my usual jokes, I'd recently added: 'What's black and white
and wants feeding? Jill Dando's cat.' It was a recycled gag that had
previously done the rounds with Mother Teresa and Rod Hull. It
probably got a laugh due to a tenuous topicality as opposed to
shock. It was a playground gag and I thought nothing of it. Two
days later I was on the front page of the *Sun*; the headline read
'BBC In Sick Jill Joke' and underneath a photograph of me. Apparently, I discovered later, the reason the headline said 'BBC In Sick

Jill Joke' was because a few members of staff from the BBC in Manchester (you know, the one opposite Greggs and the beefy ballet school) were watching the show and the *Sun* had spun the story to make it sound as if it was a private BBC party and there they were laughing at one of their dead colleagues. What got me the most was that headline saying 'Sick Joke' and then the paper went and printed it for everyone to read. They obviously couldn't have thought it was that sick.

Still, the whole thing shook me up. I felt like Barrymore, and in anticipation of a flurry of press activity outside my mum's I went into hiding at my mate Michael's house across town. According to Mary Rock over the road, nobody came round, apart from the window cleaner wanting his money, and the pop man.*

Nonetheless it was a shameful moment. I mean the closest my material had ever come to controversial before now was when I'd slagged off Rola Cola and now suddenly I was Bolton's answer to Bill Hicks. I had to ring my dad up and apologise.

'Listen, I've told a joke about Jill Dando and it's in the paper.'

'What have you done that for?' he said.

'I don't know, it just came out.'

'What was it?'

'What's black and white and wants feeding? Jill Dando's cat.'

'Seeding?'

'No, feeding?'

'What?'

---

* Did you have a pop man? We did, you could hear his wagon rattling four streets away. His rainbow bottles shining in the sunlight contained more drugs than a crack-den in Leith, he was practically a dealer now I come to think about it. We always had the same every week: two orange cordials and an American cream soda – you couldn't buy that anywhere else. He also did potatoes and pirate films but I'll save that for another book.

'What wants feeding?' I said.

'I don't get it.'

'It doesn't matter if you get it or not, it's on the front cover of the *Sun*.'

Then he mumbled the joke back to himself, there was a pause and then he said, 'That's rubbish.'

I said, 'We're not debating the quality of the gag, Dad, I'm just letting you know.' His attitude was that if you're going to go down, go down with a good 'un!

Then I had to ring up my nan just in case she wandered down to the Spar for a paper, saw the headline and had a stroke.

'Look, Nan, I gotta tell you something. I've told a joke about Jill Dando's cat and it's on the front cover of the *Sun*.'

'Oh my God,' she said.

'I'm sorry, it was just a joke.'

'And what was it?'

'What's black and white and wants feeding? Jill Dando's cat.'

'Oh Peter, Peter, Peter, why don't you think before you open your mouth?'

Then there was a long pause followed by:

'Anyway, I don't think she had a cat.'

I thought, Great, quick, I best get the *Sun* on the phone and get a retraction, she clearly didn't have a cat.

I just got another Michael Jackson joke: 'Apparently when he was fighting for his life in the back of the ambulance the doctor said "I think we should start CPR", the paramedics said "No we should start heart massage", the driver said "No, we should start an adrenalin drip". Then Jacko, gasping for breath, said "Well you wanna be startin' something." Hey, don't shoot the messenger.

Uri Geller's on the BBC news now; he's a bender, literally. He just said that Michael was a close personal friend of his and when the reporter asked him when he last saw him he said, 'I can't reveal that information'. Why not? Some 'close personal friend', he's only been dead half an hour and already he's on the phone. Vulture.

Oh bugger the book, I'm watching the news. I bet you any money they wheel Paul Gambaccini out within the hour. He does music and Barry Cryer does comedy, them's the showbiz rules.

Hang on, Paddy's ringing my mobile.

'Are you watching this, son?'

'Yeah, I can't believe it.'

'Neither can I, Micky Jackson dead. I was just lying in bed when I got a text from Bully [mate of ours from school], it just said "Jacko's dead", I texted back, "What, yer man from *Brushstrokes*, does those Flash ads?", he text back "No, Michael Jackson". It's shocking.'

'It is, he was one of the best.'

'Never mind one of the best, *the best*. I mean paedophilia aside, Pete, he was the king of pop.'

Chapter Ten

Banoffee Baskets

Fifteen minutes after I won the North West Comedian of the Year, the requests to do charity work began flooding in. How could I refuse? Worse, which ones do you choose to support when there are so many worthy candidates? Thanks to Harry Enfield and Paul Whitehouse, 'charidee' is often perceived as a bid for self-publicity in certain showbiz circles. It wasn't long before it became apparent that the worlds of comedy and charidee were inseparable. Despite being tee-total I reluctantly donated my giant prize bottle of whisky (I so wanted to fill it up with loose change) to Christie's cancer hospital in Manchester and from that moment on I pledged my allegiance to one of the most profound statements I ever heard: 'Charity is quite simply life's rent while we're on earth', and you know who said it? The late, great Jeremy Beadle MBE (thankfully he wasn't dressed as a Rastafarian traffic warden at the time).

The first charity gig that I ever did was a fundraiser for Marie Curie. I was to be the supporting act for the presenter and comedian Clive Anderson, who'd been booked to do a question-and-answer session in an aircraft hangar in Scotland (I shit you not).

As it was on Valentine's weekend I decided to take my girlfriend Susan with me. I did contemplate trying to pass the whole thing off as an impulsive, romantic weekend away but bottled it in the end.

I know quite a few comics who pull stunts like that with their partners: 'Come on, I'm taking you away for the weekend! Oh, and by the way I've got a gig on the Saturday night.' I knew I'd never get away with it. I mean how was I supposed to subtly sneak in a gig in an aircraft hangar?

We caught the train up to Glasgow and then on to Prestwick where Elvis Presley made his one and only appearance in Britain, well I say 'appearance', he changed planes there on the way back from Germany in 1960. The train driver proudly divulged this nugget of information to myself and the rest of the passengers as we pulled into the station. 'Surely he doesn't say that every time,' I said to Susan, well I whispered it to her as I'd seen *The Wicker Man* and thought, You can't be too careful in a remote place like this.

We stopped in a hotel overlooking the sea that had a suit of armour in the corner of our bedroom (I promise you I never tried to put it on, I couldn't even lift the helmet). I had no idea if every room had one but I was just happy to be sharing 'a knight' with Susan (see what I did? I frighten myself sometimes). The accommodation was luxurious and the staff were lovely, a far cry from the Scottish hospitality I'd been used to in the past – when every year my dad insisted we spent the last week of the summer holidays at the Loch Moir B&B in Blackpool.

He loved stopping there, but we all hated it. The place was without a doubt a charmless shithole. 'Come as guests, leave as friends' the felt-tip sign read in the window on arrival, and even though we tried to comply with these rules, we never could.

'Salt of the earth' was what my dad thought of the Loch Moir B&B's two owners, Lynne and Jackie McCabe. Cousins from Kilmarnock, the pair came down to Blackpool before decimalisation and had never gone back. 'As soon as we saw the Golden Mile we knew we'd found paradise,' Jackie would drunkenly confess to us every year with a tear in her eye (as she only had the one). 'They broke the mould when they made those two,' my dad used to say. I was surprised it was just the mould they broke, as they were both a couple of heifers. With matching ginger Afros, they looked like little orphan Annies on the menopause.

Neither of them were ever without a cigarette in their hands and the whole place reeked of nicotine. We used to stop in a family room in the attic and it still smelled like a nightclub up there. I have many a vivid memory of Lynne dishing out her full Scottish breakfasts with a smouldering fag permanently stuck to her lower lip. For years I was convinced fried haggis was supposed to contain ash.

The mad thing was that none of my family smoked. I'm sure the only reason we stopped there was because they used to let my dad pull his own pints behind the bar in the corner of the lounge. It was quite fashionable to have one at the time, they'd had it fitted after a pools win when they decided to give the place a makeover, but their tastes left a lot to be desired and the place looked like it'd been designed by Del Boy Trotter.

Everything was mock Tudor with fake brown leather and an endless collection of horse brasses swinging from every nook and cranny. When it rained (and believe me it never stopped) our only source of entertainment was a cheap computer game they had wired to a TV on castors. It was one of them old TVs, upholstered in a mahogany effect with sticky-out buttons that left an imprint on your finger every time you changed channel. R Julie and me would play on that computer game all the time, playing either tennis, tennis or, if we really got bored, tennis, until one of the other guests would come in and make us flick it off so they could watch *Take the High Road* or the news.

At night we liked to stay in and play tennis or watch telly. That drove my dad crazy as he wanted us to go out. 'You can watch bloody telly at home,' he'd say angrily but it was what we wanted to do. He completely lost it one year when our holiday happened to coincidentally fall on the same week as the *Brookside* siege. We never left the digs and he was going up the wall. But it was real edge-of-your-seat stuff, those two nurses and Pat Hancock held hostage at number seven, bugger the Pleasure Beach.

The one thing I used to dread the most at the Loch Moir was Friday night, as that was party night when Jackie and Lynne invited everyone to stop in for some 'sunshine indoors'. Ironically that was the one night we all wanted to go out but my dad would always insist we stayed in and joined in the 'fun'. The 'fun' consisted of us having to sit through Lynne's annual rendition of the hits of Tina Turner (complete with comedy wig and blacked-up face, it was the eighties after all), whilst Jackie accompanied her on the Bontempi (though I have to admit her pedal work was hypnotic considering she wore an orthopaedic shoe). I can remember trying to watch the last episode of *Salem's Lot* through Lynne's legs, as she paraded around the lounge to 'Nutbush City Limits'.

One year we joined forces with my Uncle Tony and his family for our annual week at the Loch Moir, and their bedroom window fell out in the middle of the night. The noise was deafening as it landed four floors below on the roof of Jackie's Allegro. Distraught, Lynne and Jackie apologised profusely as they proceeded to board up the hole. Well I say 'board', all they had was cardboard, it was half three in the morning after all. We couldn't believe it but Uncle Tony's kids were in the same room and slept through the whole thing. They didn't stir once, they just woke up at half ten the next morning to what they thought was a total eclipse of the sun, and the words 'Lambert & Butler – King Size' where their bedroom window used to be.

Anyway where was I? Oh yes, Prestwick, Valentine's weekend, about to perform on stage in an aircraft hangar. Apparently it was the largest space in the area, which meant more money could be raised for Marie Curie. I met Clive Anderson backstage; he seemed like a nice bloke, though very tall which threw me slightly. He always appeared smaller sat behind the desk on *Whose Line Is It Anyway?*

After a promising introduction from Clive, I took to the stage for my first (and hopefully last) performance in an aircraft hangar. I'd never played anywhere as big as that before and it was tough. Not just because of the nerves but the size of the room. It was overwhelmingly big, as you can imagine an aircraft hangar would be; fortunately there were no aircraft in there at the time. I began with a few jokes, which got a good response, but then I found I had to shout to compete with the noise of the huge air-conditioning units that were attached to the ceiling, blowing hot air into the room.

I asked them if they were aware that Elvis Presley changed planes there in 1960. That went down like a lead balloon; quickly I changed direction and decided to reminisce about the Scottish hospitality I'd been used to at the Loch Moir in Blackpool. Thankfully that all went down very well, phew! And continuing on that theme I decided to confess to them the real reason my dad had a penchant for holidaying in September.

It's the end of the season when things are winding down and all the end-of-the-pier acts go and play the local working men's clubs for a bit of extra money. My dad's logic was that if you went to Blackpool then you could see a top-class show for half the price. Well I say 'top class'; one of the acts we had to watch was a singer called Tony Colorado. Heard of him? No, we hadn't either. He was a cross between Barry Manilow and Barry White with an American stroke Lancashire accent: 'It's great to be over here in England by 'eck tha knows. But eee by gum the weather sure is cold.' I thought, Colorado my arse. Anyway, he sang 'Please Release Me' and he was just getting to the last line when my dad was walking back from the bar with a tray of drinks, I'll never forget it, coming to the end and his big finish, he reached the last line of the song which is 'Release me, my darling, let me . . .' and without missing a beat my dad shouted out, 'GO!' We could have died of embarrassment. Tony Colorado looked up and said, 'Thanks, dickhead' in the broadest Lancashire accent I'd ever heard.

After the hangar gig was over we returned to the hotel for some Scottish hospitality of our own. Susan and myself had a lovely meal with Clive Anderson, a few of the event organisers, Marie Curie staff and crew. It actually turned out to be quite a lavish affair; it was also my first experience of nouvelle cuisine (which I still think is French for 'sod-all'). I didn't understand half of the things that were on the menu, and plumped for chicken as it seemed safe. When it came it was the tiniest portion of chicken, I had to go searching for it under my mushrooms. And then I complained to the waiter, as there were leaves on my plate. I could have died. How was I to know it was part of the garnish? I thought the chef had left the back door open. How embarrassing.

It was a good meal, I could hardly say I was full at the end of it, but still it was a damn sight better than Dairylea Dippers and a cold Ginsters pasty from the motorway services. Mind you, all the time I was eating the meal I couldn't help but think, Who's paying for all this? I know people had to eat and we'd worked all night for free but the way I saw it, this is all coming out of the pot, surely this partially defeats the object of being here.

I was naïve to this world and also quite shocked at people's reaction when they'd ask me to do a charidee gig and I'd say I'd do it for free. Apparently it wasn't the norm, as usually there was a fee involved. I couldn't believe it when I found out people take a fee for doing charity. Some big names too whose attitude was: Well if it wasn't for me being here today you wouldn't be reaping the charitable benefits – I know but they'd be reaping even more if you weren't a greedy bastard. Shame on any showbiz turn who takes a fee for working for charity, you're either doing it for charity or you're not – simple as. The clue is in the word: charity. If you want a wage, take a proper booking.

I still feel guilty about them paying for transport and accommodation but I suppose that's fair enough as long as you don't load it up with extras. Lord help anyone who asks Paddy to do a charity gig.

I've always suffered from cynicism and perhaps it was wrong of me to be dubious about 'expenses'. Or maybe not, judging by the way things have turned out recently.* After several calls from the

* A friend of mine just sent me this he found on a news website regarding controversial BBC expenses: apparently creative director Alan Yentob's expenses include a £1,579.63 claim for an 'executive Christmas dinner' which had just twenty-seven people in attendance, £92.99 on 'hospitality for Trevor Eve' and £7.99 on a book called *The Sound of Laughter*. I have a box full of them in the shed, he could have had one for nowt.

BBC a few years ago I found myself introducing The Who at the Live 8 concert. It was an honour and a privilege to be invited to take part in such a historically important event. Yet while I was wandering around backstage I couldn't believe the hospitality and just how much free stuff there was for everybody. Not to mention free food and drink. There were marquees crammed full of almost every eat and treat you could imagine and when later I was inter- viewed by Chris Evans for Radio 2 and he happened to quote the slogan that signified the whole reason for the event: 'Make poverty history', I said, 'They should try starting backstage, you can't move for grub.' You also couldn't move for celebrities offering their support on the day. Hollywood superstars Brad Pitt and George Clooney made appearances on stage as well as Will Smith on screen, who gave out the heartfelt message, 'Every time I click my fingers a child dies.' I remember standing by the side of the stage thinking, Well Jesus, Will, stop clicking your fingers.

Bizarrely three of the most memorable charity gigs I've ever done have all been with tribute acts. The first was Muscular Dystrophy at a Masonic hall in Rotherham. A truly unforgettable night. I arrived for a sound check and was confronted by a member of the technical staff who asked, 'How would you like your lights tonight?'

'What are my options?' I said.

'On or off.'

'I think I'd better have them on then please if you don't mind.'

I was to be compère for the event, which began with a small finger-buffet, a raffle (which I'll get to later), followed by the high- light of the evening: the international tribute act Cher and Cher- a-like (you see what she's done? I can't take responsibility for that).

I did a bit of patter (love that) before I introduced her, and then sure enough a member of the technical crew flicked the stage lights off and then back on as Cher and Cher-a-like sauntered through a gap in the curtains to the theme tune from *Stars in Their Eyes*. You could hear the unmistakable voice of Matthew Kelly: 'Ladies and gentlemen, please welcome tonight, singing live . . .' And then a badly edited voice dropped in saying 'Cher and Cher-a-like'. It was truly dreadful, you could tell it had been put together at home with a tape recorder.

Dressed as Cher, complete with short black leather jacket and fishnet stockings, she opened with the classic 'If I Could Turn Back Time' but surprisingly did only two more Cher songs in the remainder of her repertoire; all her other songs were hits for Shania Twain, who she actually did sound like. In fact she'd have been better off being a tribute act to her, which I suggested to her after the show, I even came up with a stage name for her: Shania Twin.

'The problem is I sound like Shania but look like Cher.'

I feel obliged at this moment to point out that she was a black midget.

Bloody raffles, I detest calling a raffle for the simple reason the whole night grinds to a halt while a series of random numbers are read out: 'I've got a yellow ticket 457? . . . anybody, yellow 457? . . . for the luxury foot spa? . . . 457 anybody?' There'll just be this general mumbling and fumbling in the audience as people search for their tickets and look around for the winner. Oh it's painful; I'm just stood there like a numpty. '457? Come on now, where are you?' Talk about an anti-climax. Chances are they're not even in the room, they probably didn't even come on the night. It drives me insane: you work all night to get people in the mood and then they call a raffle and the whole thing goes tits-up. Sure they make money but at what cost? And don't you dare say 'A fiver a book'.

I did a gig for Cancer Research at the Queen Elizabeth Hall in Oldham once where the raffle went on for ever. I eventually lost my rag and impatiently I ended up throwing the prizes out to whoever could catch them. You want to try throwing a Weight Watchers food hamper. I almost killed a woman on the third row. The event organisers weren't too happy but we were already running behind. They had four comedians on the bill and a heavy metal band that had travelled all the way from Swansea; it was up to someone to keep things ticking along.

The other comedians were from the cast of *Phoenix Nights* and included Steve Edge, Archie Kelly, Janice Connolly and the actor and chancer Patrick McGuinness. We were standing in the wings watching Janice perform her stand-up when I had an idea.

Turning to Paddy, I said, 'Hey why don't we dive on after Janice, grab the band's gear for a laugh and have a jam session?'

'I'm up for that, son,' said Paddy, eyeing up the drum kit while myself and the other lads exchanged winks behind his back. The fact that none of us could play any instruments never even entered his head.

Janice hadn't even finished taking her bow when Paddy ran on and dived behind the drum kit. 'Come on,' he said, beckoning us on with his drumsticks. We just stood in the wings laughing and giving him the 'V's. Fair play to him, he knocked the shit out of that drum kit for a good five minutes before admitting defeat and legging it off the other side of the stage with the real drummer in hot pursuit. He'd heard the commotion three floors up and had rushed down to give the culprit a pasting. The last I saw of Paddy that night was him jumping out a bog window with a drumstick in his mouth.

*   *   *

The second tribute act I worked with was Robbie Williams, or perhaps I should really say Keith Bell. We were booked to be the cabaret after a three-course meal for spina bifida. The gig was in Hull and, misjudging the Saturday traffic, I arrived far too early. I was sitting in the dressing room with another bloke watching *You Bet!* and was just about to say 'What time's this Robbie Williams look-alike getting here?' when the door opened and a man walked in carrying some mini discs.

'I've just had a word with the organiser,' he said to the bloke sat next to me. 'You're on after the dessert in about twenty minutes.'

'Right, I better go and get ready,' he said, 'I'll see you up there, Pete,' and with that he left.

I couldn't believe it: *that's* Robbie Williams? But he's got blond hair! I looked more like Robbie Williams than he did.

Just like with corporates we were led in through the back way via the kitchens towards the stage. I have to say Keith, or rather Robbie, did look very different with his gear on, though he did look more like Ronan than Robbie. The room was an odd shape with no backstage area so we were forced to wait awkwardly in a doorway to the kitchens. It was roasting and very chaotic as waiting staff continually barged past us juggling trays piled with dirty crockery as they attempted to clear the tables before dessert.

I'll never forget this one waitress drenched in sweat, struggling to get past us in the doorway with a tray, and Keith, sorry I mean Robbie, reaching out his hands to pretend to tickle her, said, 'Y' alright darling?' and she just snapped back, 'Piss off!' right in his face. That did make me laugh a lot. Then the music started, the opening to 'Let Me Entertain You' filled the room and Keith/Robbie was handed a microphone. Standing in the kitchen he began his introduction:

'Ladies and gentlemen, welcome to the show. My name's Keith Bell but tonight I'm going to be Robbie Williams. I have only one rule and that's don't forget to drink because the more you drink the more you'll think that I'm Robbie Williams.' And with that he tipped me a wink and charged the stage, getting there just in time for the opening lines of the song. I'll never forget the audience reaction: halfway through their banoffee baskets they stopped eating, looked towards the stage, screwed up their eyes and then in unison shook their heads as if to say 'Nah, he's nothing like him' and then carried on eating.

Look-alikes and tribute acts are funny folks. I've worked with a few and the eerie thing is most of the time they actually believe they are the real people. I did a gig with a Sean Connery and a Joanna Lumley look-alike once and they insisted on being in character all the time, even backstage. Sean kept pulling out a gun and Joanna kept calling me 'sweetie' while she staggered around clutching a glass of prop champagne. I felt like grabbing them both and screaming 'YOU ARE NOT THESE PEOPLE'. But in their minds they clearly thought they were. The worst one for this was Pete Loaf (see if you can guess what tribute act he was).

Pete and I did a gig together for the NSPCC in Aberystwyth. I was scheduled to compère and he was the star attraction. We'd never met before but when we did I quickly became aware of how seriously he took his role as Pete Loaf. He was on stage with his girlfriend building his set. They were painting full-size gravestones that looked as though they weighed a ton but upon closer inspection actually turned out to be polystyrene therefore quite light and easy to manoeuvre. He had a hand-painted backcloth that was a detailed replica of the cover to *Bat Out of Hell* and then he had a Harley, that he'd loaned from a local gang of Hell's Angels on the proviso he got them free tickets for the gig.

I eyed up the audience from a slash in the curtains backstage. The place was heaving with bikers; I felt like the Rolling Stones at Altamont. Oh my Lord, what was I to do? I'd never played to bikers before. I'd done a taxi drivers' Christmas party, so how hard could it be? I came on to a few stray handclaps but mostly silence. It was so quiet I could actually hear the noise of my Adam's apple when I swallowed. I tried a few gags and they got titters but to say I was struggling would be putting it mildly: I was dying on my arse; luckily for me I was already standing in a graveyard. Then, thinking on my feet, I decided to make a joke out of that. I leaned over one of the headstones and pretended to read, 'Here lies Peter Kay, compère to Pete Loaf, Brynamlwg Social Club, June 1997.' It got a huge laugh, I was in. Luckily I'd brought my Dictaphone so fast-forwarded to a misheard lyric that I thought may suit the clientele. I played them Queen's 'One Vision' where at three minutes and five seconds Freddie begs us all to 'look what they've done to Mike Reid'. They loved it and, taking advantage of my moment in the sun, I hastily introduced the main act: 'The one, the only Pete Loaf,' and the ground shook with the cheers of over three hundred Welsh Hell's Angels.

The room plunged into darkness as the familiar strains of 'Bat Out of Hell' hit the speakers and I stood in the wings thanking my lucky stars (and feeling frisky). Now I don't know how familiar you are with 'Bat Out of Hell' but as you can gather from the title it's a monster of a song, there's a two-minute instrumental before he even sings the first line and the build-up to that point is volcanic. The place was in uproar and the cheers trebled in volume when the fire doors burst open and Pete Loaf rode in on his borrowed Harley through the club and up on to the stage. The hairs went up on the back of my neck. Then, gathering his thoughts, he raised the mic to his lips in order to to sing the opening line. Nothing. Well he was clearly singing but there was no volume. With panic in his eyes, Pete looked towards the sound desk, and his girlfriend at the controls. She shrugged her shoulders in dismay. As daylight shone upon magic, the crowd's cheers turned to boos. Pete reluctantly wheeled his Harley off the stage and back outside. There was a short pause as they searched for a member of the committee to close the fire doors (there are rules, you know). The room was then plunged into darkness as the opening bars of 'Bat Out of Hell' filled the room once again.

The long intro seemed even longer, then eventually the fire doors burst open and Pete rode his borrowed Harley through the club and up on to the stage once again. It was still just as impressive, though the hairs didn't go up on my neck. Then, gathering his thoughts, he raised the mic to his lips for a second time and . . . nothing. Oh my God! I thought, this can't be happening.

The place erupted in jeers and boos. Pete got off his bike and marched over to the sound desk.

'WHAT THE FUCK ARE YOU DOING?' he shouted at his girlfriend in a deep Welsh accent for all to hear.

'I'M DOING MY FUCKING BEST, THAT'S WHAT,' she screamed back at him, 'IT'S NOT MY FAULT THE BUTTONS DON'T WORK.'

It was excruciating to watch. Pete leaned over the sound desk and fumbled around with faders, he gave his mic a quick 'One, two' (though I'm sure he would have preferred doing it to his girlfriend at that point). 'NOW DON'T TOUCH A FUCKING THING,' he shouted to her as he wearily pushed the Harley off stage fuelled by either blind dedication or sheer stubbornness. Surely with little if any dignity intact you'd move on to the second song, but not Pete. Ignoring the chants of 'You fat bastard' from the now angry mob, he loitered near the fire door completely humiliated as the search went out again for another committee member to close the door.

I'd have laughed if I hadn't have felt so mortified for him. By the time the room plunged into darkness for a third time, people were chatting. The bar had been reopened and a queue was forming. The doors burst open to a light smattering of applause as Pete rode his borrowed Harley on to the stage for a third time. With my hands over my eyes, I held my breath. Glaring at his girl-friend, Pete lifted the mic to his lips and sang. Nothing. No, I'm kidding, his voice came through the speakers loud and clear as the whole room breathed a collective sigh of relief. Sadly, after all that, he sounded fuck-all like him.

Audiences can be tough and the fact that it's a charity event means nothing once they've got a few drinks in them. The last charity gig I did was in a marquee at York Raccs for the Spastics Society. I arrived to find there was no backstage or rear entrance which meant I'd have to come on and off through the audience, some-thing I wasn't keen to do as the people were already packed liked sardines.

'Could you not just cut a big hole in?' I said.

'Not a chance, it's off to Royal Ascot Monday.'

Sure enough, by the time I was due to go on, the audience were completely leathered and, as I suspected, it took me ages to make my way through them to get to the stage. Anyway I did my time and with the knowledge that I had to try to make a getaway at the end of my set, I came up with an idea. I just got everybody to stand up.

'Stand up, please get on your feet because you're going to see one of the best endings to a show you've ever seen! This is no expense spared, myself and the organisers of tonight's gig have got together and you're in for a real treat, ladies and gentlemen, you've never seen anything like it! Are you ready?!' Bit of a cheer. I said, 'Are you ready?!' 'Yeah!' 'OK, count down from 10, 9, 8' and when they got to 5, 4, 3, I ran. I ran across the top of the tables towards the exit, just like Roger Moore when he jumps those alligators in *Live and Let Die*. Halfway across I pulled my car keys out my pocket and kept on running all the way to my car. They were just reaching '2, 1' as I got to the door. Then I heard a boo of disappointment as I started the engine and sped off. My apologies if you were in the audience that night, but you left me with no choice.

Chapter Eleven

Home Comforts Abroad

'Good evening, Hong Kong' – four words I never thought I'd ever hear myself say but say them I did when I played The Punchline Comedy Club on Hong Kong Island in 1998. Mike Nolan (not the Bucks Fizz one in case you were wondering) was a British entrepreneur with links to Hong Kong, and capitalising on the increasing trend for stand-up he'd set up a monthly comedy night in an Indian restaurant on Hong Kong Island. I'd heard quite a few good reports from comics who'd been over and done the gig. So when the offer came up I decided to take it.

It was a great opportunity, I mean when else would I get to visit Hong Kong, let alone play there? The majority of the audience was made up of ex-pats, Canadians, Americans and Australians. I was to play four nights over the six-night trip, sharing the bill with a very funny Australian stand-up called Matt Hardy. As the rest of my time, other than when performing, was to be my own, I decided to invite Susan along with me, which they said was fine as long as I covered the cost of her flight. So off we went to Hong Kong.

Mike Nolan took care of everything: the travel, the accommodation, he even met us at the airport on our arrival, which was reassuring for me (you should by now be aware of my anxieties regarding travel). Mike was an easy-going bloke with a dry sense of humour and we hit it off straight away. What I particularly liked about him was that he took care of us without invading our space. He told us the basic dos and don'ts of Hong Kong and left us to it.

The first night we were ridiculously jet-lagged, still wide awake at half past four in the morning watching episodes of *Hi-De-Hi!* on the BBC World channel and just gazing out of our sixty-eighth-floor hotel bedroom window (the lift travelled so fast to our floor our ears popped). The view was hypnotic; I'd never envisaged the Hong Kong skyline to be so beautiful. An endless metropolis containing some of the world's tallest buildings, it was like watching a scene from *Blade Runner – The Director's Cut.*

A popular pastime for a lot of the comedians whilst playing Hong Kong was to get a custom-made suit. Mike had contacts in the business, Rocky of H.K. Fashions, a tailor based on the other side of the bay in Kowloon. We had to catch a boat over to his shop in the garment district. Apparently his bespoke suits were to die for and half the price of what it would cost back home. All the comedians went to him and, thanks to Mike Nolan, Rocky suits were fast becoming legendary on the British comedy circuit.

'Now just to warn you,' said Mike as we approached the shop, 'Rocky has got one hell of a grip, just watch out or he'll crush your fingers. Make sure you give him just as much back.'

We entered the tiny tailor's shop and were instantly greeted by a willowy Oriental man with a grin as wide as a World War II. He offered me his hand and I took it and shook it with everything I'd

On stage in Belfast, just about to introduce The Krankies. Actually I think I was talking about my Uncle Knobhead: 'He's known me since I was down there' - make of that what you will.

The panoramic crowd shot I took at the
Bridgewater Hall. Either I missed a section
or the bloke on the third row is deformed.

Interior and exterior of the Frog & Bucket,
the best comedy club (on Oldham Street)
in Manchester. Looks like there's about
a hundred and thirty-eight in.

Caught mid-Theme-along with my Yamaha-ha.

Self-explanatory. I'm very proud of this. I wonder if B*witched have kept theirs.

Patrons
Her Majesty The Queen
Her Majesty Queen Elizabeth The Queen Mother

We the undersigned
tender our sincere congratulations to

Peter Kay

on being one of the
artistes selected to appear before
His Royal Highness The Prince of Wales
on the occasion of

THE ROYAL VARIETY PERFORMANCE

Monday 7th December 1998
at the
LYCEUM THEATRE
in aid of
The Entertainment Artistes' Benevolent Fund

eabf

| Life President Laurie Mansfield | Hon. Chairman Peter Prichard OBE | Hon. Treasurer Ray Donn | Executive Administrator Peter Elliott |

Live at the Top of the Tower: a rough and final version of the DVD sleeve; and on stage, confused as to why the audience are all sunburned.

Gordon and me, joined by biscuits.

Liam and me, joined by a lady's coat...

...and if you ever need a lady's coat
or a purple suit, call this man.

JOKE: Liam and Peter

OASIS singer **LIAM GALLAGHER** left the NME awards in a huff after comedian **PETER KAY** took the mickey.

Liam refused to go up to collect his Hero of the Year award. So Peter gave it to him at his table and said of his white suede coat: "My mum's looking for that."

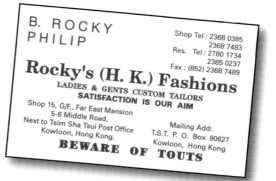

30p + delivery charge? Cheek!

Bolton Evening News

Monday, October 21, 2002   01204 522345   FINAL   30p   www.thisisbolton.co.uk

FREE INSIDE: PREMIERSHIP WANDERER

WAKEY WAKEY! Martin Sheehan and John Wright were first in the queue for tickets after spending all night outside in the cold and rain   Picture by Nigel Taggart

KAY-MANIA

It's a sell-out as 2,400 fans snap up tickets

COMIC: Peter Kay

TICKETS for comedian Peter Kay's first Bolton show in seven years went on sale today — and sold out within an hour.

A staggering 2,400 fans snapped up seats for his four-night laughter extravaganza at the Albert Halls.

Extra staff had to be drafted in to cope with the queues of people who gathered outside Bolton Town Hall, despite the freezing temperatures and heavy downpours.

Some fans of the comedian even queued through the night and, 30 minutes before the tickets were due to go on sale at 10am, more than 600 people were patiently waiting in the rain.

Manager Christine Forster said: "We knew a lot of people would buy tickets but we could never have guessed that they would buy them so fast. It was the biggest queue we have ever had outside for a show."

Turn to Page 2

PETER'S FURY

Sneak thief steals from dressing room as comic plays in his home town

EXCLUSIVE

by Ian Savage and Paul Britton

PETER Kay was furious today after a sneak thief stole from his dressing room as he performed in Bolton.

The comedian said: "I have played 141 nights all over the country and I just can't believe that now I return to my home town I have stuff stolen."

The thief, believed to be captured on surveillance cameras in the Albert Halls, took a digital video camera and a mobile phone from Peter's dressing room.

He struck just 10 minutes after the 25-year-old took to the stage to perform the second night of his four shows to an audience of around 600.

The video camera's memory card contained 'priceless' images filmed backstage at venues, which Peter intended to use as extra material on a live tour DKP. Peter said: "I am

Turn to Page 3

APPEAL: Police are keen to identify this man who was caught on CCTV in the backstage area of the Albert Halls before Peter discovered the theft

Do you recognise the thief?

The *Brothers in Arms* of stand-up comedy.

PETER KAY LIVE

AT THE Bolton ALBERT HALLS

"Mum Wants A Bungalow Tour"

The tour poster; and dressed as a pregnant steward for my final night at the MEN arena.

Back on stage briefly in 2004 introducing a guitarist friend of mine, and trying to resemble him with that facial hair. I was actually just about to film *Max & Paddy's Road to Nowhere* hence the beard.

So that's your lot. Now either buy this book or get out of the shop. Look, it's either this or Alan Carr's and that came out last year.

got. But I was confused: contrary to Mike's caution, Rocky's hand felt as light as wet leather and he crumpled to his knees, clearly in some pain, so I immediately let go. Confused, I spun round to find Mike red-faced and hysterical with laughter. Some practical joke, I thought as I helped Rocky back to his feet.

'All your comedian friends got mighty strong grip, Mr Mike.'

I couldn't apologise enough. Mike obviously knew what Rocky's handshake was like and clearly did this every month. He was a tailor, Godammit man, those fingers are instruments.

I removed my shorts and he measured me at length, then we discussed styles and pockets. I wasn't used to such treatment as the few suits I'd ever owned had been off the peg in either Topman or C&A.

Then Rocky got out his selection of swatches. Now I'd always dreamt of owning a purple suit. Don't ask me why. I think it may have been a Jack Nicholson Joker thing, anyway Rocky showed me a huge selection but my eye was immediately drawn to the colour of my dreams.

'That's the one,' I said without hesitation.

'Are you sure?'

'I am.'

'OK, Mr Peter, it shall be ready for you Friday.'

As he was still nursing his hand I opted not to shake it again, choosing to bow to him instead in my ignorance and excitement; how classy was I going to look on stage in my new purple suit?!

Aimlessly we wandered around taking in the sights and sadly the smells of the city. It stunk, a combination of what appeared to be burnt salmon and condensed milk (Tip Top as opposed to Carnation Cream). We stumbled upon a street market, which gave a whole new meaning to the word 'miscellaneous'. They had one bloke selling what appeared to be second-hand Tonka toys next to another stall which had a bloke slicing up live eels then wrapping them in cling film for his customers as they still squiggled. The world had gone mad. What was wrong with a bit of order?

Then Mike took us out for a traditional Chinese lunch. I was starving and genuinely fancied the idea of sampling some authentic Chinese cuisine. We got round a lazy Susan (and I'm not referring to my girlfriend) with our chopsticks in our hands and then our food slowly began to arrive dish by dish. But what arrived was a far cry from the chicken in black bean sauce I was used to. It was, quite literally, an eye-opener, as I'm still convinced to this day some of the food winked at me as it sailed past. I discreetly sniffed and licked a few things but I wasn't smitten; it was like the banquet scene in *Indiana Jones and the Temple of Doom*, and ten minutes later we admitted our defeat with a Family Bucket over the road – at least with KFC the shit we were eating was familiar.

I found I was helplessly turning into my dad again. He was the same every time we went abroad when the subject of foreign food inevitably came up. Even something as insignificant as garlic bread would get the third degree. 'Garlic bread?' he'd say, his brain unable to compute such a radical combination. 'Garlic? And bread? Together? Am I hearing you right? Garlic bread? No thank you, I don't want any of that foreign muck, I'll stick to me baguette, stick to what I know.'

My first night on stage at the Indian restaurant in Hong Kong (an equally radical combination), I felt compelled to share my dad's shameless Anglophilia with the audience of ex-pats:

My dad only wanted two things abroad: hot weather and home comforts. We went to Lloret De Mar in '82 and he was so chuffed at finding a British pub. 'You'll love this place, it's called the Red Lion. Here it is, look they've got a British phone box outside. Come inside, look at this, they're serving Tetley's bitter! And normal food too, egg and chips, chips and beans, it's all here, look they've even got yesterday's Daily Mirror and Only Fools and Horses on the television. It's like being back home but you've got the weather. They're a lovely couple, retired with emphysema; she won't see Christmas, it's heartbreaking. Here, bring that Connect 4 over, son, I'll have you a game.'

My dad would also try and take everything from home with him on holiday. The suitcase would be stuffed with things like a sink plunger, digestive biscuits, a washing line.

'Dad why have we got a washing line in the case?'

'You never know,' he would always say, 'they might not have them out there.'

Surely they've got washing lines in Spain, we didn't invent them.

He'd take tea bags and that powered milk stuff, Coffee-Mate, and wrap them up in a polythene bag, his logic being: 'You arrive at four o'clock in the morning and you're thirsty, what do you do? Come and see your dad. He'll make you a brew.'

'Dad, are we going to be alright going through customs with a bag of white powder?'

Nineteen hours we spent in that Spanish cell, it was like a scene from Midnight Express. My dad trying to make brews for the guards in an effort to prove his innocence. 'It's Coffee-Mate,' he'd say. 'Hey, I'm not your fucking mate,' they replied.

I don't know if the Yanks and the Aussies got my Coffee-Mate references but the ex-pats lapped it up. Mike was made up with their response, so much so that he swapped the bill round for the rest of the week so now I headlined the show. But then I came down with the flu, not man flu either, just proper bad flu in my head and chest. I ended up in bed for the remainder of the week, only venturing out for the gig each night and to the local KFC when I could stomach it. Mike suggested I should perhaps try some local herbal remedies; after all I was in the Far East.

Feeling like shit and with nothing to lose, I took another trip over to Kowloon on the boat. Lordy, I was as rough as the sea we were sailing on. Desperate for something, anything, I meandered down a few back alleys in search of a local apothecary (all right then, chemist). It was like Diagon Alley in *Harry Potter*, then I found a small shop with jars and medicines in the window – also the universal sign of the green medical cross was a giveaway. There was a wizened old Chinese man behind the counter and I tried the best that I could to describe my ailments to him, taking the liberty of shouting of course as he was foreign. 'FULL OF A COLD,' I said, gesturing my hands around my face, 'ALL IN MY HEAD AND CHEST.' He looked a little bewildered but then the penny appeared to drop. 'AH-A,' he said, reminiscent of Alan Partridge, and headed off through some beads hanging over the doorway into the back of the shop. I heard some shuffling about and banging, which sounded promising. Then after five minutes or so the old bloke emerged back through the beads carrying a big bottle of Night Nurse. Bloody Night Nurse, I thought he was in the back grinding up some crushed elephant's dick or some-thing. You know I was that desperate I bought it, then I later worked out the exchange rate to discover it had set me back about twenty-five quid, the robbing herbalist bastard.

I told that story on stage that night and it also went down a storm with the audience. In fact I received one of the nicest compliments I've ever got after the show from an American lady who said, 'I didn't understand half of what you said but you made me laugh so much.' Which I suppose you could take either way but I chose to take it as a compliment.

The flu was getting me down but every night I'd struggle over to the gig and sweat it out on stage, as the performance adrenalin kicked in and masked the symptoms. We'd loiter after the gig, helping ourselves to as much Indian food as you could shake a stick at and then salsa dancing until the adrenalin wore off at which point Susan would bundle me into a taxi home.

On the Sunday morning Mike kindly drove us to the airport, we said our goodbyes and he presented me with my bespoke purple suit. Because of the flu I'd been unable to make it back over to Rocky's tailor shop for a final fitting and this was the first time I'd clapped eyes on the finished article – oh my God the suit was purple! I couldn't believe that tiny little swatch could be so deceptive in comparison to this. It looked like something I'd sent away for with Ribena tokens! I felt like the whole passenger terminal was staring at me, so I quickly bundled it back into the suit carrier where it remained for the next eight years until I shot the video to 'Amarillo'.

Also, to my surprise, Mike paid me in Hong Kong dollars instead of sterling, which nobody had mentioned to me, and with the exchange rate I came home with about £350. Anyway what the hell, I put it down to experience and was glad we'd gone out there. Despite getting the flu it was a hell of an experience and I doubted I'd ever have the chance to repeat it. Saying that, four weeks later I found myself in Las Vegas. Only this time it wasn't a working holiday.

*　　*　　*

Having spent the previous few years constantly gigging, I decided that a dream holiday was in order and so after countless mind-numbing hours and what seemed like several lost weeks sifting through holidays on Teletext, Susan and I eventually found and booked a fortnight at a three-star hotel just off the Sunset Strip (well the lady on the phone said it was just off the strip but we still had to catch two free shuttle buses and a rickshaw to get within spitting distance of Caesars Palace).

The Americans certainly know how to go that one step further: it was a three-star hotel like I'd never seen before, with its very own ice-cream parlour, a three-screen cinema and a twenty-two-lane bowling alley – the three-star accommodation in Blackpool was never like this. They also had two outdoor Olympic-size swimming pools, which unfortunately we never got the chance to use as the weather changed on the second day. I'll never forget the weather reporter proclaiming, 'It's the first time it's snowed on the strip for twenty years.' Snow! In Vegas, how could this be? I could have cried, having brought only one pair of jeans each and no long-sleeve tops. Well you wouldn't, would you, it was the middle of a desert.

We headed off to the nearest mall in search of winter wear but it was spring and all I could find was an 'I (Heart) Las Vegas' sweatshirt. Well it was either that or pneumonia. I attempted to ease the embarrassment by wearing it back to front but ended up just looking like a freak with my head on the wrong way round. If you happen to have any photos of me in said sweatshirt please do keep them to yourself.

The decline in clement weather was caused by El Niño, which is a global coupled ocean-atmosphere phenomenon (well that's what it's just said on Google). Which in layman's terms means it turns freezing cold every March and tips it down for a fortnight, something they'd failed to mention on Teletext.

Gazing at the temperature back home with envy, we spent our days wandering around the hotels in an effort to keep dry. Ironically, just like Blackpool. The hotels in Vegas were so humongous and extraordinary we were able to stay in them for hours. One of the things I loved the most about Las Vegas was the tackiness. We were in Caesars Palace and suddenly I heard a commotion followed by a loud trumpet fanfare and chants of 'Hail Caesar! Hail Caesar!' then coming through the centre of the casino was a man dressed as Julius Caesar flanked either side by four Roman soldiers. They marched towards me and up a set of stairs on to a small stage that sat above the slot machines. The fanfare ceased then Caesar said, 'My name is Julius Caesar and this is my palace and for only five dollars you can play lotto or bingo this afternoon.' Only in America. Another hotel we visited was the one shaped like a pyramid called the Luxor. There were numerous attractions including one of the world's very first Imax cinemas – we watched a film about fish (the sea kind as opposed to the ex-lead singer of Marillion). They also had one of these revolutionary 'new' (at the time) motion-sensor rides which was supposed to simulate the feeling that you were plummeting to the depths of the earth and The Secret of the Tombs, which was the title of the ride. It cost fifteen dollars each to have a go and before you could say 'Suckers' we were in the queue.

Ten or twelve of us filed into a replica lift, sorry elevator (hey, when in Rome) where an actor playing the part of an archaeologist tried in vain to make the whole thing appear real. It was embarrassing. Everybody was so reserved and shy and there he was in the corner of the elevator acting his arse off. The prop elevator was encased in screens that had moving images projected on to them giving the impression the elevator was plunging downwards at great speed. This, combined with a hydraulic jolting, which only succeeded in making me nauseous, as well as the dramatic use of lights, music and sound effects of screaming, not to mention the actor screaming 'HELP US! HELP US! WE'RE FALLING TEN THOUSAND FEET TO THE SECRET OF THE TOMBS' all added up to a believability level of zero as far as I was concerned. Eventually we 'supposedly' reached The Secret of the Tombs with an almighty hydraulic thud, which sent the acid reflux that I'd acquired from an all-you-can-eat $5 breakfast buffet out through my ears.

'We're OK, we're safe,' said the actor-ologist, 'Welcome to The Secret of the Tombs. If you'd like to make your way down the corridor and out that way, ladies and gentlemen . . .'

That was it! Fifteen dollars each and that was it? What a load of old shit. Angry at the result, I decided to do a bit of acting myself and approached the actor-ologist.

'How do we get back up?' I said, acting all traumatised and scared.

'Excuse me, buddy?'

'How do we get back up to street level?' I said.

'We are at street level, sir, just go down the corridor and out the door.'

'But we can't be, we dropped ten thousand feet, you were there, how do we get out of here?' With a look of confusion I started to hyperventilate. Susan was not amused. And the humour was completely lost on him too. Linking my arm, the actor-ologist escorted me down the corridor towards a door that opened on to the hotel ground-floor mezzanine.

'Here, sir, look we're on street level, sir, it was just a ride, sir, just a ride.'

I hugged him so tightly. 'THANK YOU!' I shouted, then I high-fived him and ran off, whooping and cheering like George Bailey when he's back in Bedford Falls.

Like most holidaymakers abroad, we felt obliged to go on a few excursions and see the local sights. As we flew into Las Vegas, the pilot came over the intercom (the dirty bastard):* 'Just to let you know if you take a look out your window on the right-hand side of the plane you'll get an amazing view of the Grand Canyon.' I thought, Cheers for that, mate, you've just saved me three hundred dollars on a trip. One of the other popular excursions was to Lake Mead, where you took in lunch on board a sailboat and then a trip to Hoover Dam, as seen in the film *Superman*. Feeling obliged, we booked for the Hoover Dam/Lake Mead but what they failed to mention was that we'd have to make two other stops en route, the first being Cranberry World, where they allowed us forty-five minutes to sample over sixty different types of cranberry products – not suffering from cystitis, I stayed on the coach. The next was Ron Lee's World of Clowns; now I don't hate much but I hate clowns. Ever since Mr Twinkles thought it was funny to chase me round the room at a children's party at the Anglers' Club and pop a balloon in my face. I was collecting glasses at the time and he could have taken an eye out. So help me God, I would have gladly shoved a glass in his face had the room not been full of five-year-olds.

They allowed another forty-five minutes to stroll round a clown shop. I wouldn't be bothered but they rushed us round Hoover

* Bit wrong that.

Dam in just under an hour and as for Lake Mead, well I hadn't so much as got the top off my thermos when the captain dropped his anchor back in the harbour.

I should know better by now but I fall for the excursion scam every time: the reps are on a kick-back and by the time you've found your feet on holiday you realise it's cheaper and easier to just do it yourself. Gavin, our rep, who was clearly sporting eyeliner, tried to flog us some excursions to some shows but after the Hoover Dam debacle I refused point-blank to get involved.

'You can't come to Las Vegas and not see a show,' said Susan and she was right but what to see? Siegfried and Roy? (It would have been an historic visit with hindsight as two months later Roy had his throat ripped out by a white Siberian tiger.) Michael Crawford was going down a storm at the MGM Grand with a new show called F/X but with tickets starting at $150 a pair he could F/off as far as I was concerned and besides I hadn't come all this way to watch Frank Spencer kick his legs. I wanted glitz, I wanted glamour, and I wanted a show for less than $30 each – and we found it with a show called *Legends*.

It was a bit like *Stars in Their Eyes*, which I'd never really been a big fan of, as Matthew would always say, 'So tell us, when did you first discover you could sing like the person you're going to be tonight?'

'Well, Matthew, I was singing in the bath and my mother shouted "Turn that CD down" and I shouted, "That's not a CD, Mum".'

'You've got a lot in common with the person you're going to be tonight, haven't you?'

'Yes I have, Matthew, as we've both got heads.'

And that's where the similarity ended. Then they cut their hair and shave them, what a transformation.

'The incredible look-alikes and sound-alikes in *Legends* are so sensational that even some of their biggest fans wonder if they are the real McCoy', well that's what it said in the leaflet. Boasting a legendary cast of over thirty iconic singing sensations in its repertoire, they could also offer us two free vouchers for an all-you-can-eat Cajun buffet and as many free drinks we could down within the interval. Now that was the kind of Vegas show I'd been searching for; granted none of the 'thirty iconic singing sensations' were anything like the originals, the food on the Cajun buffet was lukewarm and the interval only lasted eight minutes, but hey, we weren't going to let that ruin our big night out in Vegas.

We'd got friendly with a couple from Bradford and they came along with us for a laugh. Arriving early, we were seated at some trestle tables right at the front of the stage, so close we could literally touch it. I remember thinking, This is gonna be good.

The huge stage was book-ended with giant screens on either side which showed continuous footage of the real artists as if enticing the audience to 'spot the difference' – believe me, you really couldn't, well you couldn't if you were sat at the back of the room or suffered from glaucoma. We, on the other hand, could see their nose hair and the look-alikes we saw were Bad with a capital B.

Diana Ross looked more like Rusty Lee, Neil Diamond was Chinese and Ritchie Valens was so bad they didn't even bother showing footage of the real one, they just showed Lou Diamond Phillips in *La Bamba*. By the time the interval came round I was ready for a drink. Now you all know I'm tee-total but with eight minutes of free drinks on offer I decided to try a few glasses of Baileys, as I'd tried some Baileys ice cream at the Häagen-Dazs down the mall the day before and it had rocked my world.

Eight minutes later I'd had my money's worth and was just

starting to feel oddly giddy when The Four Tops came on singing 'Loco in Acapulco' and they certainly looked like the real Four Tops to me at that point. I was ready to party and was straight up on my feet, singing and shuffling. Susan had to yank me back into my seat.

Then when they went into 'Reach Out (I'll Be There)' I was unstoppable, moon-walking and gyrating, I was having a ball, then The Four Tops split up and one of them (I think it was Top number two) came over to the front of the stage to sing the chorus, 'Reach out, reach out' and so I did just that and I grabbed his hand. I don't know what for and I don't know why but I wasn't for letting go. I could see the look of terror in the whites of his eyes as he sang 'I'll be there', and I thought, You *will* be here, pal, because you're going nowhere.

The other three Tops were back centre stage and starting 'Bernadette' when I still had hold of his hand. He was getting desperate now, bent over and wriggling. I had Susan pulling me back helped by the couple from Bradford. What a palaver. And with a glimpse of security guards approaching in the corner of my eye I finally let go, sending Top number two crashing to the floor along with the rest of us and me in hysterics. I still blame the Baileys.

The night after, I decided to play it safe and have a night in the digs (just like my dad at the Loch Moir in Blackpool). There was karaoke on, it was all the rage at the time and everybody was into it. But they were are all singing bloody maudlin songs that night like 'Hello' – Lionel Richie, and that one from *The Bodyguard* by Whitney Houston. I was thinking, Come on, I'm on holiday here. So I put my name down, I'd had a few Baileys (now I'd acquired a taste) and thought, It doesn't matter if I make an arse of myself as I'm not on home turf.

I had to wait my turn and in the meantime this German air-conditioning salesman called Hans got up to sing an Elton John song, he even looked like Elton John. I was ready to slit my wrists. Then thankfully the MC said, 'Next up, all the way from England we've got Peter to sing a song for us.' So I got up and made my way to the stage.

'What part of England are you from?'

'I'm from Bolton.'

'You mean like Michael Bolton?' he said, which got a laugh.

'Yeah, if you like,' I said. I thought, I'm going to give them one they won't have heard, I'll give them a British classic, and as they didn't even have backing tracks I thought, I'll have to sing it Acapulco. Fuelled by Baileys, I launched into an unforgettable rendition of 'Agadoo', complete with actions, and they loved it. The place went nuts and by the time I got to the second chorus the whole place was doing it, bar staff, the lot. They'd obviously never heard of Black Lace stateside.

Then after I'd finished, Hans got up again and killed it stone dead with another Elton John track. What made it worse was that he sang 'Candle in the Wind' and it wasn't even the Marilyn Monroe version, those words came up on the screens but he sang the other version, the one about Princess Diana – The Queen of Hearts, 'Goodbye English rose' and all that. I was speechless.

Well I'd never seen a reaction like it: the Americans were crying and sobbing, I even saw two eight-foot cowboys remove their Stetsons with tears in their eyes. Because they love her over there, they have her on fridge magnets and everything. And when he finished, silence, you could have heard a cockroach fart. Then the MC said, 'Ladies and gentlemen, that was a truly beautiful, beautiful rendition of "Candle in the Wind" from Hans. I can't honestly think of a more fitting tribute.' I thought, What, than an air-conditioning salesman from Düsseldorf? And then he said, 'And I'd especially like to dedicate that song to Peter from Bolton over there in the corner. I'm sure he'll appreciate that heartfelt rendition more than anybody else in here tonight.' Mortified, I just raised my glass of Baileys. 'Cheers, Hans.'

The next day we packed our bags and left Las Vegas for the warmer climate of Bolton. Back to reality, with at least an hour's worth of new material, and back to the stand-up too.

Chapter Twelve

Groundhog Month

Two years after my first appearance at the Edinburgh Festival I was back, this time with my own show. I'd spent the months leading up to Edinburgh rehearsing and structuring the best of my material into a one-hour show, which I was to perform each night between 9 and 10 at the Pleasance Over The Road, which consisted of two venues, a large theatre where the actor Steven Berkoff was performing *Shakespeare's Villains** (and he always complained about the noise from my show); I had the smaller theatre which held about a hundred or so. Thankfully due to a loyal build-up of fans from working on the comedy circuit, the show was pretty much sold out for the first few nights. The hard part would be sustaining that demand for the rest of the month.

I was also concerned at how much I'd be able to sustain the demand on myself as I'd been booked for a formidable run of twenty-eight consecutive nights, a feat I'd never attempted before;

---

* Never mind Shakespeare's villains, I thought, he'd have been better off reviving some of his own from *McVicar*, *Octopussy* and *Beverly Hills Cop,* oh, and *Rambo: First Blood II.*

the most I'd ever done was three in a row. With the daunting prospect that lay ahead I knew I'd have to pace myself and spend my days recharging if I intended making it to the end of the festival with my sanity still intact.

A management company called Off The Kerb had booked my run of shows at the festival. They'd also booked the accommodation and it was standard practice to share a flat with other comedians. My flatmates were Junior Simpson and a Canadian comic called Phil Nichol, both lovely, naturally funny blokes but who sadly I saw very little of as we were always out working.

Flat-leasing during festival time can be quite a lucrative venture for some Edinburgh residents. Swapping the annual disruption for the peace and tranquility of some faraway shores probably becomes much more appealing if you know your empty property back home could be offsetting your holiday costs. It can be a win-win scenario: comics and turns get digs while the owner cleans up, or not in our case as the flat we got landed with was a shit-hole. I was beginning to think I was jinxed with bad accommodation in Edinburgh; this place made my previous Edinburgh accommodation at the crack-den in Leith look like a penthouse overlooking the Thames.

Kim and Aggie would have had a field day with this place. I'd never seen stains like it before; it was inches thick in dust and grease. There were bare wires hanging out of wall sockets, not to mention a cooker that looked like it'd come straight out of a charred flat on *London's Burning*. It was a disgusting death trap and, worse still, I was paying for it.

'Well we can't stay here,' I said to Junior and Phil four minutes after arriving.

'But this is where they've put us, they said everywhere is full.'

Full my arse, that Mary and Joseph bollocks never washed with me.

'Well we can't stop here, it's disgusting.'

I got straight on to somebody in charge and lost my mind.

A representative from Off The Kerb came over with an agent from the leasing company and concurred, it was a shithole. Unfortunately they wouldn't be able to source an alternative until after the weekend.

I'd driven for five hours and was completely disheartened. So with my trusty Fiesta bursting at the seams with home comforts, and hotel rooms as rare as rocking-horse shit, I decided to let my OCD take over and began scrubbing the place. I knew I shouldn't have but I couldn't let it lie. Besides I've always found cleaning very therapeutic and I hadn't experienced such an inner calm since I'd scrubbed the staff canteen when I worked at the Cash and Carry. Thankfully on the Monday they moved us to a beautiful flat across town – granted it was smaller but at least we didn't stick to the floor when we walked.

The whole palaver became a blessing in disguise as during the hasty move I forgot to hand in my keys for the first flat. I had a lot of friends and family wanting to come up and offer their support during the festival; the only problem was them finding digs, and cheap digs at that. Problem solved, and with the first flat now spick and span from forty-eight hours of elbow grease, I decided to do a little bit of leasing of my own. It felt like the whole of Bolton stopped in the first flat over those four weeks, and we had some great times. It was just what I needed to keep me going and make the long run bearable. I'd heard tales from comedians of how playing the festival could send you batty. Each day blurring into the next, it felt more like Groundhog Week.

But I managed to keep going by having a daily routine, just like I had at home on a Saturday night. I got myself ready: shower, shave, then ironed my clothes, shined my shoes and packed my gear. My fondest memory is of walking to the gig each night. It was then I came alive, synchronising my pace to the pounding beat of the festival. The energy relentless, spilling out of every doorway, on every street, it felt like Hogmanay every day, the whole city buzzing just like it had the moment I'd stepped off the train for my first festival.

By the time I arrived at the theatre I was psyched. Each night the same routine: with no backstage area I'd have to stand outside of the gig with the rest of my audience. We'd chat as the previous act to mine came to an end, then I would go in and set up while the festival staff quickly cleared and cleaned the room, which was always roasting hot. Less than five minutes later my show would begin.

I went round my grandma's flat, I walked in, she said, 'Guess who's dead?'

I've gotta guess, I mean where do you start with a question like that? Guess who's dead?

'You'll never guess.'

'I will. Chuck me the phone book.'

'She got knocked down by a bus.'

'Who did?'

'Connie.'

'Who's Connie?'

'You know, Connie in the flat upstairs.'

'I don't know no Connie.'

'You do know Connie! Her husband had a beard, emigrated

to Canada. Remember her son joined the RAF, big lad. Her daughter Donna, grand-daughter, used to be at nursery with you. She ate crayons. She's in the police now, she's a desk sergeant. She used to work at Warburtons. Her other son Jimmy was in borstal, he knocked a nun down in Green Lane in a three-wheeler. Kelly and Angela live over at the dry cleaner's together, they're both lesbians.'

'I don't know her.'

'Well anyway she's dead. I only saw her an Tuesday an' all and she looked alright to me.'

She got knocked down by a bloody bus. What do you want her to look like?

Worrying about the inevitable monotony of performing the same material every night, I came up with a solution that I hoped would alleviate the boredom. A series of alternative endings that could be voted for by the audience via a home-made clap-o-meter. It was quirky, it was different and it would at least keep me on my toes for the last ten minutes of the show.

My friend Gordon worked as technical crew on the shows at Salford University and together we designed and built a big clap-o-meter that moved around on a set of castors we stole from a hospital trolley.* It looked fantastic and was also collapsible so it could fit into the back of my Fiesta.

Fortunately, through a bizarre twist of fate, Gordon also happened to be working on a show at the Edinburgh Festival that year and I asked him if he'd like to work on *my* show too, taking charge of the technical side of things. I was delighted to have a

---

* Don't worry, there wasn't a patient on it at the time.

familiar face and someone I trusted working alongside me during the run. Plus he'd also be able to see the clap-o-meter in action every night.

The different endings I came up with were: 'Environmental Song' – where I sang along to a self-penned track called 'O-Zone Layer' in the style of Oasis; 'TV Theme-along' – which relied upon my extensive knowledge of TV themes randomly chosen by the audience, accompanied by myself on a drum machine, which I bought from a Cash Generator; 'Mystery Duet' – where a random member of the audience joined me for a romantic Sing-along to 'I Know Him So Well', the only snag was they had to dress up as a woman round the back and the success of this ending depended on how much they were up for it; and my final ending was 'Arse Fireworks', which I never actually ever did but the clap-o-meter always came dangerously close to picking it.

Of course the clap-o-meter was rigged. I worked it from behind, whilst resting a false mannequin's arm (wearing a different-coloured shirt) on the top of the clap-o-meter, in order to make it blindingly obvious what I was up to. The endings did succeed in keeping me on my toes but as the inevitable fatigue kicked in over the run I did have a tendency to always choose the easiest and most convenient ending, TV Theme-along.

By the middle of the second week the show was starting to take its toll and I began to have problems with my voice. I'd never experienced that before and it sent me into a state of panic and stress, which did little to help my throat. It was deeply frustrating having the main tool of my trade at half-mast and it left me feeling exposed and vulnerable on stage each night. I tried every remedy available, from gargling salt water to hot honey and lemon, which I used to make up in a thermos flask and drink during the show.

It knocked me sick, and to be honest none of the remedies ever worked. People meant well but the advice I got was so contradictory: 'Whatever you do, rest your voice', while others said, 'You've got to keep talking.' I didn't know what to do except go home and hide.

To be honest I don't think the audience even noticed. The reviews I'd received were excellent and not only was the show selling out but I was also given the news that I'd been nominated for the Perrier award at the festival for best comedian. I couldn't believe it, bloody hell! Now that was an honour and there I was with no voice. Suddenly everything seemed to notch up a gear, and thanks to the nomination the show instantly sold out right through until the end of the festival. Which was reassuring as I think I was the only comedian who ever went to Edinburgh and actually made some money.

With even more attention now focused on me, it was more important than ever for *me* to stay focused. I gave it everything I'd got at night but during the day I tried to take it easy, either sleeping or relaxing, anything to take my mind off work. I did go to see a few other shows, plays mainly as watching stand-up was a bit of a busman's holiday. One was called *The Wrestling*, which had been adapted from a book by a comic actor called Alex Lowe.* He played a wrestler in this amazing one-person show, who chats to the audience and transforms into so many other characters that I couldn't quite believe I was just watching one man for the whole time. The story basically followed the success and decline of the old school of British wrestling from its peak on *World of Sport*, when characters like Big Daddy and Giant Haystacks were national

* Alex would go on to appear in almost all of my work for television, most notably as the disastrous psychic Clinton Baptiste.

icons, through to its eventual decline due to the arrival of the American style WWF.

The show was brilliant and I went to see it several times. I found it fascinating and touching, as well as incredibly funny, and Alex Lowe was brilliant, so believable.

One of the times I went to see it I was in the audience with the actor and professional wrestler Pat Roach, who played Bomber in *Auf Weidersehen, Pet*. I'd struck up a friendship with Alex, and after the show I invited Pat Roach back behind the curtain to say hello. Incredibly Pat thought Alex really was a struggling wrestler, the irony had been completely lost on him. It was painful (and funny) to listen to Pat giving Alex advice and wrestling tips, as well as writing down contacts for promoters who could possibly get him a match. Alex was so taken aback; he didn't have the heart to tell him the truth. The funniest bit was as Pat reminisced and said, 'I still see some of the old gang, we lost Tiger Ryan on Tuesday', Alex was just nodding while I was hid behind the curtain, laughing so much that I ended up with snot on my t-shirt. But in a way it was a real compliment and a testament to Alex's acting ability – either that or Pat was just thick.

I'd taken my trusty Fiesta up to the festival, but as the flat only had residents' parking the spaces where like gold dust so the car mostly stayed parked up. Occasionally though I just needed to get in it and drive, just to catch my breath. I'd drive to the sea or the countryside for a few hours. I even found myself driving through the crack-den in Leith with a nostalgic tear in my eye. I visited a multiplex to see *Armageddon* (that was two hours I'd never get back) and I also became a regular at the 24-hour Asda, where I frequently stocked up on throat-healing remedies and ice cream.

Into my final week and with the end of my run now in sight, things began to ease up a little, the muscles in my throat found the strength that they needed and now with my voice back there was no stopping me. The media attention both at the festival and back home in Bolton was intense (my mum would send me copies of the *Bolton Evening News*, who as usual were throwing the town's full support behind me, which meant a great deal). I was fortunate to have my family and friends there for me; well when I say 'there', I mean they were all in my knock-off 'first' flat across town, but at least they were near.

Then one morning I got a whispered call from one of my mates telling me, 'The owner is back.'

'What?'

'I think the owner's come back, some bloke has let himself in with a key and is in the kitchen brewing up, what should we do?'

'Shit! He's not supposed to be back until after the festival, mind you I'm not supposed to still have his key and you're really not supposed to be there.'

'What? You never told us that!'

'Oh, it must have slipped my mind,' I said.

'Slipped your mind? You're charging us twenty quid a night.'

(I wasn't really, I just added that for comic effect.)

'Hang on, I think he's going out . . . [*sound of a door closing*] . . . he is, what should we do?'

'GET OUT!' I shouted, cue the *Benny Hill* theme.

He told me later it was like a scene from a bad sitcom, as he frantically ran round the flat trying to wake everybody up. They were half asleep, as he was trying to explain the situation whilst rolling up their sleeping bags with them still inside.

Forsaking my parking space, I screeched across town, meeting them moments later on the street corner in their pyjamas, with their clothes hanging out of hastily packed suitcases and stuffed into bin bags. Lord knows how I managed to get six of them and their gear into my Fiesta but I did, and as we sped away I saw a man in my side mirror walking back up the steps of the flat with a paper under his arm. I never heard anything from anybody ever again, mind you I did scrub the flat from top to bottom so perhaps if the man in question happens to read this one day, he'll understand what exactly happened and he might even end up thanking me. I mean let's be honest, mate, it was a shithole.

The last Saturday of the festival the Perrier awards took place. It was also my last show, and when it was over Susan and myself were whisked across Edinburgh in a white stretch limousine to join the rest of the guests at the prestigious Perrier nominee party. I'd never been to anything like it in my life. On our arrival we were blinded by camera flashes and stepped out of the limousine and on to a red carpet, it was completely overwhelming. Once inside, we were seated in an area designated for the nominees and their family and friends (I had plenty of those, as they were all currently homeless and had nowhere else to go).

I didn't win the Perrier award, Tommy Tiernan did, and to be honest with you I was gutted, which I found very disconcerting. But Tommy is a fine comic and was a well-deserved winner.

Being nominated for the Perrier award really was a double-edged sword. I mean I was just ticking along doing my job and then suddenly there was all this pressure: will he or won't he win? I was genuinely just chuffed to be nominated and have my work singled out in the first place. But before I knew it I was caught up in the whole shebang and then when I didn't win I was more crushed than I ever imagined I would be. What made it worse was having people who meant well telling me 'You should have won' or 'You was robbed' and spitting in my eyeball as they shouted it to me in the noisy party. I just wanted to crawl into my shell and hide, like a typical Cancerian, but instead I stayed, had a big glass of Baileys and danced my pain away (I think the healing powers of S Club 7 have been seriously underrated).

All my friends got incredibly drunk, including Gordon who stole a plethora of official Perrier merchandise such as ashtrays and cutlery from the party, smuggling them out in the turn-ups of his jeans. He still swears blind he didn't do it and yet when I called round the other week he unwittingly served me lunch on an official Perrier plate.

We staggered out of the party and across Edinburgh, which was still pulsating as the sun came up. With a crepe each from the van in Grassmarket, we headed back to my flat, seven of us to an airbed.

The next day I collapsed my clap-o-meter and headed home, and by the time I reached Carlisle it became clear to me just how insignificant the whole festival was in the grand scheme of things. Don't get me wrong, I don't wish to be disparaging to the Edinburgh Festival, it's just that I was relieved to be heading back to normality.

As I drove down my street I could see coloured balloons in the distance. My first thought was, Shit, whose birthday have I missed? but then it all became clear: my mum had thrown a surprise party for me and the house was packed with family and friends. Frail and weary from a five-hour drive and twenty-eight nights of alternative endings, I threw my arms around my mum and cried like a baby.

*　　*　　*

News of my success in Edinburgh spread fast and the bookings came in just as quick. The following week myself and Gordon found ourselves on a train to London as I was booked to play both Her Majesty's Theatre in the West End and some other place you may have heard of called the Royal Albert Hall! Utter madness of the first order.

A lovely lady called Nica Burns organised an event called *The Best of the Festival* – a series of shows in London that each week featured a different Perrier nominee's one-man show, and it was my turn. Basically all I had to do was the same thing I'd been doing for twenty-eight nights, which wasn't hard, you'd think. But playing a West End theatre was incredibly intimidating and a lot different than a hundred-seater venue in Edinburgh. I was terrified as I wheeled my collapsible clap-o-meter on to the enormous stage and made the simple mistake of looking up at the three tiers of seats that towered above me. 'What the hell am I doing here?' I said to myself as I groped around for my false arm.

I'll never forget the sound man's face when I handed him my Sainsbury's carrier bag full of tape cassettes and then attempted to explain my complicated configuration system.

'I've lined them all up for you. You start with this red cassette which is labelled tape A, then you go to the green cassette which is labelled tape B . . . Cassettes C, D and E depend on what ending I'm having but I'll get to those in a minute.'

He looked at me like I'd strolled into his house on Christmas Day and pissed on his tree.

It was pitiful when I think back now. I mean rolling up in the West End with a carrier bag full of cassettes, what was I thinking? I mean it's not as though CDs hadn't been invented or anything. The cassettes were also so knackered and worn that when he played one there was this awful noise of hiss from it. How embarrassing.

I can't remember much about my performance; the whole thing is still a blur. I'd never worked with a spotlight on me before and I found it difficult not being able to see anybody; it felt like playing to an enormous black void. The show seemed to go well though, and the audience laughed loudly in all the right places, but not having any eye contact completely threw me and I wasn't comfortable at all.

After playing a small venue for so long, my whole show seemed small-scale and amateurish in such a large space. Looking back now, I think I overanalysed it all a bit too much and I got overwhelmed by where I was playing. Consequently I felt out of my depth and I deemed the gig to be a failure before I'd even opened my mouth, which was a shame as it probably wasn't as bad as I thought. Anyway, if I thought playing a West End theatre was intimidating, things were about to get a whole lot worse.

We went back to the Regent Palace Hotel and I hardly slept a wink what with thinking about my performance and Gordon's snoring – 'Never again will I share a room with this man,' I repeatedly chanted along to each snore as the whole room rhythmically shook in the darkness. It was like listening to a midget drill through a sofa.

The following night we made our way over to one of the most famous venues in the whole world, the Royal Albert Hall. All the great comedians had played there, Billy Connolly, Victoria Wood, Michael Ball. Now it was my turn to add my name to that long list of impressive names.

I'd been invited to appear there as part of a Stonewall equality benefit, which was a charity event promoting equal rights for gay people and minorities. I was booked to perform ten minutes' stand-up at the event and was so daunted by the sheer scale of the building from the outside that I simply couldn't speak on arrival and instead I just nodded and grunted to everyone I met.

A member of the crew immediately led me out on the stage for a brief soundcheck. I almost keeled over, it was breathtakingly beautiful and I'd never seen anything like it in my life. He literally had to link my arm and lead me through my positions. Where to enter and exit, where the mic was etc but I wasn't listening to a single word he said because, for the second time in twenty-four hours, I made the simple mistake of looking up. This place made Her Majesty's Theatre look like a bloody wigwam.

There was a stellar line-up on the night including Martine McCutcheon, who sang the Donna Summer track 'I'm Coming Out', Mika, who was about fifteen years old at the time, Paul O'Grady as Lily Savage, Elton John and Bobby Crush, who I happened to share a dressing room with (Bobby Crush that is, not Elton John). Although I did meet Elton John after the show; well I say 'meet', he skirted past me with his entourage and mumbled, 'You're a very funny man' without actually giving me any eye contact.

Bobby Crush was nice; you know his favourite film is *On Golden Pond*? It's amazing the conversations you have when you're trapped in a dressing room and apoplectic with fear.

'Mr Peter Kay, five minutes to stage, Mr Peter Kay, five minutes to stage.'

I stood up and was about to leave when Bobby said, 'Where do you think you're going?'

I pointed to the speaker and then the door.

'Not like that you're not,' and he span me round, sat me down and gave my face a powder. 'You'll look like death warmed up out there,' he said. Bless him.

The MC on the night was the actor and politician Michael Cashman who played Colin in *EastEnders* and was the first actor to openly kiss another gay man in a British soap. Standing in the wings, we shook hands and he said to me, 'Peter, my name's Michael and I'm going to be introducing you. Could you tell me, did you win this year's Perrier award in Edinburgh?' God knows why but I nodded yes. It was just a little white lie and perhaps I said it in fear, and I was just about to retract it when he exited through the curtain.

Two minutes later in front of six thousand people: 'He's the winner of this year's Perrier award in Edinburgh, please welcome Peter Kay.'

Well, I won't tell if you won't.

Chapter Thirteen

One Hundred Pounds a Minute

Watching stand-up was always more than just a hobby to me. I spent hours listening to delivery, days studying techniques. I watched *Robin Williams – Live at the Met* twice a week. Steve Martin – I could recite every word of his live albums. Ben Elton – his live album *Motormouth* became a yardstick for a whole new generation of British stand-ups, and of course, the greatest stand-up comedian of them all in my opinion, Eddie Murphy. He was just twenty-one when he performed *Delirious* and for me that is why he earns that title. That concert had everything in it: amazing impressions, brilliant gags and observations, but most of all it had incredible structure. My life after school and college was absorbing these masters. Did I know that one day I would be a stand-up comedian? Well no I didn't, but like Dr Martin Luther King I too had a dream.

Stand-up has always been popular on television. But I believe its resurgence started with a show made by Granada TV in the early nineties called simply *Stand-Up*. Using the same structure as *The Comedians*, *Stand-Up* attempted to offer a similar platform for new comedians to its groundbreaking predecessor. Screened late on Friday nights, it featured up-and-coming comedians such as Steve Coogan, Jo Brand, Sean Hughes and Lee Evans, to name but a few. And just like the stars of *The Comedians*, they all went on to become household names and define the new era of stand-up comedy.

I'd watch and tape it religiously, I even clumsily edited together my own personal highlights via two video recorders. I used to borrow the second one from Kathleen (she lived over the road). I would spend hours putting together a compilation of personal highlights. I've still got the VHS in the shed. I saw it the other day, it's on the same tape as *Who Will Love My Children?** It says 'The Best Of Stand-Up' in coloured felt-tip. I've said it before and I'll say it again: I didn't waste my evenings.

Next came the BBC's offering, *Paramount City*. Presented by comedian Arthur Smith, it too showcased new comedy talent such as Jack Dee, Caroline Aherne and Frank Skinner, all of them performing to an audience in a cabaret style. Both series were recommissioned and it wasn't very long before the trend spread to every channel. Before you could say 'Cheap television' they all had their own stand-up show. *Paramount City* morphed into *The BBC Stand-Up Show*, which was probably the most successful of them all, Channel Five launched *The Comedy Store*, which was the first stand-up show to actually film in a real venue, and then ITV followed suit in a similar style with *Live at Jongleurs*. And it *was* cheap television. It was completely self-contained – all the producers needed was a microphone, a stage set and a bunch of comedians itching to get on TV. Well they certainly had plenty of those to

*Christ, have you seen that? Now that is a sad film.

choose from. Fortunately for me, I'd arrived just in time to appear on them all.

Channel 4 were auditioning comedians in Manchester for a new stand-up show called *Gas*. Word spread like wildfire on the circuit as the producers put together a showcase of local talent. After a few desperate calls pulling in favours I managed to bag myself one of the lucrative six-minute audition slots on the night.

It was tough going back down to such a short length but I'd done it before and knew I could do it again. Packing in some of the very best lines I had, I hardly stopped for a breath as I raced through my set that night. After the showcase I hung around with the other stand-ups, hoping to hear if I'd been successful. Loitering nervously by the bar, I was eventually approached by the producer, Sandie Kirk, who told me there and then that I had a slot on the new series. Then casually I enquired about the fee, and she said, 'It's a thousand pounds.'

'For ten minutes? But that's one hundred pounds a minute?'

She may have nodded but I was already gone, on my way to the payphone to ring to tell the world and his wife. Well, Susan and my mum.

'Hello, it's Peter, is Susan there?'

'Er . . . I think she might be asleep,' Susan's mum replied. She did have a point – it was half twelve on a Tuesday night. 'Is everything alright?'

'Yeah, everything's fine, could you tell her it's an emergency please?'

There was a bit of fumbling and banging as the receiver went on the side and Susan's mum headed out into the hall. I could hear the theme tune to *Nash Bridges* on the television as I waited. Then I heard someone approaching the phone, there was a click as Susan picked up the other phone upstairs and shouted, 'Right, Mum', almost deafening me. Then the theme from *Nash Bridges* ended abruptly, as the other receiver went down.

'Hello?'

'Hiya, it's me, I'm sorry for ringing so late but I got the gig, they want me to do the show in London and you'll never guess how much it is?' There was a pause, where I obviously didn't want her to guess, I just wanted to build the anticipation. Pause over. 'A thousand pounds for ten minutes! Can you believe that?' I said.

'A thousand pounds for ten minutes . . . but that's a hundred pounds a minute.'

I tried ringing my mum but it was engaged. I tried again as I went for my last train and it was still engaged. I rang again on the platform payphone – engaged, now I was worried. I tried again when I got off the last train in Bolton – engaged. By now I was pretty sure she was lying dead with the phone off the hook. Being a tight-arse, as you know, I'd usually walk up the hill but given the emergency I hailed a black cab, I even cheekily asked the driver if I could use his mobile – engaged. I counted out the fare as he was still speeding up my street. Diving out of the cab and into the house, I ran up the stairs two at a time to find my mum startled, sat up in bed watching the end of *Nash Bridges*.

'I'VE BEEN RINGING YOU,' I shouted in block capitals.

'When? Why, what's the matter?'

'When? About five hundred times! Your phone's engaged.' (You're allowed to exaggerate when you're worked-up.)

She checked the phone by the side of her bed and sure enough it was in its 'holster' as she affectionately calls it. Then I traced the phone down the wall to discover that one of her castors was sat on her main junction wire (sounds painful).

'You've got your castors on the phone wire,' I said, all flustered.

'Oh, I'm sorry. I wondered why nobody had phoned all night, anyway what's the matter?'

'I got it! I got a spot on the stand-up show on Channel 4 and you'll never guess how much? A thousand pounds for ten minutes!'

'A thousand pounds for ten minutes . . . but that's a hundred pounds a minute,' she said. 'Hey, a few more of those and you'll be able to buy me a bungalow.'

It's been twelve years since I first did *Gas* (that sounds well) and watching it back just now it seems very dated. The studio set was all cutting-edge at the time, enormous green screens showing surreal images, and the stage had all this gas, well steam, coming up through it. It looked really trendy at the time, though now it looks dated to buggery.

I was the first comedian on the very first show, sharing the bill with the real Perrier award winner Tommy Tiernan. Susan and myself headed down on the train and after checking into a dodgy hotel near Euston we were driven over to the London Studios.

There was a lot of hanging around as they organised the set and everybody went through their cues for the show. Once again I was very nervous but I was also confident with my material, having spent the previous fortnight honing it at various gigs I'd done. It was a big deal doing stand-up on TV. I know I'd appeared on the BBC New Comedy Awards and then on *Edinburgh Nights* but this was different, this was me performing as a professional stand-up comedian and I'd been waiting for this moment my whole life.

In order to reduce the risk of alienating anybody in the audience, I deliberately chose material that went right across the board and I opened with a fail-safe that was also one of the first routines I ever wrote, right back in school, 'The A-Team'.

Every week the baddies would lock The A-Team in a barn in the middle of nowhere and that's when they'd start making stuff and they'd use anything they could find: bit of old drainpipe, knackered lawn mower, paper clips, anything they could lay their hands on. Then we'd hear the A-Team theme over a montage of close-ups. B.A.'s hands bending the old drainpipe, while Hannibal managed to conjure up some kind of welding gear from out of nowhere. Then it would cut to outside and the baddies would be getting very curious

'It's gone very quiet in there, Hank.' [Deep south accents.] 'Those A-Team boys gone very quiet, what they doing in there?'

'I'm-a gonna check it out, boss.'

Then just as he walks close to the barn: BANG! The doors burst open in slow motion and out comes Murdock straddling this contraption on wheels that fires hot paper-clips out through a drainpipe.

The baddies would fall to their knees in agony screaming, 'God damn those A-Team boys.'

The other thing that used to wind me up was B.A.'s fear of flying. Same thing every week: 'I ain't getting on no plane, fool.'

'Hey, B.A., fancy a glass of milk?' He'd drink it and then ten seconds later he'd be unconscious. Then eight hours later he'd wake up in another state. 'How'd I get here?'

Next week, same thing: 'I ain't getting on no plane, fool.'

'Here you go, try this hamburger.' Then out he goes again, then he wakes up.

'How'd I get here?'

How do you think you got there, you thick bastard, you just
ate a burger and then woke up a day later at a destination they
all wanted to go to, can you not see a pattern evolving?

After an agonising two-month wait, my episode of *Gas* was finally shown on Tuesday 26 August 1997 at 11.30 p.m. A date that will stay etched into my memory for ever as sadly I had to gig that night and so left the video-recording in the capable hands of my mum who of course taped the wrong channel. I rushed home to watch the end of a documentary about the fated IRA hunger striker Bobby Sands. Luckily the producer, Sandie, sent me a copy and that's what I've just sat and watched. I haven't watched an actual video for so long, it's mental how big they look now.

After my appearance on *Gas* (still sounds like solvent abuse) the floodgates opened. I got a call from a production company called Open Mike; they wanted me to appear on *The Comedy Store* for Channel Five. This was actually a better atmosphere than *Gas* as it was filmed in a real comedy club and there is no way of faking that vibe. It was good to be back at The Comedy Store and I made sure my performance was timed right down to the last millisecond.

My slot was edited down and shown over a number of episodes – in fact if you happen to suffer from insomnia it'll probably be on one of those comedy channels tonight, as they appear to show it ad infinitum, every bloody week.

I kept in touch with Sandie, who then moved over to the BBC to work on *The Stand-Up Show* and she managed to get me a slot on that too. It was presented by Ardal O'Hanlon, who I'd met briefly when he'd hosted the BBC New Comedy Awards in

Edinburgh. They used the same standard format as the other shows, three comedians over thirty minutes, which worked well, particularly if they booked comedians with contrasting styles, for example a comedian who did characters, an absurdist and an observational type of comedian – this last category was the one I fell into.

Took me mum out for her big shop last Friday, 'cause Friday is big shop day, it's the law – big shop Friday evening, chippie tea when we get home. We've just spent a small fortune buying food and then we have a chippie tea! We always park in that parent and child bit at the front of the supermarket. Well why not? I'm with my mum and they don't put an age range on it. It's great because you're right at the front of the shop. At least we know where our car is parked when we come out. I love seeing dads with no short-term memory struggling to find their car and thinking it's been stolen, you see them dashing round the car park: 'The car's gone! Jean, the bloody car's gone, someone's had it . . . oh no, there it is.' Panic over.

I'll be for ever grateful for the profile these shows gave me and the work they generated; I can honestly say I wouldn't be writing this book now if it hadn't been for my appearances on them. Just pull out ten minutes of material, pick up my cheque and that was it. I honestly believe if it had been just two years later I would have missed the boat completely – they were gone. Like anything fashionable, tastes change, especially when producers discovered that reality television was an even cheaper route to go down.

There are some amazing comedians I know who just haven't had the breaks because there hasn't been an outlet for them to perform on TV for the last ten years. All we've got now is *Britain's Got Talent* or if they're really desperate *Big Brother*, or worse they could go on *Embarrassing Bodies** and try and crowbar their act round some doctor examining their genitalia. There has been a slight resurgence in the last few years with the series *Live at the Apollo* but nothing on the same scale of what happened a decade ago.

After doing almost every stand-up show at least twice, the novelty was starting to wear off so I jumped ship and the second series of *The BBC Stand-Up Show* was to be my last. In an effort to liven up my final appearance I dug out my trusty lion costume and took it along to Television Centre.

During the afternoon I did a camera rehearsal with Ardal O'Hanlon and the other comedians. Then as the time to record the show drew nearer I got into my lion costume. You've got to understand at this point I hadn't told anybody, not any of the crew, not the producer, not anybody. It's not like I was secretive about it either, sitting in the BBC canteen eating a tuna baguette in my full feline regalia. Nobody said a word and then they wonder how those lesbian activists got on the *Six O'Clock News*.

Eventually I was called from my dressing room and brought through to the studio where the show had already started recording. Again nobody said a thing, it was as if I always dressed that way. I was led to the corner of the set as Ardal was just finishing his introduction: 'So, ladies and gentlemen, please go wild and crazy for a very funny man – Peter Kay.' And then I walked out dressed as a lion. If you ever get to see it, watch Ardal O'Hanlon's reac-

---

* Don't get me started on that show. 'Gavin's had his condition for four years but hasn't been to see his local GP for fear of embarrassment.' No, but he'll whip his manky cock out on national TV while I'm eating my supper. He deserves his STD, the sexual deviant.

tion, he literally jumps back in shock and then glances over his shoulder as he leaves the stage. Then I did my entire set as planned and as usual I never referred to my costume once.

Everybody took it in good spirit, including Ardal. I don't think Sandie, the producer, was as keen but as my performance went down well they left it in the show. Later in the dressing room, I was getting changed and there was a knock at the door; it was a man called Kevin Bishop who was a producer on the *Royal Variety Performance* and having heard good reports he'd come along to *The Stand-Up Show* specifically to see me. He thought I might be suitable to appear on the bill, well that was until he saw my lion costume.

'I'm sorry if this sounds rude but what's with the lion costume?'

'Oh this, I don't normally wear this, I just wore it as a bit of a prank, you know, comedy an' all?' I said, desperately trying to gloss over it whilst still dressed as a lion. Of all the nights he could have seen me, he had to pick the one when I was dressed as a bloody lion. I bet he was thinking, What's the Queen going to make of this? 'Er . . . you've no need to worry, I wouldn't be dressed as a lion if I got the *Royal Variety*.'

'That's good,' he said, 'because you've got it. It's the first week in December and please leave the lion costume at home.'

And with that he left the dressing room, and me in shock, dressed as a lion. I remember looking at my reflection in the mirror and letting out a huge cheer (should have been a roar).

In preparing for this book (because it's not just thrown together, you know) I was sorting through all of my memorabilia and souvenirs from my years doing stand-up and I found a note in the back of a jotter that I wrote to myself on the 22.10 back to Manchester Piccadilly that night:

I'm doing the Royal Variety, the <u>Royal Variety Performance</u>, and I can't believe it. I've done some amazing things so far in my life, I've done warm-up for Michael Parkinson, I've played an Indian restaurant in Hong Kong, I've even shared a stage with a Meatloaf tribute act in Aberystwyth and just when I think there's nothing left for me to do I get offered a spot on the Royal Variety Performance, the biggest variety show in the world, and I'll never forget how happy I feel right now.

Sadly I didn't get to meet Her Majesty the Queen; it was Prince Charles' turn that year. He came with Camilla and the King and Queen of Greece. The show was filmed at the Lyceum Theatre in London, and sitting in the stalls watching the rehearsals it resembled organised chaos. 'There's no way this is going to be ready in time,' I said to myself as Barry Manilow and Ronan Keating rehearsed their Frank Sinatra tribute medley. Their stage set consisted of seven giant letters, each cleverly brought on by the dancers who revealed them in time to the music to spell the word 'SINATRA', or in this case 'A RATS IN' as they were all in the wrong positions. Mr Manilow wasn't best pleased and I don't think I helped matters: 'What about the dyslexic fans, Barry?' I shouted from the darkness.

As well as Barry and Ronan, the producers had assembled a stellar line-up including Jim Davidson, the cast of *Stomp* and the heavily pregnant Spice Girls, miming all the way to the top of the bill, what more could the licence-paying public want? I was scheduled to go after B*Witched and as usual I was shitting a brick.

Now please hear me out as I feel like I'm repeating myself when I tell you how overawed I get. But you've got to understand things just kept getting bigger and better for me. Playing the West End was big, then the Royal Albert Hall was better but appearing on the *Royal Variety Performance* was the top of the tree. Not just in show-business terms, but for me personally, as I'd watched it my whole life and now I was about to be on it.

I managed to blag a couple of tickets for my mum and my nan; well I say 'blag', they cost me £170 each but the money went to charity and as it was my nan's birthday the next day I couldn't let her miss it. Anyway they were both back at the hotel as I stood nervously in the wings waiting for B*Witched to finish their rehearsal.

For my act I'd decided to go with my misheard lyrics routine, you know the ones I usually did for corporate events, as I'd never performed them on television before. I thought it was important to do something special, plus I knew it was a winner on the laughter front. Poised with my Dictaphone in my hand, I waited for Ulrika Jonsson to say my name and then it was my turn to rehearse, back in the blinding spotlight, which thankfully didn't come as such a shock to me this time after playing Her Majesty's Theatre.

'Hello, how are you?'

Silence, well apart from the sound of hammering and the back-stage crew barking orders at each other. Then a voice shouted from the darkness, 'Just top and tail it.'

'Just what?' I said, with my hand blocking out the spotlight.

'Just give us an overview.'

'Oh right, well I say it's great to be here, then I mention bringing my mum and my nan, then go into a bit about *MasterChef* and then I play these.' Then I pulled out my Dictaphone and pressed play. I put my microphone to the speaker on the side as I normally did; this relayed the sound through the theatre speakers. I'd performed this routine many times and knew it off by heart but the sound that I heard completely threw me. Sure enough it was 'Drive' by

The Cars, which is what I expected to hear, but it was sped up. They sounded like Pinky and Perky. Panicking and confused, I quickly pressed fast-forward to the next track, 'One Vision' by Queen, but that was the same, Freddie Mercury sounded more like Mickey Mouse. I heard some of the stage crew laughing, and I shouted to them, 'This isn't right', but obviously they think everything you say or do on stage is all part of the act, including the look of terror on my face.

By now I was in a right state. I fast-forward again to 'Turn, Turn, Turn' by The Byrds where at two minutes and five seconds it sounds like the theme tune to *Crossroads*. But it too was sped up. Shit! What was going on? It was like a bad dream. I tried to protest but my mic was faded down as they played the walk-off music.

Reluctantly I left the stage and was greeted in the wings by a girl in a headset who hurriedly took my mic from me. 'That was very funny,' she said without giving me any eye contact. 'OK, can we have Bryan Adams to the stage please.'

'But that wasn't right,' I pleaded, 'you don't understand, it's not supposed to sound like that.'

'Well it sounded good to me. Where's Bryan Adams?' she snapped into her headset. I was nearly in tears, as Bryan Adams' band launched into 'Summer of '69' over my shoulder.

What was I going to do? I went down to the stalls and found Kevin Bishop, the producer I'd met at *The Stand-Up Show*; he was all smiles.

'Peter, Peter, what can I say? That was fabulous.'

'But it's not supposed to sound like that, all sped up.'

'Well they're gonna love it tonight, it's very funny.'

'I DON'T GIVE TWO SHITS IF IT'S FUNNY. SOME-THING'S WRONG!'

Finally he paid attention.

We went back on stage and checked the Dictaphone with a sound man; again it was sped up. They tried it with another microphone, they replaced the batteries, they turned the sound up and down but it was still too fast. The only explanation the sound man could come up with was static interference. I thought, Jesus, I'm about to die on my arse on national television and this prick's giving me science fiction.

'Haven't you got a spare Dictaphone?' said Kevin.

'Er . . . well I have but it's broke.'

I always carried a spare for moments such as these but, and what are the odds, I'd dropped it in the Frog & Bucket car park the night before and basically it wasn't playing at all. I rushed back to the hotel to get it so the sound man could have a go at fixing it over lunch. Kevin and his assistant said they'd try sourcing another but other than that I was goosed.

In a state of depression I headed back to the dressing room. I was sharing with the male cast of *Oklahoma!** and the comedian Phil Cool, but even he couldn't raise a smile with one of his many faces. I couldn't believe it was happening: my big moment on the *Royal Variety* was about to be ruined by a defective Dictaphone. I mean it wasn't as if I could rewrite my act, the Dictaphone *was* my act.

The producer, Kevin, had people searching for Dictaphones everywhere and eventually he arrived at my dressing-room door with one in his hand but unfortunately it wasn't the same as mine.

'But won't it do?' he said, forever the optimist.

'I'm not being awkward, Kevin, but you've got to understand

---

* Which included Wolverine himself, Hugh Jackman, who offered to take me out and get me drunk, his twisted logic being 'Everything sounds like it's at the wrong speed when you're pissed'. God love him.

I've been using my Dictaphone for years. I know it inside out, I could use it blindfolded. I can't go on stage with a new one, I won't have a clue what I'm doing!'

With the clock ticking and the audience taking their seats, I was beyond inconsolable. Phil Cool was in the corner doing Rolf Harris and just as I was about to commit hara-kiri the door burst open; it was the producer Kevin telling me that they'd found me a Dictaphone and it was on its way from Milton Keynes on the back of a motorcycle. Oh the joy! The relief! Then the associate producer burst in and said she'd just had a call to say they'd found one reduced in Harrods. Then a researcher burst in and told us that one had been found up Tottenham Court Road. Then Hugh Jackman burst in drunk. It doesn't rain but it pours, I ended up with five Dictaphones in the end, all courtesy of the BBC. Stick that on your expenses.

With my mum and my nan seated on the back row of the top tier, facing a pillar, I took up my position in the wings once again as B*Witched performed a medley of their 'hit'. God, they were good. And despite the unbridled joy of finally feeling a Dicta-phone in my pocket, my nerves were in pieces. Cue Ulrika Jonsson, 'Please welcome award-winning comedian Peter Kay', and on I walked.

My misheard lyric routine went like a dream and I have to say I handled my new Dictaphone beautifully. I think the reaction I got was very much divided; downstairs in the stalls the laughter was quite gentle and slightly delayed. Then after adjusting my eyes to the spotlight I could see some of audience: pensioners with hearing aids and walking sticks – no wonder it was delayed with the cast of *Cocoon* gawping up at me. The majority of big laughs came from the top half of the theatre where the audience mainly consisted of family and friends of people in the show, not to mention my mum and my nan who were probably up there egging everybody on.

Six hours later it was all over and as I stood in between Phil Cool and Hugh Jackman singing 'God Save the Queen' (I think the Spice Girls might have mimed that one too) I couldn't help but get emotional. It was a moment to treasure.

Then immediately after the curtain came down the whole cast turned around in order to greet the royal party. I could see him, there he was, Prince Charles, and as he approached all I kept thinking was, I've got him at home on a tea towel. In fact I almost said it to him I was that overwhelmed. We shook hands and I can't honestly remember what we said to each other, pathetic I know and not what you want to hear – sorry, reader – but sadly it's the truth.

I do remember the Queen of Greece asking Phil Cool if he wore some kind of special mask. I thought, That's his act, you stupid bitch, he pulls faces, 'Do you wear some kind of a mask?' indeed. How embarrassing. She was clearly too busy opening her Terry's All Gold when he was on.

After the show I met my mum and my nan in the foyer and we hugged like we'd just been reunited at the end of *Surprise, Surprise*. They seemed so proud of me, and as we headed back to the hotel all they wanted to know was one thing: had the Spice Girls been miming?

Chapter Fourteen

Elkie Brooks' Dog Hairs

One thing I'd never embarked on at this point was my own tour, but after my success at the Edinburgh Festival and on the *Royal Variety* it seemed like the next logical step. I decided to call it the 'Greatest Hits Tour', as that was something you usually associated with someone at the end of their career as opposed to the beginning; well it made me laugh anyway. In an effort to test the waters I kept the tour dates to a minimum: twenty nights over three weeks, which was more than enough for my first national tour; well I say 'national' but I never actually went any further than Newcastle or Rugby.

In fact I'd played a lot of the venues many times before, like The Glee Club in Birmingham where I was a regular, Just the Tonic in Nottingham, and Hyena Comedy Club in Newcastle. So I was established in those places and the tickets sold well. But I also ventured to new territory like Lincoln and Leicester, where I was surprised to find they too sold out, despite not having played there before.

The Leicester gig was at a venue called The Y Theatre, which looked more like an old church than a venue for comedy, with its brightly coloured walls and high-beamed ceilings. A young buck called Jason Manford accompanied me on the night and sat in the wings watching my performance. We'd become very good friends after meeting on the circuit and he too had recently won the North West Comedian of *that* Year. Jason is a fantastic comedian and a naturally funny bloke* who'd also performed his first gig at The Buzz Club after being enticed into having a go whilst working behind the bar. His and my styles are very similar – friendly, chatty observations about everyday life, in particular family and childhood. Jason was just eighteen and he confessed that he was a bit unsure about where his stand-up career was headed at that point or even if he wanted stand-up to be his chosen career at all. I suggested he should maybe apply for the HND in Media Performance that I'd done at Salford University, which he eventually did and immediately loved – in fact he even stayed to get himself a degree.

Several years later he returned to stand-up comedy once again and hasn't looked back since (due to the fact that he wears a surgical collar).† He replaced my *old* friend Dave Spikey as team captain (or whatever it's called) on the Channel 4 show *8 Out of 10 Cats* and has just completed his very own stand-up tour, where I went to watch him at the Lowry in Salford, only this time it was me who was sitting in the wings on a chair.

The major difference doing a tour was that this time people had specifically come to watch me and I didn't feel as if I had to vie for attention like I did in the clubs. Being on tour also brought back the excitement I used to get in my early days at the Frog & Bucket and I couldn't wait to get on stage each night and give it

---

* You may have noticed that all the comedians I know are naturally funny blokes.
† Just jokes.

my all. Which is exactly what I did give: with the show weighing in at just under two and a half hours, it was both completely exhilarating and exhausting but the way I saw it, that was the deal. They buy a ticket; I give them a night to remember. Sounds corny, I know, but it felt like my duty.

Being on tour meant I was also able to work with my friend Gordon again, extending his role from sound and lights this time to tour manager (although he still did sound and lights, and catering, and drove, in particular when I'd just come off stage and was still high as a kite from adrenalin, as I would have just ploughed into a tree had I been behind the wheel). He claims he was delighted with the arrangement, and so was I, as having a friend to share it all with made touring a joy and not a chore.

The tour also gave me some of my first experiences at playing proper theatrical venues, like the beautiful City Varieties theatre in Leeds, where they used to record *The Good Old Days* for the BBC. The thing I remember most about playing there was that it had a sloped stage, as for my finale I had a Christmas tree on castors which almost ended up in the orchestra pit.

I also played Sheffield City Hall where I was designated the smallest room, which has a capacity of about five hundred, unlike the main room across the corridor which holds two thousand but happened to be occupied that Saturday night with an all-black adaptation of *Pinocchio*. The cast were a nightmare, as they kept coming in when I was on stage and popping their heads round the curtain for a nosey (and what a big long nosey it was too). If that wasn't bad enough, the singer Elkie Brooks had been playing in the main hall the night before and had apparently used the smaller room for her two golden retrievers to run around in, hence my red-carpeted stage being covered in several thousand dog hairs.

Luckily I managed to find one of those huge industrial sit-on floor cleaners and made my grand entrance on that at the start of the show, hoovering up Elkie Brooks' dog hairs.

Home to the Hallé Orchestra and Choir was the then not-long-opened Bridgewater Hall in Manchester, which is an incredible venue, definitely the largest and most impressive of the tour – one thousand, seven hundred and forty seats to be precise. That was an extraordinary night. Walking out on to the stage, I was completely flabbergasted by the response the audience gave me and the place looked magnificent. I was so overawed by the experience that I immediately ran back off stage to the dressing room to get my camera. I then returned and took photos of the audience, I even did one of those crappy panoramic ones where you take individual photos and then put them in a line when they're developed so you can see the whole view. Then the first thing I said was, 'What the fuck are we doing in here?', as I was humbled to be playing such a prestigious space.

I performed for over three hours, which was the longest I'd ever been on stage. I felt as if I owed it to the audience, just to say a thank you to everybody for supporting me over the past few years. Gordon had organised the hire of a snow machine from a place in Halifax for my finale, and as Christmas was approaching I decided to perform a special festive song called 'Christmas 2000', which I'd written and recorded for my first television series called *That Peter Kay Thing*.*

Unfortunately the glorious winter wonderland I'd imagined ended up a bit of a disaster, as after performing for much longer

* The title just came to me in frustration after racking my brains thinking of one. I thought, Whatever it's called, people are still going to say, 'Did you see that Peter Kay thing last night?' and thus the title was born.

than I'd anticipated the light fluffy snowflakes had been transformed into the kind of muck you used to see on *Tiswas*. With white slush enveloping the stage, I almost broke my neck (the audience seemed to find this most amusing) but I managed to successfully slip and slide my way to the end of both the song and the night. And with a standing ovation that brought tears to my eyes, I reluctantly left the stage. I was extremely proud of that night, and was even more chuffed when the show received a Manchester Evening News Theatre Award for best comedy show.

In the bar after the show I was overwhelmed again by the amount of family, friends and fans that had come to offer their support. Some of them I hadn't seen for a long time, in particular my old teachers from Mount St Joseph: Mr Fitzpatrick (Art), Mr Donaldson (PE, banged his arse on a wing mirror) and Mr India (Craft and Design). They looked a bit older and greyer but other than that they hadn't changed a bit. They invited me and a few of my other mates from school to go for a curry in Rusholme. That was a funny meal. I don't know if you've ever had the chance to have a meal sitting opposite some of your old teachers but it was a very awkward experience because we reverted to behaving like we were back at school again. Paddy said to Mr India, 'What are you having, sir?', well that started us giggling and once we started we couldn't stop. Oh it was bad. You know when you know you shouldn't laugh and that makes it even worse? I was just going to say 'just like when you were at school', which is exactly how it felt.

Undecided, Mr India said, 'I don't know, I don't know' then turning to Mr Fitzpatrick hc said, 'What do you fancy, Graham?' Simultaneously we all buried our heads in our menus, whispering behind them, 'He just called him Graham, did you hear that, he just called him Graham?!' out the side of our mouths.

'Well I don't know what to have; there's fuck-all on here,' said Mr Donaldson, chipping in. The laugh came so fast that a bit of sick came up with it. Him swearing was just way too much for us to handle and both Paddy and me just slid under the table in hysterics. We were laughing that hard we had to excuse ourselves and go to the toilet. Surely they must have known.

'Did you hear what he said: "There's fuck-all on here?"' we recounted in the bogs with tears rolling down our cheeks.* It was very, very funny. I'd like to tell you that our childishness subsided after a while but it didn't.

Touring changed my perception of stand-up completely; it felt good being on a bigger stage in front of a bigger audience. I'd been performing for four years at this point, I'd done over six hundred gigs and the time felt right to now move on. Although it was never a conscious decision to stop playing the clubs, it just seemed to happen. The last club gig I ever did was at The Funny Farm in Liverpool where I'd been booked to be the resident compère one weekend in every month. I was coming to the end of my six-month contract and my final Saturday night saw me being compère for the heats of a regional comedy competition.

I was in the toilet during the interval and the bloke next to me turned round mid-piss and said, 'Hiya' in an abnormally high-pitched voice (which turned out to be real). 'I'm Nicky Martine.'

'I'll not shake your hand if you don't mind,' I said.

He was an odd-looking fella, a cross between an old Wayne

* Face cheeks.

Rooney and a young Chuck Norris (and that's when Chuck was in his prime – *Silent Rage, An Eye for an Eye,* none of that *Delta Force* shit).

'Listen, I'm glad I've caught you,' he squeaked. 'I'm on next and I do impressions, could you please tell them I do impressions?'

'I will.'

And with that he left without washing his hands (the dirty bastard).

Five minutes later I was back on stage.

'Now then, we've got a very special act for you, I've just bumped into him in the gents'? and he told me to tell you he does impressions, so I'm sure you're in for a treat, although he didn't wash his hands, please welcome the many faces of Nicky Martine.'

He charged on stage and the dirty bastard grabbed the mic and squealed, 'My name's Nicky Martine and I did wash my hands thank you very much but see if you can guess who this is!' Then he reached for a chair in the corner of the stage and pulled it towards him; unfortunately the microphone cable was caught around the leg of the chair and as it swung round it knocked over a pint of beer that some punter had rested on it. It smashed and someone shouted, 'Stevie Wonder?' which got a massive laugh.

'No, no I haven't done it yet, I've not done it yet . . . just wait,' said Nicky, the comedy completely lost on him. Then he sat down on the chair and painstakingly he pulled out a pair of black National Health framed glasses, he put them on and proceeded to do a piss-poor impression of Ronnie Corbett.

'So the producer said to me, "Ronnie, Ronnie, Ronnie, Ronnie,"' he said.

Silence. Even though he said the name Ronnie four times, everybody struggled to think who it was. More silence.

'NO? . . . No guesses? It was Ronnie Corbett!' he said, slightly put-out.

But it had sounded more like Joe Pasquale doing Ronnie Corbett on helium, if you can imagine such a thing. I'm sure all the dogs nearby got it. They were probably scavenging for food two streets away saying, 'It's R-R-R-R-R-Ronnie Corbett, the dirty bastard's doing R-R-R-R-R-Ronnie Corbett.'

'Anyway, moving on,' he said, 'here's another one for you.'

Then, adopting a new stance, he proceeded to rock back and forth on his heels as he did another piss-poor impression, this time it was supposedly Sir Terry Wogan.

'Hello and welcome to another *Children In Need*, it's been twelve months since we last . . .'

Then interrupting him somebody shouted out in a thick Scouse accent, 'Hey, mate, do Wogan!'

He said, 'I'M DOING WOGAN, THIS IS WOGAN, YOU THICK PIG! I'M DOING HIM NOW!' Again the humour was completely lost on poor Nicky, who in a fit of anger threw down his microphone and left the stage. The place was in uproar and I have to admit it was a very witty put-down. But then again they always were in Liverpool; it's the only place I've ever played where 90% of the time the audience is funnier than the comedians themselves.

The Funny Farm wasn't supposed to be my final club gig, I had been booked to play the Frog & Bucket on New Year's 'Millennium' Eve but as the night approached, things changed. With club and taxi prices escalating, the British public decided to do an enormous U-turn and stay at home, thus reinventing the house party (and New Year's Eve fireworks from there on in for everybody). With the cash and carry and the off-licence making a killing as people stocked up, Dave Perkin reluctantly had no choice but to pull the gig at the Frog & Bucket and, with it, my chance to say farewell to the end of the century at my local comedy club. Ah well, at least this now meant I shared my final club gig with Nicky Martine (the dirty bastard).

With my New Year's Eve now free (for the first time in years, as previously I'd always worked New Year at the Frog & Bucket) I found myself at a bit of a loose end. Thankfully I was invited to a family house party (my girlfriend's family that is, just in case you think I accepted any random invite). The theme was fancy dress and as it was a special night I felt compelled to try a little harder than my obligatory lion costume, so I went as Gary Glitter. A slightly controversial choice, I know, but all I needed was a few rolls of foil and a manicured Afro wig. (It could have been worse, it could have been Michael Jackson . . . Question: if Gary Glitter had Michael Jackson's back catalogue would he have got away with it? I'll leave that with you.)

Being tee-total, I spent most of the night in the way I always do at family gatherings: as resident taxi driver. I appreciated I could have had a Baileys but I'd have felt mean-spirited in the wake of taxis charging quadruple fare.

My first port of call was to pick up my girlfriend's cousin and his wife who were on the other side of Bolton at another house party which had started very early. In anticipation of their second social engagement of the evening, both were already in fancy dress. By the time I arrived, Sister Sonia was more than a little worse for wear, in fact I've never seen a nun do a forward roll across a lawn and stagger to her feet without spilling so much as one drop of Lambrusco from the glass she was carrying.

Her husband, Father Barry, wasn't in a party mood. 'Fucking stupid bitch,' he said as she staggered over to the car and got in.

'I'm pissed and I don't give a shit, excuse my language, Father,' she screeched and laughed so manically my foil vibrated.

We were quite a sight to behold – an irate priest and a drunken nun having a domestic whilst Gary Glitter chauffeured – we got a few stares at the traffic lights, I can tell you.

We saw in the new century with a drink and a dance and a rocket so big that we all had to dash back into the house for health and safety reasons. We then ran back out into the garden just in time to see the last remaining embers glitter out, a bit like Gary's career.

Then before you could sing another drunken verse of 'Auld Lang Syne' I was back behind the wheel of my trusty Fiesta, ready to ferry revellers round Bolton and beyond.

'Can you get another in?' came a shout from the front door.

'Not really, it's going to be a bit tight with seven as it is,' I shouted, cursing Princess Diana's death for distracting me into buying a hatchback.

One of the seven included another cousin, Michelle, who earlier, when realising it was imminent that she was about to vomit, ran to the front door, opened it and missed. It went straight down and into the UPVC door frame (which incidentally is a bugger to get vomit out of, we went through four rolls of Bounty, sorry Plenty). I mean how can you miss the outside?

Thirty minutes later she was spreadeagled behind my gear stick, with the heel of her stiletto repeatedly twatting the back of my head every time I hit a speed bump. Desperate for the journey to end and in considerable pain, I pleaded for somebody, anybody, to give me directions.

'I know it's near a bus stop,' came a slurred voice from the back.

'Oh good, well we're almost there then aren't we,' I snapped, tired and ratty whilst trying to avoid any speed bumps.

'Straight on,' said Michelle in her semi-conscious state, followed by 'Straight on', followed some time later by 'Straight on' again.

'I think I'd better stop now, Michelle, as we're near Hull.'

The fact she had her eyes shut should have given me a clue.

It was half four when I did my last run. Some relation dressed as one half of Salt-N-Pepa took the liberty of opening my rear passenger door at 40 mph and threw up on Crompton Way, the dirty rapper. Now I had vomit all down the side of my car and no Bounty (sorry Plenty). I left her propped up in a garden still searching for her house keys as I reversed down her cul-de-sac. Then as I headed home to the remains of some lukewarm chilli and a well-earned glass of Baileys I glanced in my rear-view mirror only to find another bloke sat in the back dressed as The Real Slim Shady – Christ, where did this one come from?

'Where do you live, mate?'

'Anywhere me, pal, anywhere.'

I thought, Great, I've got Paul Young in the back of my car: open the window and chuck your hat out, you're home. I left him at the Texaco garage, with a four-litre bottle of windscreen wash as a pillow. After inspecting my interior to ensure there were no more stray pissheads in fancy dress lurking, I headed home, shattered. It was on nights like that I wished I had been gigging.

Things would change for me in the dawn of the new millennium; well that's what Russell Grant said and he wasn't wrong either. By the end of January I'd found myself a manager, Phil McIntyre, a kind and lovely man who originated from a place called Rufford which is about half an hour from Bolton. We got on extremely well but the thing I liked most about him was that he always put his family first. That was the greatest of all priorities as far as I was concerned.

He agreed with me that the time was right for me to make my first live stand-up video and so we set about choosing a location. I wanted the theatre to be somewhere special, somewhere that would make the event unique. I'd never been keen on nameless, faceless stand-up videos, I preferred shows like *Robin Williams Live at the Met* or *Billy and Albert – Billy Connolly at the Royal Albert Hall.* I had so much affection for Blackpool, it seemed to be the perfect place. My initial idea was to film at the end of the pier; it seemed fitting considering I was regarded as more of a traditional comedian. Sadly, when we visited the North Pier it was already on the way to rack and ruin and apparently it would have cost a small fortune to run cables down from the promenade. So it was a no-go.

We then investigated the Tower Circus, which as a child I'd always thought was at the top of the tower. That's what my grandad had told me when I was a boy. I'd never been up the tower, as I was scared of heights, but always believed that all the entertainment was right at the top. I'd had no idea of scale, it looked huge from a child's perspective, like anything could have gone on up there.

The setting was perfect, a gorgeous Victorian circus space, with actual working fountains, that I ended up using in the show to create a Busby Berkeley-esque finale. And in an effort to perpetuate my childhood belief, I decided to pretend the show was actually at the top of the tower. The venue was booked; all I had to do now was sort out a structure to my material.

Seven consecutive nights of warm-up gigs were booked as a lead-up to shooting the video. Doing these allowed me to hone my material quite quickly and try out any new bits and there were plenty as the week before the gigs I spent a fortnight in Egypt (sorry t'Egypt, as my nan called it and even that became part of my act). My spontaneous trip to t'Egypt proved to be the catalyst for the entire show. What better theme than holidays for a live video in Blackpool?

It gave me the opportunity to perform some of my very best material on subjects close to my heart. Family holidays as a child to Blackpool and beyond, my dad's home comforts abroad, 'garlic bread'. School trips, big summer holidays at home which incorporated my mum's crap pop and having sales outside the house selling rose perfume, airport baggage carousels, even our recent trip to Las Vegas and the *Legends* show got an airing.

The whole show just fell into place and the material just poured out of me as I scribbled down my thoughts beside the pool in t'Egypt. Mind you there was absolutely nothing else to do except lounge by the pool soaking in the sun's rays and getting bitten by mosquitoes.* At night we had a choice between watching Hollywood blockbusters such as *The Fugitive* and *Young Guns II*, dubbed into Arabic for some reason, or sitting in the bar listening to the resident musical act, Mr Fabiola, murdering The Carpenters' back catalogue each and every night (except on Thursdays when it was Tropicana night at the New Winter Palace Hotel and guests were allowed to limbo through reception, while Mr Fabiola wore a grass skirt and murdered the hits of Bob Marley instead).

Once again Gordon accompanied me during my week of brief warm-up shows which took in consecutive nights in Nottingham,

---

* You can actually still see the mosquito bites on my arms on the video.

Southport, Stockport, Liverpool, Oldham and a double bill at the Citadel in St Helens. By the end of an exhausting week of honing I felt as if I'd never been more ready for anything in my life.

Two nights were booked at the Blackpool Tower Circus, the first as a rehearsal show, the second was to be the one that was filmed. Apparently it's normal for both shows to be filmed but as this was my first live video the budget was tighter than usual. I actually think that decision helped my adrenalin to focus on the one performance – when it's make or break, people always tend to pull it out of the bag.

My *old* friend Dave Spikey came down for both nights and acted as compère. I even had a couple of other acts supporting me: a brilliant comedian called Steve Royle and Archie Kelly, who plays the character Kenny Senior in *Phoenix Nights*.

The Tower Circus looked spectacular that night, the audience was packed out with family and friends – my mum had come with my Auntie Pat (well she wasn't my real auntie, she was just a friend of the family). The cameras were set and everything was ready to roll but there was one thing missing: me. I was on the other side of Blackpool having my tea in The Cod Cottage. Well I couldn't break an age-old family tradition and not have fish and chips at the seaside. Phil McIntyre had been going on about what beautiful fish they did over at The Cod Cottage all afternoon, so in a break before filming, Phil, Paddy, Gordon and myself took a taxi ride across town in order to indulge ourselves. Phil was right, the fish melted in our mouths, but alas we got so engrossed in gorging ourselves we completely lost all track of time. As we were unable to wait for a taxi, the owner ended up giving us a highly illegal lift over to the tower in the back of his fish van; it stank. Thankfully we arrived just as Steve Royle was finishing his act. So there I was, poised beside the stage about to film my first ever live stand-up video and stinking of haddock.

Welcome to the top of the tower. We're filming this tonight; hope it makes some bloody money, my mum wants a bungalow. Right, I'd better tell some jokes, hadn't I? William Shakespeare went into a pub, the landlord went, 'Get out, you're barred.' A friend of mine got knocked down by a mobile library and he was lying in the road screaming and the driver got out and said, 'Shush.' Another mate of mine went into the doctor's with a steering wheel down his underpants. The doctor said, 'What happened?' 'I don't know but it's driving me nuts.'

I had to open with a few ticklers, it would have been criminal not to. Then it was on to the rest of the show. After a minute or two I forgot the whole thing was being filmed and completely relaxed into it. The audience were all that mattered that night and I gave them everything I'd got, including the new stuff I'd just written on holiday:

Just been away, just been t'Egypt. That's how they pronounce it in Bolton: t'Egypt. Me nan said, 'When you going t'Egypt?' She said, 'Did you get it on t'internet?' On t'internet? I actually got my holiday from a travel agent but then I made the mistake of telling my mate; he said, 'No, bollocks to the travel agent, you want to get on Teletext if you want a good deal. We saw a holiday on there, me, Sheena and the kids, we went to Skiathos, we saw it that afternoon. We put Teletext on, up it came, we got on the phone and booked it and then we were off, we were on the beach that night. Booked it, packed it, fucked off. I'm telling you, get on Teletext.'

But you go on and there's four hundred pages of holidays and you're just mesmerised by them all. 'That's a good one there, Corfu, what's that half-board? Oh now it's changed. Hang on, that looks like a good one there, self-catering, Malta for a fortnight, where's "hold" on this remote, quick where's "hold"? I don't want to make it bigger, what are you making it bigger for? I've not got cataracts, oh now it's gone off.' Three hours we were on there. 'Get ready, it's coming round again now, wait, page eighty-five, any second now, page eighty-six . . . take them matchsticks out your eyes and get that pencil ready, it's coming on now. Oh it's gone now! It's gone, it's sold. Forget about it. Booked it, packed it, f . . .

All comedians doubt they can create new, good material. They cling to their old material for dear life; it's so easy and safe to wheel out the gear that works week-in, week-out. But there's no better feeling than discovering a new bit, especially when it goes down a storm; it's life-affirming, knowing you still have the ability to make people laugh.

My favourite bit from *Top of the Tower* is right at the end when the credits have almost come to an end. There's a shot of me just about to flick off the light as I leave the dressing room and it cuts to a shot of Blackpool Tower and the lights go out, then it cuts back and clearly I've flicked the wrong switch. The music is playing: 'Run For Home' by Lindisfarne stops right at that moment. I love that bit, for me it was a great end to both the show and the video.

*   *   *

Live at the Top of the Tower was released in the autumn of 2000 and got some fantastic reviews, the most complimentary of which compared it to *An Audience with Billy Connolly*, which was a huge deal for me as that was exactly what I aspired to achieve. Something that the whole family could watch together without fear of it really offending anybody.

The success of the video grew and grew. It even launched catchphrases such as 'Get on t'internet', 'Put big light on', 'It's spittin' and of course, the bizarrest of them all, 'garlic bread', which even managed to make it into the *Oxford Dictionary of Modern Quotations* and was voted the funniest one-liner of all time in a national poll. I mean I'm not knocking it but 'garlic bread'? Garlic and bread? It's just food, and it's hard to comprehend that a simple comment made by my dad as he sat in the Red Lion pub in Lloret de Mar has gone on to become a national catchphrase.

Then funnily enough I discovered that *Top of the Tower* had started being played in bars abroad for holidaymakers, which totally freaked me out as the whole thing had come full-circle and it is now itself considered a kind of home comfort abroad. *Top of the Tower* went on to become the second-biggest-selling stand-up video in Britain, something I'm still extremely proud of.

But with my first live video complete I was left with a dilemma: what was I to do next? Well, there was only one thing left as far as I could see: get my mum a bungalow.

Chapter Fifteen

This Time It's National

After the release of *Live at the Top of the Tower* I spent the following couple of years making both series of *Phoenix Nights* back to back. I also became the new face of John Smith's bitter and filmed a few adverts for them, which I found ironic, as I don't drink* (obviously I neglected to mention that to them). Apart from the occasional corporate or charity event, stand-up was completely relegated to the sidelines.

Much as I enjoyed creating and making television, it was a completely different process to stand-up, and with so many people involved and other factors to take into consideration I'd often find myself yearning for the simplicity of being back on stage. So once filming was complete, I set my sights on doing a second stand-up tour, only this time it would be a national one. Besides I'd already publicly promised my mum a bungalow, so if ever I needed motivation I had it.

* Apart from the nectar of the gods, Baileys.*

  * Which is actually more of a dessert than a drink.

I spoke to Gordon, who was still working at Salford University, and asked him would he like to get involved as tour manager again. He was really keen and so organised, taking some time off from work so we could start putting the show on the road (quite literally). The tour was scheduled to start in September and run for a total of forty nights – taking me through to the end of October. But what it eventually turned into was something nobody ever expected.

A few warm-up shows were booked in preparation for the tour, as it was important for me to put the structure together and try out new material. Problem was I hadn't got any new material. So I did what anybody else would do in my situation – I went on holiday for a fortnight.

In between sunbathing and swimming I began to piece the show together, from a collection of crib sheets, scraps of paper and notes scrawled down on things like the back of old beer mats that I'd built up over the previous five years. I was notorious for always scribbling, noting down things people said on anything I could lay my hands on. I still do it now. What a sight I must have looked, sitting beside the pool with my Netto carrier bag crammed full of notes.

Believe it or not, I actually had a lot of fun and found it a very therapeutic process. Obviously it's not something you'd normally do on holiday, but being away gave me a chance to focus, and by the end of my fortnight at Center Parcs I felt confident I had the makings of the new tour.

Next up came the warm-up shows. I was conscious that a lot of my material was parochial and so wouldn't be as popular in other parts of Britain. I'd also started having panic attacks in the middle of the night with thoughts like, Who the hell wants to see me in Plymouth? and, What business have I got trying to play a one thousand, seven hundred-seater theatre in Ipswich? So trying the material out in new and varied places was just what I needed to ease me in gently and it also allowed me to hone the show. I played a variety of venues during the warm-ups, just two-hundred-seat theatres in places like Maidenhead, Jersey and Oxford, to see if the material would travel and potentially work all over the country.

It did prove my theory that funny remains funny wherever you go. Ironically what I did discover though was that the further I went away from home the better my material seemed to go down, which was very reassuring. I think I got a lot of ex-pat Northerners who'd relocated or who were working away so a lot of my act reminded them of home.

A big national tour also meant a few changes in terms of now using my own lights and a PA. On the first couple of tours I'd had to resort to Gordon doing the sound and lights (and both simultaneously in the case of the Barracuda Club in Lincoln) or having a local crew ruin the show as I'd only be in town for one night and so they had no vested interest in even attempting to get anything right. Most of them couldn't even work a CD player and any subtle sound cues from me were often missed, resulting in me screaming, 'WILL YOU PRESS PLAY NOW FOR F***'S SAKE!' at a sound man barely awake at the back of the theatre.

This time we were going to get it right and have a proper travelling sound and lighting rig and our own man to operate them each and every night. His name was (eventually, as we sacked three before we got it right) Pete the Hat, because he wore a hat,* and

* He arrived with that nickname. It had nothing to do with me.

he had a hard job, travelling round in his lorry, setting up the show hours before Gordon and myself would arrive to do a soundcheck. It made a huge difference to the quality of the tour and I was also able to relax knowing I had a competent sound man watching my back every night.

I had a lot of ideas for the show that I never actually used in the end. One idea I had was using a ventriloquist dummy of myself. I don't know why, or where the idea came from. There's a marvellous man in Sheffield called Shaks who invents and makes a lot of stage props for people like *Little Britain* and *French and Saunders*. I asked him to make a working ventriloquist dummy of me, and when it arrived it was so lifelike it was terrifying, like the one in that film *Magic* with Anthony Hopkins. In the end I chickened out of using it as it was a little bit too eerie for my liking; it never even made it to the warm-up shows. In fact it never even made it out of my wardrobe in the back bedroom until I needed an emergency dummy for R Wayne's special skills performance in *Britain's Got the Pop Factor*. We blacked it up and used it as the other half of his duet during 'Ebony and Ivory'.

Another idea that got dropped was using giant letters that spelt my name in lights on the back of the stage. I even had them made. They were about 8ft by 6ft with big bulbs round them, and they cost a bloody fortune.

I thought it would be funny at the start of the show if I came out to find them spelling 'Peter Gay' at the back of the stage. Horrified, I'd then proceed to drag this huge heavy 'G' into the wings, where I'd have an argument with some backstage crew. But again I bottled it, as the gag felt too convoluted, and moving the enormous letters from one venue to another would have meant hiring another lorry just for the privilege. As far as I'm aware they're still in a lock-up in Sheffield so if anyone fancies a couple of 'E's they can have them at a very competitive price.

The warm-up shows went well. They allowed me to ditch a lot of material that wasn't working and stick with the stuff that was. That was the hard part. There's no getting around trying out ideas and thoughts for the first time. There really is no grey area with comedy – they either laugh or they don't. Give it a second chance and if they don't laugh again, it's out. But having to stand there while something doesn't get a laugh is, as you can imagine, one of the most excruciatingly embarrassing things you can do. Really it should be enough to put you off doing it but, amazingly, it doesn't. I believe there's a masochistic streak running through all stand-up comedians that keeps us coming back for more.

Over the course of the warm-up gigs a theme naturally developed: family weddings. I liked it because it was universal and had great potential for allowing me to pull together all the characters I'd developed throughout the show. Plus it also gave me the chance to involve music, which as you know (or should do by now) I live for. I'm that bad, these days I can't even nip for a bottle of semi-skimmed without knocking up a playlist on my iPod.

Another thing I love about family weddings is at the start of the night you always get little girls up dancing, and there's always little boys stuffed tightly into waistcoats and bow ties who always spend the first half hour of every wedding sliding on their knees across the dance floor. Why? It sends their mums crazy.

'Just look at your trousers, they're filthy, get up, come and sit down, you're roasting, look you can't get your breath, you're like a bull mastiff.'

'But I wanna go and play.'

'*You're best man for Christ's sake.*'

You always get aunties and grandmas doing their bent-over dance and grandmas always go early as well.

'*Sandra, your grandma's going. It's ten to eight.*'

Grandma's like Yoda from Star Wars. *She's about three foot tall, with her anorak on.* '*Going now am I, going now. I'm gonna go home and get settled. Get curtains drawn. That disco's too loud for me. That's not music, it's just noise. Here, give us a kiss.*' *[Kiss noise.]*

'*Here you go, Grandma, you get home. You get home, get a shave.*'

Tickets went on sale for the first forty nights and they sold out in less than a week. I was completely gobsmacked. And after the success of the first forty, my manager suggested doing more dates, so another forty nights were quickly added, taking the show right up to Christmas 2002. Whether they'd like me or not in Plymouth and Ipswich remained to be seen, but I would definitely be going there to find out.

The *Mum Wants a Bungalow* tour started quite quietly on September the 16th at Buxton Opera House. I invited a few friends for the opening night. Ian Savage, the editor of my local paper the *Bolton Evening News*, came along, and my mate Pete Hallworth who'd edited both series of *Phoenix Nights* (and won an award for it) came down with his family and I sang 'Happy Birthday' to his wife Cheryl. I received lots of flowers and cards from family and friends offering their support but they didn't come on the first night, as I was far too nervous. And the last thing I needed was my mum giving me a detailed critique of the show.

Being on stage that night felt like heaven and I know I've blathered on about how good it feels but that first night, in fact that whole first week, I was walking on air. In fact I remember driving home with Gordon after the shows and all I could do was smile. The show was weighing in at two hours and forty-five minutes and was receiving a standing ovation every night. Everything was going great but unbeknownst to me those first few weeks were completely fuelled by adrenalin but once that wore off I came back down to earth with a serious bump.

Performing six nights a week, I took the show to Kendal (where the dressing room was a toilet – no, quite literally it was, a disabled one), Rhyl, Preston, Blackburn, Stoke-on-Trent, Southport, and by the time I reached Sheffield I was officially knackered. It just hit me like a train: Bang! I was out for the count. My new friend Mr Fatigue moved in and he was taking no prisoners. I also started suffering with my voice, just like I'd done previously at the Edinburgh Festival. In an effort to heal myself I resorted to sleeping in the car on the way to the gigs (Gordon was driving, I hasten to add) and dosing myself up on honey, lemon and anything else I could suck before I went on stage.*

Whilst I was in Sheffield, my friend, the comedian Toby Foster (who played Les in *Phoenix Nights*) invited me on to his afternoon show on BBC Radio Sheffield. During the show he took some calls from listeners and one guy phoned in who'd been at the opening night in Buxton. He said he'd enjoyed the show but his arse was numb by the end of it. It confirmed a suspicion that I'd had for a while: that the show was way too long.

Less is definitely more when it comes to stand-up as there's only

---

* Cheeky.

so much an audience can take before they start to get tired. I'd always subscribed to the Ken Dodd school of comedy, of giving them a night to remember, but I now believe you can do that and leave them wanting more. Ken Dodd is without a doubt the greatest front-of-cloth comedian there has ever been and the fact that he's still regularly touring at the age of eighty-two and doing a five and a half hour show (yes, that's right) each night is incomprehensible. I urge you to go and see his *Happiness* tour when it comes your way, as the man is a legend and the last of the truly great British comedians. Now that's a night you'll never forget, and some of the morning too.

So I decided to give the show a dramatic overhaul and cut out forty minutes. It felt like a painful decision at first but I knew it was the right one. With a much lighter show I was able to give more and also cope with the fatigue a bit better – don't forget I did have another sixty-seven nights to go and needed as much help as I could get.

Embarking on a big tour like that was a huge learning curve. I couldn't really compare it to anything else I'd ever done. I was shocked at how gruelling the whole thing was and I certainly wasn't prepared for it. It was the daily cycle that drained me. Being on the road, travelling all the time – I thought I'd done some driving but those journeys were like a trip to the seaside compared to this. I also had the pre-show nerves to contend with: they never ever subsided and arrived with such precision each night I could practically set my watch by them. That was followed by the rollercoaster ride of emotions that was the show itself. You're basically walking out on your own each night and saying, 'Right, I'm going to make you laugh.' That takes its toll and affects you in ways you never imagined possible. Then after surviving on your wits for ninety minutes, the adrenalin crash arrives and reminds you just how mentally and physically exhausted you are. I can understand how and why performers resort to drugs as a form of consolation. It's a very bizarre juxtaposition: one minute you're on stage entertaining two thousand people and then twenty minutes later you're on your own. Fortunately I had my music, a packet of digestives and the knowledge that I was travelling home to keep me sane. Or when I wasn't able to get home, I had the next best thing on the road: a Holiday Inn Express.

They'd started opening them all over Britain around that time, so that meant everything in them was brand spanking new, clean and pristine. They were revolutionary! And they also did duvets, which was a godsend for me, as I hate layers of thin sheets tucked under a mattress. I just want to get in and pull a big duvet up over me and sleep, end of. The layouts of the rooms were always the same, which meant you had familiarity and weren't staggering into solid walls or wardrobes in the middle of the night when you needed a wee. Things like this matter a lot when you're on the road. What I also loved was that the TVs in the rooms all had scart-lead connections at the back which meant I could plug in my VHS recorder (that I always took with me) and set the timer to tape *Corrie* while I was out performing. What more could you want for less than fifty quid a night? (I sound like Lenny Henry flogging Premier Inns.)

Paddy came on the road with Gordon and myself and he used to insist we book him one of the disabled rooms at the Holiday Inn Expresses because they always had twice the space to kick about in, as well as a massive shower and handrails everywhere. Paddy loved them as he could pull himself up from the floor when he rolled in drunk at four in the morning. Thankfully they didn't have any mini-bars, which was a relief with Paddy joining me on tour as I'd have been picking up the tab.

So basically every night after the gig we'd drive to a Holiday Inn Express within a thirty-mile radius of the following night's show. We'd arrive blurry-eyed in the early hours, just in time to watch the signed version of *Des and Mel* before we hit the hay.

Having Paddy on the road was also handy as we'd just started writing the spin-off from *Phoenix Nights*, called *Max & Paddy's Road to Nowhere*, and travelling around Britain gave us a lot of ideas for the series. Like the time we almost knocked a cow down in Norfolk – that ended up in episode five – or the time we had our TV themes quiz whilst we were travelling. Paddy is very competitive and he would get incredibly irate, screaming out the titles like '*BAGPUSS*', '*T.J. HOOKER*' and '*PLAY YOUR CARDS RIGHT*', which I disqualified him for as it's actually *Bruce Forsyth's Play Your Cards Right*. He overreacted slightly by trying to push me out of the car as we thundered down the A14 towards Cambridge. Like I said, he's a very competitive man.

Despite the exhaustion of the travelling and the hanging around for shows, I like to think my level of performance never waned. Though I do think I peaked one night in Grimsby. For some unknown reason it was the perfect performance: every syllable was seamlessly delivered and every gag was rewarded by the perfect amount of laughter. It truly was a fantastic show, honestly in my opinion the best I've ever given. I'd hit the bullseye with one dart but my work was far from over. It was only night number twenty-one. I realised if I'd been making a film or a TV programme my performance that night would have nailed it: CUT! But that's the bitter pill you have to swallow when you're a stand-up: no two shows are ever the same and you've got to do it all again the following night. It can be soul-destroying and you can't help but draw comparisons between audiences' reactions. The night after, the show went down well but it just wasn't in the same league as Grimsby.

Another thing that constantly bugged me about touring was having an interval. I felt obliged to have one as it was deemed standard practice in the theatre world, but it always messed me up. I would just be hitting my stride, the adrenalin kicking in, and I'd have to come off. I found it frustrating, like running very fast and then suddenly having to stop. I'd go and sit in the dressing room for twenty minutes, eat a Boots meal deal and watch the end of *The Bill* which always seemed to be on at that point wherever I was. The mad thing was I didn't even watch *The Bill* at home. Sometimes if it was a good episode I would extend the interval for a few minutes just so I could find out who'd done it. Oh the power I wielded. Then I'd have to go back on stage and start building up the momentum again.

As the tour headed towards Christmas I played fourteen nights at the Lowry theatre in Salford, which I enjoyed not only because it was a lovely venue but I could also see my house from the roof. Being able to go home every night made life on the road much easier, in fact touring would be much easier altogether if you didn't have to tour at all. Many family and friends came to the Lowry shows. I felt comfortable enough to finally let them see it. Though it had changed considerably since my first night in Buxton. I'd been constantly self-editing my material and changing it, I had to, otherwise I think I would have gone mad. That is the beauty of being up there alone, you can do or say whatever you like and you don't have to worry about other actors missing their cues, or letting anybody else down.

It was during one of the nights at the Lowry that I uncovered the crowning jewel of my show completely out of the blue. You've got to remember I'd done this material over seventy-odd nights by this time so nobody was more surprised than me. I used to do a bit all about the game show *Bullseye* with Jim Bowen and at the end I'd mention how we all used to watch it as a family on Sunday afternoons. My mum would come into the front room carrying a tray with a pot of tea, a cake and some biscuits and we'd religiously watch *Bullseye* and then *The Love Boat*. That was it. Then for some reason after seventy-odd nights I poked the material a little further, I talked about dipping your biscuit in your tea and it breaking and falling back into your cup. Well, it was like opening a secret door and finding a room full of treasure.

Do you ever dip your biscuit in your tea and it breaks? Do you ever do that? I swear to God, no matter how old you get in life, you never quite get over that. And you panic, when it falls in? It's like slow motion. 'MUM, GET A SPOON QUICK, MY BISCUIT'S FALLEN IN MY BREW, HURRY UP, IT'S SINKING.' Ahhhhh! Bastard thing's burnt my fingers.

 Rich Tea are bad for that, Rich Tea should be called 'One Dips' because that's all you get, one dip. You've got to be like lightning with Rich Tea 'cause they just fall straight in your cup, they don't even try. I'm willing them to have a bit of backbone, just try, come on . . . 'Oh I can't, I can't . . . Oh it's too hot', you're a biscuit, it's your job. You have to get four together to get a good chance at dipping and they're cocky, they don't even fit into your cup. You've gotta bite a bit off to get them in your brew, Rich Tea. They're not like HobNobs, now that's a biscuit made for dipping. HobNobs are like marines, they're like the

Steven Seagal of the biscuit world. When you dip a HobNob they're like 'Is that it? Again! Go on dip me again 'cause I'm going nowhere, me son, dip me!' And they drink half your brew. Where's the brew gone? 'If you don't dip me I'll drink it again!'

The tour saw out the end of the year with a two-night stint at the Hammersmith Apollo in London and once again, due to the prestigious history of the venue, I was bricking it. Led Zeppelin, David Bowie, The Wiggles, they'd all played there over the years and now it was my turn, and to top it all not only did I have to perform in front of three and a half thousand people but I also had one of rock's greatest icons in the audience come to see me: Eric Clapton.

We had become good friends since I'd met him backstage after one of his shows in Manchester the previous year. I had always been a massive fan and I'd seen him live about five or six times; in fact my favourite song of all time is 'Badge' by Cream. Then I got a call from a friend of mine called Ian Day, who was working as his production manager on tour. He told me that Eric would like to meet me after the show. I thought, This has got to be a wind-up. Anyway I stayed in my seat, I waited and I waited, and eventually Ian turned up and took me backstage. I thought, Watch this, there's going to be no one there and it's just going to be a door into the car park or something.

Anyway I followed him into one of the dressing rooms and there he was, Eric Clapton eating a sandwich. 'Hello,' he said and we shook hands. He turned out to be a massive fan of *my* work, he loved *Phoenix Nights*, but he particularly loved *The Top of the Tower* and then I watched in utter amazement as he re-enacted the bit where I held on to one of The Four Tops in Las Vegas.

Madness. He knew it word for word, apparently it was a firm favourite on the tour bus and in the dressing room with the band.

We exchanged email addresses and kept in touch. He'd tell me he was ice fishing in Quebec or on tour in North America and I'd tell him I'd been round my nan's flat for my tea. But it was the start of a beautiful friendship that has remained strong over the years. He came to the show in Hammersmith with his lovely wife Melia. Because some of the tour was being filmed for archive, my friend Karl caught the moment after the show when they both came backstage to say hello while I'm on the phone to my mum, who I used to ring every night. In fact the footage later turned up on a 'behind the scenes' tour documentary. Eric and Melia had just had a baby girl, and my mum had made them a cushion. She was into her cross-stitch at the time and went to a craft class at High Street Library on Monday mornings. It's really funny because I happened to mention I'm on the phone to my mum and then she says she wants to say hello to them; 'Oh my mum wants to speak to you.' So I hand the phone to Eric: 'Oh hello, Mrs Kay . . . sorry, Deirdre', which always makes me laugh as my mum has clearly said 'No, please, call me Deirdre'.

'Thanks very much for the cushion,' said Eric, 'and by the way Peter did really well tonight, in fact he got a standing ovation which is very hard in London, because they don't normally do that kind of thing down here.'

It was a moment to treasure: Eric Clapton chatting to my mum about a standing ovation I'd received at the Hammersmith Apollo. Absolutely marvellous. Then my mum completely embarrassed me by asking him to give her three rings when he got home. She's still waiting.

Chapter Sixteen

Hello Darkness My Old Friend

My mobile rang, the theme from *The Love Boat*. Hastily I flicked it on to silent, so as not to disturb the other mourners; but it was too late, I was already being glared at. The call was from my manager, Phil, wanting to know if I fancied extending the tour yet again. 'Do you think the demand is there?' I whispered as they lowered the coffin.

'Yes, I do,' he said.

And so a third leg of the *Mum Wants a Bungalow* tour was added in the New Year with an announcement scheduled to be made via an appearance on *Parkinson*. Can you believe that? The same show I used to warm up every week and now I was back.

'My next guest used to be warm-up comedian in this very studio for this very show. Since then he's gone rapidly downhill to the point where now he has his own television show and is currently touring to sell-out audiences and standing ovations. Ladies and gentlemen, Peter Kay.'

Then Laurie Holloway and the band began playing the theme from *Phoenix Nights* and I was on. How surreal is this? I thought as I walked down that iconic staircase, taking my time as I'd already had a few nightmares in which I tripped and fell the full length of it, hence my precautionary speed. I walked over to Parky and we embraced like the old friends we really were and then I took my seat next to Lulu.

Parky: So you're back, and how are you finding it?

Me: It's strange, it feels very weird.

Parky: Did you ever think you might be walking down those stairs one day?

Me: I used to clean them. That's why I left – I thought, I shouldn't be doing this before each show, running round with a duster and a Dyson.

My appearance must have gone down well because when the tickets went on sale for the third leg of the tour the following Monday morning they went through the roof. Sixty nights sold out in less than four hours. Something I still can't comprehend and all I can say is: if you were one of the people who bought a ticket, thank you.

In order to try and alleviate the fatigue of touring, most of the new dates added were to be in residency at each venue for a few nights as opposed to the usual one-night stands. This gave me a chance to catch my breath and meant that I was able to actually unpack my case at the Holiday Inn Expresses rather than just live out of it.

The new dates saw me taking in a week at the Grand Theatre in Leeds, followed by a week at the lovely Liverpool Empire and a fortnight at the Hammersmith Apollo in London, which I found funny after my initial fear of playing such an historic venue and now I was back doing a residency. Don't get me wrong, it was still an incredible thrill to play for 3,632 people every night, I just wasn't intimidated by the building any more. The show would start at eight o'clock so every night at half seven I'd walk from the Holiday Inn Express Hammersmith to the theatre, calling at Boots where I'd pick up my usual meal deal, and then straight through the crowds queuing outside to get in. Amazingly, nobody ever saw me – perhaps this was due to the fact that I always wore a woolly hat that was made from the same material Harry Potter uses for his invisible cloaks.

Backstage life is very deceptive and I apologise for casting daylight upon magic yet again, but it really was a far cry from the coke-fuelled orgy people perceive it to be. Most of my time backstage was spent either searching for an ironing board (I did have one on tour but had it stolen in Liverpool. How anybody can steal an ironing board is beyond me. It's not like you can just casually walk out with it under your jacket) or trying to get a picture on the portable TV in the dressing room. I never had much of what they call a 'rider' – which means that basically you can request anything your heart desires and have it delivered to your dressing room, from blue M&Ms to Filipino prostitutes. Unfortunately it all gets knocked off your money at the end of the tour, which is why my rider consisted of a family bag of Mint Imperials and twelve bottles of Volvic. Noel Gallagher wasn't too impressed with either when he called backstage to see me after one of the Hammersmith shows. 'Bottles of water? Is that it? It's not very rock'n'roll.' I was just grateful he hadn't brought his dickhead of a brother with him after the run-in we'd had at the *NME* Awards.

I was compèring the ceremony in London when Liam refused

to come up on stage and collect an award he'd won. If that wasn't bad enough, he'd turned up for the event wearing what resembled a lady's fur coat – it was a bright white, fluffy affair that made him look like a bleached Womble. Still refusing to budge from his table despite jeers from the audience, he raised his hand and beckoned me down from the stage. Bring the award to me, he gestured. So I did. Taking my time, I sauntered down the steps leading from the stage and slowly walked over to his table where I placed his award right down in front of him. 'There you go,' I said, then turning to walk off I added, 'Oh and will you let my mum know when you've finished with her coat?'

We don't text.

Part of the new leg on the tour also saw a return to my hometown of Bolton where I hadn't ventured since the unforgettable night I'd had at Sub Zero (used to be Sparrows), you remember the gig where I got heckled with the truth in Chapter Two? Tickets went on sale for a week of shows at Bolton's Albert Halls, where I decided to shoot my second live video at what was scheduled to be the end of the tour.

Once again, demand for tickets was so great, people actually camped out overnight in the town hall square in order to get them, can you believe that? Because I still can't. This was the town I'd grown up in, shopped in, went to the dentist in – that kind of support at home blew me away.

Saying that, on my first night back, somebody robbed my dressing room. I was gutted, well you would be after playing the length and breadth of Britain, then you come home and get robbed. Whoever did it let themselves in while I was on stage performing and helped themselves to my camcorder (which unfortunately had some precious backstage tour footage), money and my mobile.

Which I should have probably just rung in hindsight and then listened for the theme from *The Love Boat*.

The following night the *Bolton Evening News* ran the story on the front cover with a photograph of the robber taken from CCTV. It was a completely unrecognisable image of a figure walking down a corridor inside the building, and that night I walked on stage at the start of the show holding a copy of the newspaper and said, 'Well look at that! We've as good as got 'em.'

I can't convey to you the joy and relief it was to play in front of a home crowd and look out on so many faces I knew each night. Though I'll not say it was easy, in fact they were probably some of the toughest gigs I did on the whole tour as I felt I had a lot to prove. On the last day the film crew arrived and took over the theatre in order to film the show for DVD.* Wires and cables everywhere, the place was in pandemonium. I was also stressed as I had a guest list as long as my arm, probably longer – in fact it was written on a roll of wallpaper. It seemed like everybody and anybody I'd ever brushed past wanted to come to that final show.

Watching the DVD of the show now, it was worth all the hassle of organising the guest list as almost every shot has at least someone I know in it. It's packed with family and friends, some of whom aren't around any more, and so it's lovely to look back now and see them all laughing. My mum's there – well she had to be, the tour was named after her – and my nana, who apart from my appearance on the *Royal Variety* had never seen me perform live before. I love the sections where I refer to her in my act, as her face is a picture.

* Videos were now a thing of the past. You can't fight progress; mind you, I still can't bring myself to get rid of any of mine but what I'm going to do with ninety-three episodes of *Mork & Mindy* I'll never know.

My nan now lives in a warden-controlled flat. Oh yes, there she is. [Peter gives her a wave.] Warden-control means you get a piece of red rope hanging from the ceiling in your front room, with a red plastic triangle on the bottom. There's one in the bathroom but she has that tied up. And when she pulls it, it goes through to Duggy, her warden, who's fourteen miles away doing a word search. Every time I go round she'll say, 'Don't pull that, it's for the warden' but when I've had my tea and I'm going in the kitchen I'll forget and . . .

'Oh Nan, I've pulled it.'

'Oh bloody hell, that's for the warden.'

The alarm goes off, shutters come down on the windows, laser beams.

Then Duggy comes on the intercom: 'Is everything alright, Mrs Kay, is everything alright? It's Duggy, do you want th'ambulance, do you want th'ambulance, are you on the floor, are you breathing, are your lips blue?'

'I'm alright, Duggy, it was just an accident, me grandson pulled it, he thought it was the big light.'

I take her out sometimes, I don't mean with a rifle, I mean in the car. But she won't put her seat belt on, she just holds it round her.

'I'll just hold it round me, we're only going up the road.'

'That's just lazy, Nana, you're about an inch away from clipping it in.'

'No, I'll just hold my lifebelt round me.'

'Lifebelt? We're not at sea, Nana.'

After the show we had a party in the town hall where everybody came and my friend Karl did the disco, with a few interruptions from me (once a DJ, always a DJ). During the party my manager Phil had a suggestion.

'You could carry on, you know? Do one more run, only this time do arenas,' he said, chewing on a mushroom vol-au-vent.

'Do you think the demand is still there?'

'I do.'

And he was right, it was. So after a four-week break, the final leg of the tour was added, though this time the plan was to play arenas.

The thought of playing them excited me, not knowing if touring a stand-up show in arenas would actually work. Other well-established comedians such as French & Saunders and *The Fast Show* had been successful but apart from that no stand-up comedian had ever toured these huge venues before, and embarking on that final leg meant I would be the first.

Honestly, I wouldn't have carried on with the tour if I didn't want to, but I was still really enjoying the show. And as the whole thing was still up and running it seemed like too good an opportunity to waste. Of course the financial implications were enticing but I wasn't doing it for the money – if I was, I would have been on tour every year since.

The shows were pencilled and the dates slowly put on sale. I was being careful as the last thing I wanted was to be playing these huge half-empty venues with egg on my face. However, I got a call from Phil within ten minutes of the tickets going on sale telling me that both nights in the Birmingham and Cardiff arenas had already sold out and would I like the rest of the dates to go on sale? I did, and two hours later the whole lot had been sold! So now I was scheduled to do weeks in arenas. But deep down I knew this was definitely going to be the final leg, I knew I had to get out while things were going good. Perhaps I could have carried on, who knows? What I do know is that I really wanted to end the tour in style and so I decided to look into the possibility of playing the Manchester Arena for my final night.

I liked the idea of coming full-circle, back to Manchester and the days when I was doing stand-up at The Buzz Club and the Frog & Bucket and when I was still working part-time as a steward at the arena. Plus technically I'd never actually left my job there, so I may have been able to wangle some extra cash for working the same night. I'm joking of course. We spoke to the powers that be and fortunately the Manchester Arena *was* available, the night before my thirtieth birthday too. It felt like the perfect way to finally end the tour and get my mum her bungalow once and for all.

I'll never forget my first night at Birmingham NIA, the arena was so enormous I was actually able to drive my car in through the back doors, right up to the stage – how cool was that? I got out and peeped my head round the curtain. 'Oh my God! So that's what eight thousand people looks like.' I found it unbelievable that so many people had actually bought tickets and turned up. You know, I'd heard people talking about the size of the arenas I was playing, their capacities and numbers, but until you're actually stood looking at eight thousand people, you can't possibly comprehend it, it takes your breath away. I played to more people in the last leg of the tour than I had over the previous ten months and it was at that moment I realised just how far everything had come since my warm-up shows in two-hundred-seat venues the previous summer.

Initially I was worried about how intimate playing an arena

might be but, to be honest, once I was up on the stage it was just like anywhere else. When the spotlight's shining on you, you can only ever see the first five rows anyway. I seemed to have spent the whole tour playing to the exit signs.

A few weeks before the end of the tour I started developing headaches. Thinking it was just a normal headache brought on by fatigue and hot weather, I downed a couple of Anadin Extra and got on with the show, but four days later when the headache hadn't subsided I started to get concerned. In my typical Catholic way I assumed this was the beginning of the flipside of the good fortune I'd been having.

My doctor said quite casually that he was sending me for an MRI scan 'just to be on the safe side and not to worry'. Don't worry? He was sending me for a brain scan and I wasn't to worry? I'm a bloke – as far as I was concerned I had a tumour in my head the size of a football and it was time to put my affairs in order.

Arriving at the hospital, I was redirected out into the car park to what looked like one of those mobile hot-dog vans that you see outside football stadiums. Slightly dubious, I climbed up some steps round the back of the van and, lo and behold, I was actually in the right place.

The nurse took my details. 'Any allergies?' she enquired to which I replied, 'Face paints and cats, although I did enjoy *Phantom of the Opera*.' I thought I'd inject a bit of levity into the situation, Lord knows it was needed. Then the nurse asked me if I would like a CD on.

I said, 'What, while I wait?'

'No,' she said, 'while you're having your scan.'

I thought, How bizarre. But then she explained that the noise of the machine can sometimes be quite unnerving and I immediately recalled the scene in *The Exorcist* when young Linda Blair has a scan and the noise is actually quite deafening. And that was just watching a pirate copy on headphones on a portable telly under my duvet. If my mum had ever found out she would have pasted me for bringing Satan into the house.*

I browsed the nurse's zip-up CD wallet as she plugged the machine in. I didn't think Steps was appropriate or *The Essential Gipsy Kings.* I plumped for a childhood favourite: *The Best of Simon & Garfunkel,* though with hindsight it probably wasn't the best choice I could have made as the opening track was 'The Sound of Silence'. I'll never forget sliding into the scanner in the back of that hot-dog truck and the opening line: 'Hello darkness my old friend, I've come to talk with you again'. Why didn't I pick Steps? I thought to myself as I lay helplessly on my back, listening to the sombre warblings of S&G. And then as if things couldn't get any worse, the second verse kicked in with 'silence like a cancer grows'. Jesus, where's Mrs Robinson when you need her?

When the scan was over I told the nurse about my inappropriate choice of CD.

'Oh I know,' she said, 'but some patients make the mistake of choosing *The Best of Frank Sinatra* thinking it's going to be all big-band swing and the first track's "My Way".'

---

* People forget *The Exorcist* was banned for years and that getting a pirate copy was the only way you could watch it. Don't get me wrong, I'm not condoning pirate copies; like the advert says (you know that really annoying one that's at the start of every DVD you watch these days, that won't allow you to fast-forward past it), 'You wouldn't steal a car, would you?' No I certainly wouldn't, but come on, there's a big difference between hot-wiring a BMW and watching a knock-off copy of *Wolverine.*

That perked me right up when I thought of all those people sliding in to 'and now the end is near'.

After a lot of praying and several lit candles on my mum's makeshift window-sill altar, which sits underneath a statue of the Virgin Mary with her head glued back on after an overindulgent throw of the dishcloth one Boxing Day, my scan came back fine and it turned out I had severe sinusitis, brought on by playing all those big dusty theatres six nights a week. By the end of each show I'd be drenched in sweat so Gordon would have a big pile of tissues waiting for me in the wings. I'd blow my nose and head straight back on for the encore. So with all those open pores, what did I expect? It was an accident waiting to happen.

A prescription of strong antibiotics kept things at bay as I headed into Liverpool and my last eight consecutive nights of the tour. Normally that many nights in a row would have crucified me but knowing it was all coming to an end the adrenalin kept me going, as well as the people of Liverpool – they really made those last few shows a joy.

Then it was a short trip over to the Manchester Arena for the last night of the whole tour. An incredible six thousand tickets had initially been sold in twenty minutes, then after arriving at the venue and weighing up the seating arrangements, the audience views of the stage weren't as bad as I'd anticipated and so I decided to put another three thousand on sale that afternoon. We rang a local radio station who made the announcement and by five o'clock the whole lot had gone, bringing the total to an amazing nine thousand people.

Now you can no doubt tell by the thinness of the pages in your right hand that we're coming to the end of the book. I have to say, even though it's been time-consuming, writing this book has been a very enjoyable and therapeutic experience (just like cleaning the canteen at the Cash and Carry and the flat in Edinburgh). And like I said in Chapter Nine, it's allowed me to look back and realise just how much I actually achieved during those five years doing stand-up. I had such a wonderfully happy time – OK the past has a way of distorting the truth and I'm pretty sure it wasn't all sweetness and light, but I wouldn't swap a thing, from every crap gig to every standing ovation. Now I'm sure you're wondering where am I going with this paragraph? What's the point? The point is that at every stage of my career I've thought, It can't get any better than this – winning the award in Edinburgh, doing warm-up for *Parkinson*, then actually being on *Parkinson*, doing the *Royal Variety*, selling out the *Mum Wants a Bungalow* tour – it's all been an unbelievable adventure and the grand finale came on the last night at the Manchester Arena.

The show was being filmed for a Channel 4 special which made it even more nerve-racking but, to be completely honest with you, I had nothing left to prove or give. I had that glorious feeling you get when you reach the end of something that you've worked at long and hard (which ironically is exactly how I feel right now, knowing that my last few hundred words are coming up. I've even got a celebratory bath running upstairs as I type, with Fenjal, Lush bath bombs and a *Saturday Night Peter* completion playlist waiting in my docking station, which is perched on the bog cistern). Having worked at the Manchester Arena, I thought it would be funny to dress up as a steward, and so, taking the audience completely by surprise, I bounded down the steps in my bright yellow jacket at the start of the show. What a response and what a view as I stood on the stage, looking out at that epic sight with a mixture of sadness and relief. Before I went on stage I'd recorded a message in the dressing room to camera:

> *It's Tuesday the 1st of July 2003 and tonight is the last night of the tour. It started last September in Buxton and the warm-up shows started on June the 26th so it's almost been a year and after a hundred and eighty nights it's time to say goodbye. I am sad it'll be over but I'm also relieved because I'm very tired, but I've had a wonderful time and it's been the hardest and best thing I've ever done.*

As I performed my material, I took a breath after each section and bid farewell to the material. That probably sounds very odd but for me it was like saying goodbye to a dear friend who'd been through so much with me. That's the huge difference between stand-up and performing music. If you go to see a band like U2 or Del Amitri, you want them to do their hits and usually head to the bar when they announce 'This is off our new album' (or not, in Del Amitri's case). But it's the complete opposite for a comedian. You wouldn't dream of repeating your old material, which is just as well because all the audience want to hear is the new stuff.

Ending the show as I always did, with a rousing version of 'Danny Boy' (an emotional song at the best of times), I stood on a chair in the centre of the stage and looked round at nine thousand people smiling, singing and swaying. It doesn't get any better than this, I thought and then I recalled the very first time I encountered that feeling, when I played the inn-keeper in the school nativity and offered Mary and Joseph an en-suite with full English. Hearing that laughter and knowing I was the cause, I felt happy,

I felt safe. Twenty-three years later I felt exactly the same.

Family and friends sang happy birthday as the clock struck midnight, and as I turned thirty the release and realisation that it was all over finally hit me and I cried. I was tired beyond comprehension. Tired of being in the spotlight and tired of standing up – it was time to sit down for while. So I did; and now it's been close to seven years I often wonder if I'll ever do it all again. Could I ever do it all again? Well I'll tell you something: after all those Saturday nights it'd be a shame not to.

Shit! I've left my bath running.